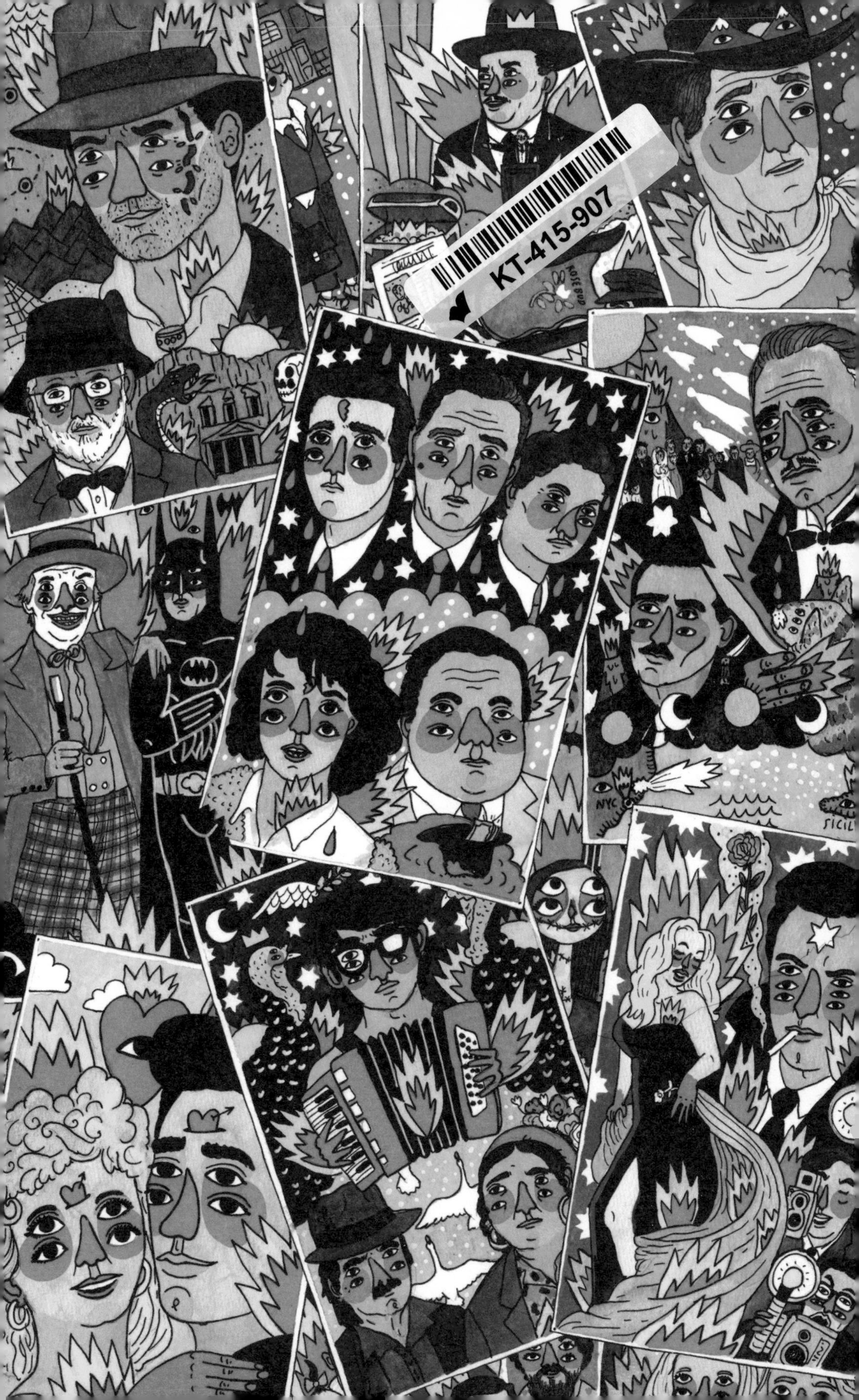
NYC
SICIL

101 MOVIES TO WATCH BEFORE YOU DIE © NOBROW 2017.
THIS IS ~~NOT~~ A FIRST EDITION PUBLISHED IN 2017 BY NOBROW LTD.
27 WESTGATE STREET, LONDON E8 3RL.
TEKT AND ILLUSTRATIONS © RICARDO CAVOLO 2017.
RICARDO CAVOLO HAS ASSERTED HIS RIGHT UNDER THE COPYRIGHT,
DESIGNS AND PATENTS ACT, 1988, TO BE IDENTIFIED AS THE
AUTHOR AND ILLUSTRATOR OF THIS WORK.
TRANSLATION BY SOPHIE HUGHES.

PRINTED IN POLAND ON FSC ® CERTIFIED PAPER.

FSC
MIX
Paper from
responsible sources
FSC® C001693
www.fsc.org

ISBN: 978-1-910620-25-0
ORDER FROM NOBROW.NET

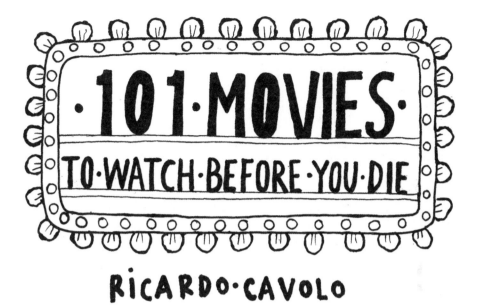

· 1 0 1 · MOVIES ·
TO · WATCH · BEFORE · YOU · DIE

RICARDO · CAVOLO

TRANSLATED BY SOPHIE HUGHES

NOBROW

LONDON | NEW · YORK

CONTENTS

INTRO

A LONG TIME AGO, I WROTE A BOOK ABOUT THE MUSIC I LISTEN TO. OR RATHER, I MADE AN X-RAY OF MYSELF USING MY MUSIC, MY PERSONAL SOUNDTRACK. AND FOR THAT BOOK, I TOOK PAINS TO MAKE IT CRYSTAL CLEAR THAT I'M NO EXPERT IN THE SUBJECT. I'M A MUSIC CONSUMER, AN ENTHUSIAST EVEN, BUT A MERE FOOT SOLDIER. AND AS SUCH I DON'T CLAIM TO HOLD THE UNIVERSAL TRUTH ABOUT THE MUSIC I WROTE ABOUT BACK THEN (OR ANYTHING ELSE FOR THAT MATTER... OK, MAYBE FOOTBALL, HA).

AND THE SAME THING IS TRUE OF MOVIES. THIS BOOK IS REALLY AN OUTPOURING OF MY CINEMATOGRAPHIC LOVES, REGARDLESS OF HOW THEY'RE REGARDED BY THE CRITICS. DON'T EXPECT A SYNOPSIS OR ANY KIND OF CRITICAL ~~ANAL~~ ANALYSIS IN THIS BOOK. THE ONLY THING YOU'LL FIND HERE IS ME GENUINELY LOVING EVERY SINGLE ONE OF THESE MOVIES. THIS IS A LOVE STORY TOLD IN 101 INSTALMENTS.

THE GOOD THING ABOUT CINEMA IS THAT YOU CAN MAKE IT YOUR OWN, HOWEVER THE HELL YOU WANT. ONE MINUTE I MIGHT BE WRAPPED UP IN KUROSAWA'S SEVEN SAMURAI AND THE NEXT HAVING A BELLY LAUGH WATCHING AMERICAN PIE. I GET THAT THERE ARE A LOT OF PEOPLE WHOSE GATEWAY TO CINEMA ARE CHEESY MOVIES, AND OTHERS WHO REFUSE TO WATCH ANYTHING WITH A CRITICS' RATING UNDER 8.5. I RESPECTFULLY ~~AGREE~~ DISAGREE WITH BOTH OF THESE POSITIONS, AND I THINK YOU COULD EVEN END UP HAVING A REALLY SUBSTANDARD CINEMATOGRAPHIC EXPERIENCE IF YOU ADHERE TO EITHER ONE. YOU MIGHT HAVE GONE THROUGH EVERY ONE OF THE TOP 100 MOVIES ACCORDING TO FILMAFFINITY, BUT YOU'D STILL ONLY HAVE WATCHED THAT 100. I'D LIKE AT LEAST TWO MOVIES A DAY. IN FACT, MY BRAIN AND BLOOD CRY OUT FOR MOVIES OF ALL GENRES. I WAS A PRETTY SOLITARY KID. MOVIES FULFILLED ME TO THE EXTENT THAT AFTER

WATCHING THEM I'D IMAGINE MYSELF IN EVERY ONE, RELIVING WHAT THE CHARACTERS WENT THROUGH. IT'S NOT THAT I WANT TO LIVE IN A MOVIE. BUT SEQUENCES, CHARACTERS, AND DIALOGUES JUST RUN AROUND IN MY HEAD, WHETHER I ASK THEM TO OR NOT. SO MUCH SO THAT SOMETIMES I'VE BEEN FREAKED OUT, WORRIED I MIGHT BE DEVELOPING SOME KIND OF PSYCHOPATHY. BUT UP UNTIL NOW AT LEAST, IT'S NEVER CAUSED A ~~PROBLE~~ PROBLEM OR HURT ANYONE, SO I THINK I'LL JUST CARRY ON LIVING IN MY OWN MOVIE.

AND IF I AM WHO I AM BECAUSE OF THE MOVIES I'VE WATCHED, THEN IT GOES WITHOUT SAYING THAT MY ART IS PART OF THAT. I TAKE A HUGE AMOUNT OF IDEAS FROM MY CONCEPTUAL UNIVERSE – FORGED OUT OF HUNDREDS OF MOVIES – AND APPLY THEM TO MY ARTWORK. THERE MIGHT BE ONE DETAIL IN A PIECE THAT COMPLETELY FLUMMOXES YOU, AND MAYBE IT'S BECAUSE THE STORY I WANT

TO TELL TAKES ME TO SOME DETAIL FROM
GOODFELLAS, OR THE GOONIES, OR TOY STORY.
SOMETIMES I DON'T EVEN KNOW THE ANSWER
MYSELF. I'M A REAL LOVER OF IMAGES — I WORK
WITH THEM. AND MOVIES ARE A STEADY, CONSTANT
STREAM OF IMAGES. HOW COULD I NOT LOVE THEM?
I'M PRETTY SURE WE'RE GOING TO AGREE ON A LOT
OF THE MOVIES IN HERE, BUT I ALSO SUSPECT THAT
YOU'LL BE THINKING "WHY ISN'T THIS OR THAT ONE
ON IT?". BUT THIS LIST LOOKS LIKE IT DOES
BECAUSE IT'S THE DNA OF JUST ONE PERSON — ME.
AND EVEN THOUGH WE MIGHT BELONG TO
VERY SIMILAR - LOOKING PLANETS IN OTHER
RESPECTS, EACH PERSON'S MOVIE LIST IS
AS PERSONAL AS THEIR GENETIC MAKE UP.
THAT'S THE MOST BEAUTIFUL PART OF ALL
OF THIS — DIVERSITY.
AND THAT'S EXACTLY THE REASON WHY
THERE ARE MOVIES OUT THERE FOR ALL OF US.

VIVA THE FLICKS !!!

RICARDO. CAVOLO
☺

LE·VOYAGE·DANS LA·LUNE

(1902)

(A TRIP TO THE MOON)

THE EARLY DAYS OF CINEMA WERE ALL ABOUT MAGIC AND ILLUSION, AND MÉLIÈS WAS THE PERFECT MAGICIAN. THIS FRENCHMAN USED CINEMATOGRAPHIC ADVANCES TO IMPROVE ON THE SPELL THAT OLD THEATRICAL PERFORMANCES CAST. BEFORE HIM, THIS KIND OF MAGIC WAS IMPOSSIBLE TO ACHIEVE BECAUSE THEY DIDN'T HAVE THE TECHNOLOGY, AND AFTER HIM, TECHNOLOGY ADVANCED SO ~~FAST~~ QUICKLY THAT FILMMAKERS LOST THIS THEATRICAL ELEMENT. MÉLIÈS'S SPECIAL BRAND OF CINEMA REMAINS INTACT IN THE SNOW GLOBES FILLED WITH LITTLE STARS THAT YOU SHAKE. THE MOVIE IS AN EXERCISE IN DELICIOUS MELANCHOLY THAT YOU DON'T EVER WANT TO END. I GET COMPLETELY SWEPT UP IN THE STORY, LETTING MYSELF BE FULLY IMMERSED IN IT LIKE A ~~THREE~~ THREE-YEAR-OLD PLAYING WITH PUPPETS... WHEN I'M WATCHING THAT TRIP TO THE MOON, I CAN FEEL MY EYES FILL UP WITH LITTLE STARS AND I SMILE, OPEN-MOUTHED, THE WHOLE WAY THROUGH.
MÉLIÈS WAS REALLY A LITTLE KID WITH A GENIUS' ABILITY TO MAKE US FEEL LIKE KIDS AGAIN.

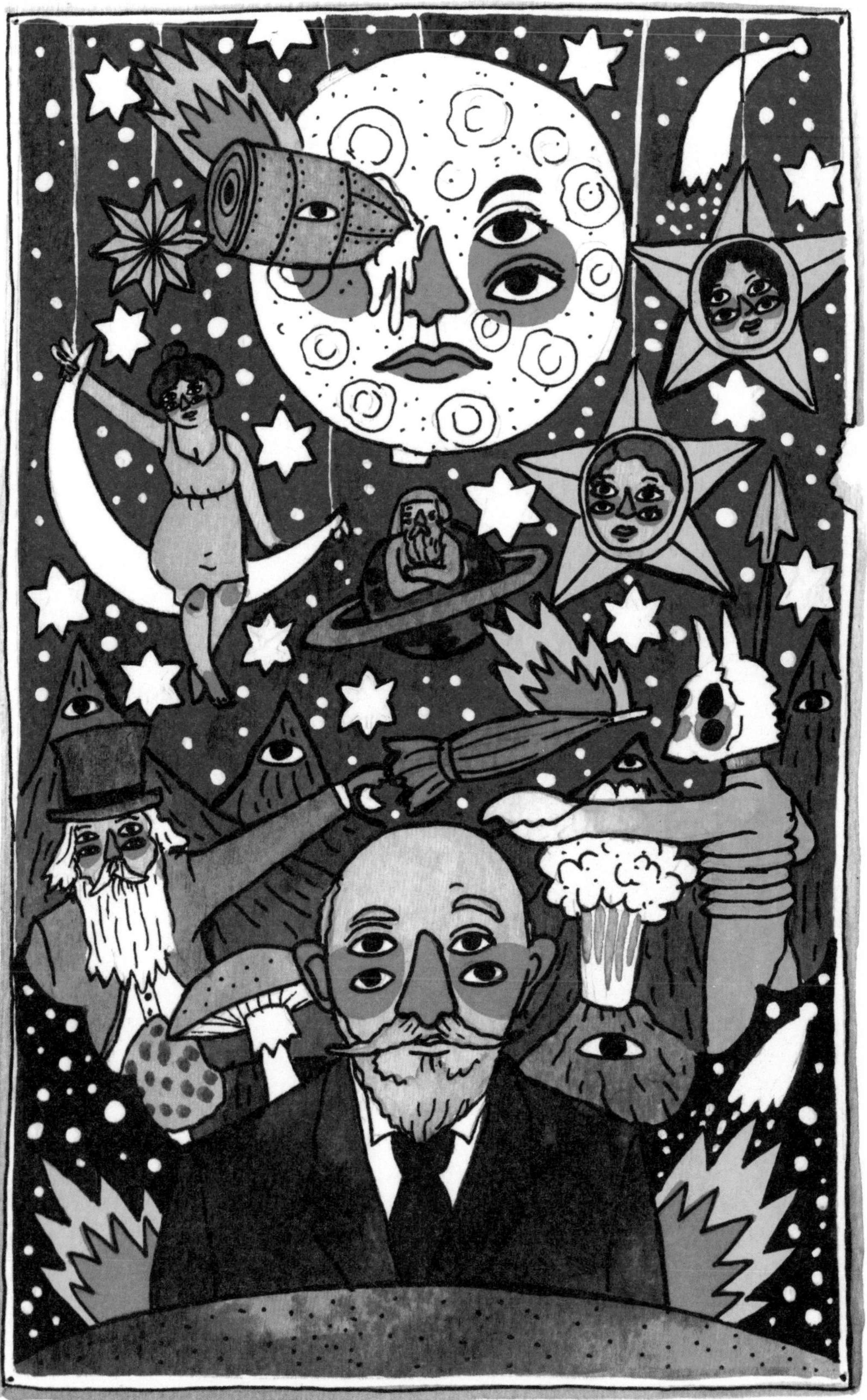

·LE·VOYAGE·DANS·LA·LUNE·

CHARLIE · CHAPLIN'S
MODERN·TIMES

(1936)

AS I WROTE IN MY INTRO, I WAS A PRETTY SOLITARY KID SURROUNDED BY IMAGINARY FRIENDS ~~...~~ (WHETHER ~~...~~ I'D INVITED THEM OR NOT). I SHOULD SAY THAT ALL OF THEM WERE BASED ONE WAY OR ANOTHER ON CHAPLIN. WHENEVER I WATCHED HIM, THE WORLD OUTSIDE CEASED TO EXIST. "THE LITTLE FELLOW" DANCED ABOUT AND CAUSED ALL THAT MISCHIEF THAT WOULD HAVE ME ROLLING AROUND ON THE FLOOR LAUGHING. AND IN MODERN TIMES, CHAPLIN IS PERFECTION. I WAS WITH HIM THE WHOLE WAY: FALLING HEAD OVER HEELS FOR PAULETTE GODDARD; WINCING IN PAIN WHEN HE HIT HIS FINGER WITH A HAMMER; JUMPING EVERY TIME HE DID AS HE STROLLED ALONG. I LOVED HIS FINAL PERFORMANCE IN THE BAR SO MUCH THAT I LEARNED THOSE IMPROVISED LYRICS OFF BY HEART. EVEN TODAY I GO BACK TO THAT SCENE, AND THE SECOND THE MUSIC STARTS UP A BIG SMILE SPREADS ACROSS MY FACE, LIKE THE ONE I WORE AS A BOY.

16

CHARLIE·CHAPLIN'S·MODERN·TIMES

FREAKS

(1932)

THIS MOVIE IS A MILESTONE IN MY LIFE AND CAREER. I'VE LIVED WITH ROMANI PEOPLE EVER SINCE I WAS A LITTLE BOY, SO I'VE BEEN ~~SINCE~~ LUCKY ENOUGH TO SEE A WHOLE OTHER SIDE OF OUR SOCIETY. AND EVER SINCE THEN, THE DRIVING FORCE BEHIND ALL MY WORK HAS BEEN THE DESIRE TO APPRECIATE AND HONOUR THE PEOPLE WHO MAKE UP PART OF THAT OTHER SIDE. AND FREAKS IS LIKE THE BANNER FOR THIS MOVEMENT. ALMOST LIKE THE HOLY BOOK OF MY IDEALS. I'M MORE ~~INTEREST~~ INTERESTED IN SHOWING HOW DIFFERENT PEOPLE LOVE AND LAUGH, THAN IN THE REVENGES THEY EXACT. AND THAT'S WHAT TOD BROWNING SHOWS US. HIS GREAT CLAN OF PEOPLE HAVE ALL BEEN UNCEREMONIOUSLY REJECTED FROM SOCIETY, BUT ARE TAKEN IN BY THE TRAVELLING ~~CIR~~ CIRCUS FAMILY. IN THE SAFETY OF THEIR NEW HOME, THEY FORGET ALL ABOUT THE SO-CALLED "NORMAL PEOPLE" WHO RIDICULE THEM, AND THEY BECOME ONE BIG HAPPY FAMILY. THEY'RE MAGICAL. I ALWAYS KNEW WHAT I WANTED TO TALK ABOUT IN MY WORK, BUT SEEING THIS MOVIE GAVE ME EVEN MORE REASON TO DO SO. IT'S TERRIBLE TO HATE AND FEAR THINGS OR PEOPLE THAT ARE DIFFERENT. DIFFERENT IS MIND-BLOWING ~~AND~~ FAULTLESS. LET'S EMBRACE IT

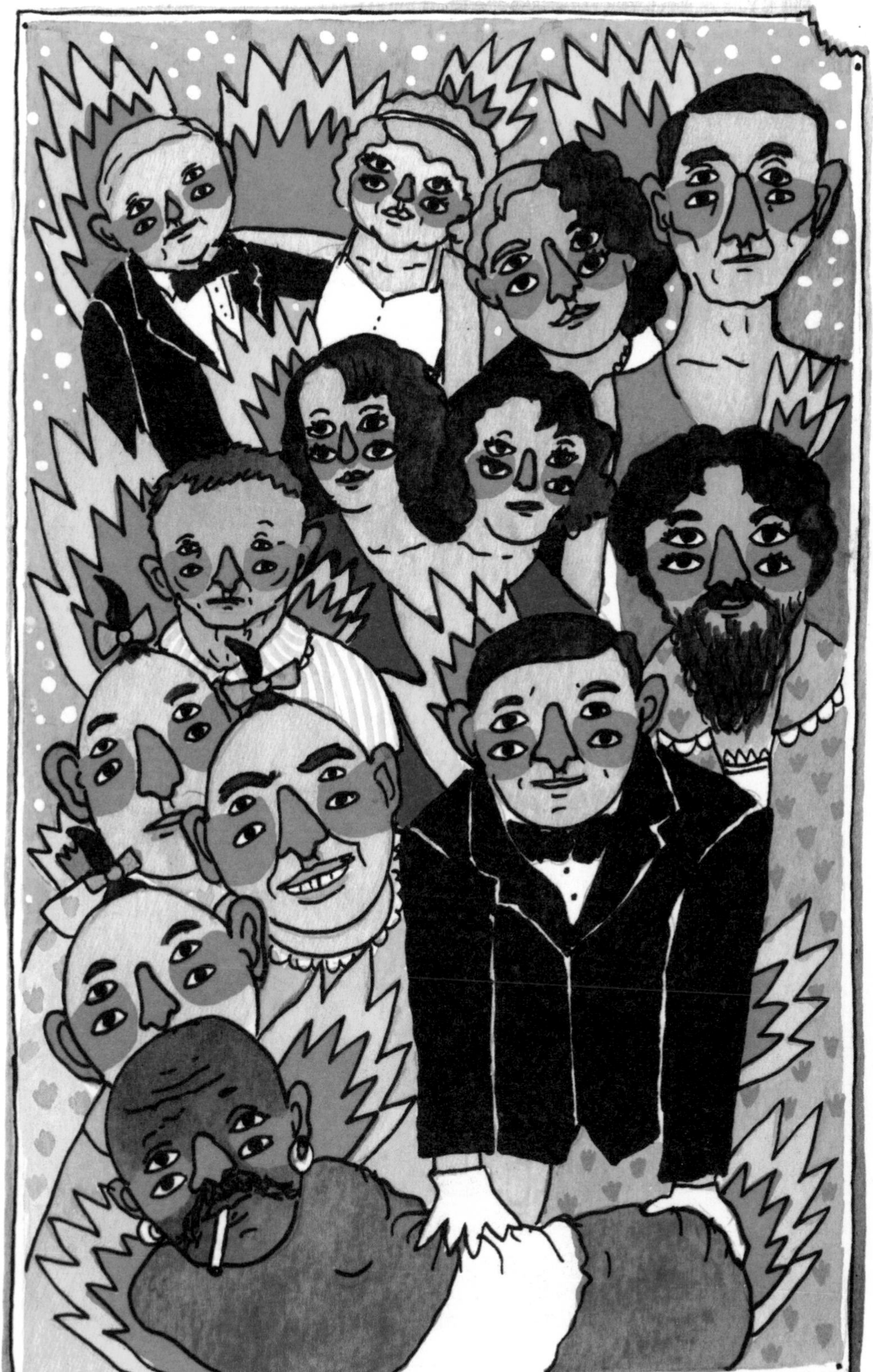

FREAKS

A·NIGHT·AT THE·OPERA

(1935)

THE MARX BROTHERS MADE ME VERY HAPPY AS A KID. I MIGHT NOT HAVE GOT ALL OF GROUCHO'S RISQUÉ JOKES, BUT I WAS COMPLETELY MAD ABOUT HARPO. I FELL RIGHT INTO HIS CLUTCHES. I WOULD SPEND THE WHOLE MOVIE WAITING FOR HIM TO APPEAR AND DRIVE ALL THE STUCK-UP, PO-FACED ~~CHUMP~~ CHARACTERS TO DISTRACTION. EVERY TIME, I SWEAR. I EVEN DESIGNED MY OWN HARP TO COPY HARPO WHEN HE TOOK A BREAK FROM THE HORN AND OFFERED US A MINUTE OF ANGELICAL, SWEET HARMONY, PLUCKING THE STRINGS OF HIS HARP. WHEN I WAS A LITTLE OLDER, I WAS FINALLY ABLE TO SEE THE REAL FUNNY SIDE OF GROUCHO AND CHICO'S RUTHLESSNESS. NOW I COULD ENJOY THE MOVIE IN ALL ITS LUSHNESS. I COULD HAVE CHOSEN ANY OF THE MARX BROTHERS' MOVIES FOR THIS LIST, BUT THE JAM-PACKED CABIN SCENE STILL MAKES ME FALL ABOUT LAUGHING, AND THAT'S WHAT SETTLED IT.

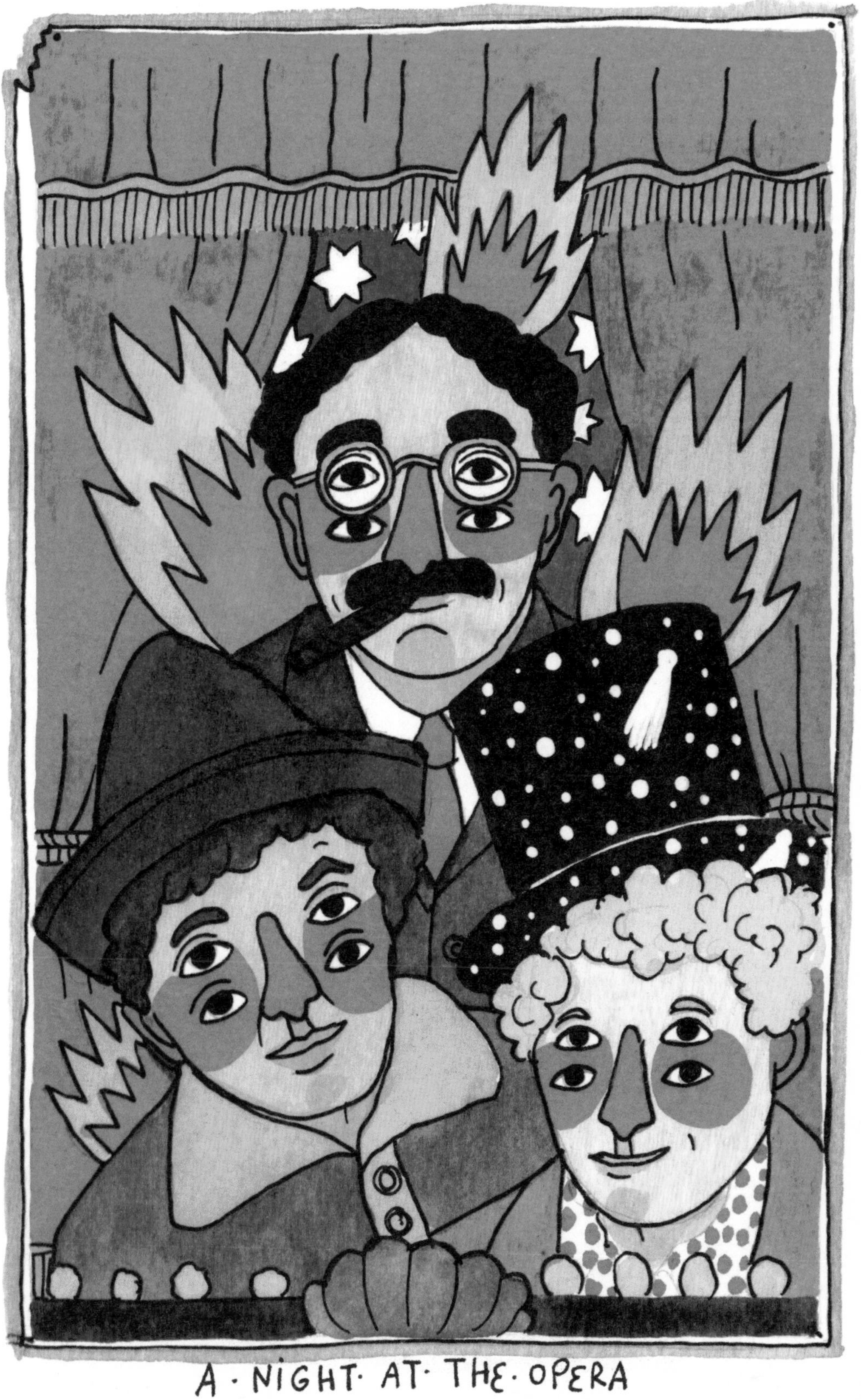

A · NIGHT · AT · THE · OPERA

"Casablanca"

(1942)

MUCH OF THE CLASSIC CINEMA I'VE SEEN, I SAW FOR THE FIRST TIME WITH MY FATHER. HE PROVIDED ME WITH AN ENTIRE UNIVERSE OF PERFECT, TIMELESS MOVIES. BUT IN THIS CASE, HE GAVE ME SOMETHING EVEN BETTER. MY FATHER HAS ALWAYS CALLED ME JAMFRY, WHICH IS THE SPANISH VERSION OF HUMPHREY. MY MY AFFECTIONATE NICKNAME CAME ABOUT BECAUSE APPARENTLY AS A BOY I WAS TOUGH, SERIOUS AND BRAVE, LIKE BOGART. AND FROM THEN ON MY LIFE BECAME INEXTRICABLY LINKED TO THE ACTOR'S. I COULD NEVER SEE HUMPHREY BOGART ANY OTHER WAY — HE HAS ALWAYS BEEN A KIND OF PROJECTION OF MYSELF. AND IN CASABLANCA WE LOOK PRETTY GOOD.

I'M LUCKY ENOUGH TO HOLD NOT ONLY THE MOVIE IN MY HEART, BUT ALSO A GREAT MENTOR.

TO THE BITTER END, JAMFRY!

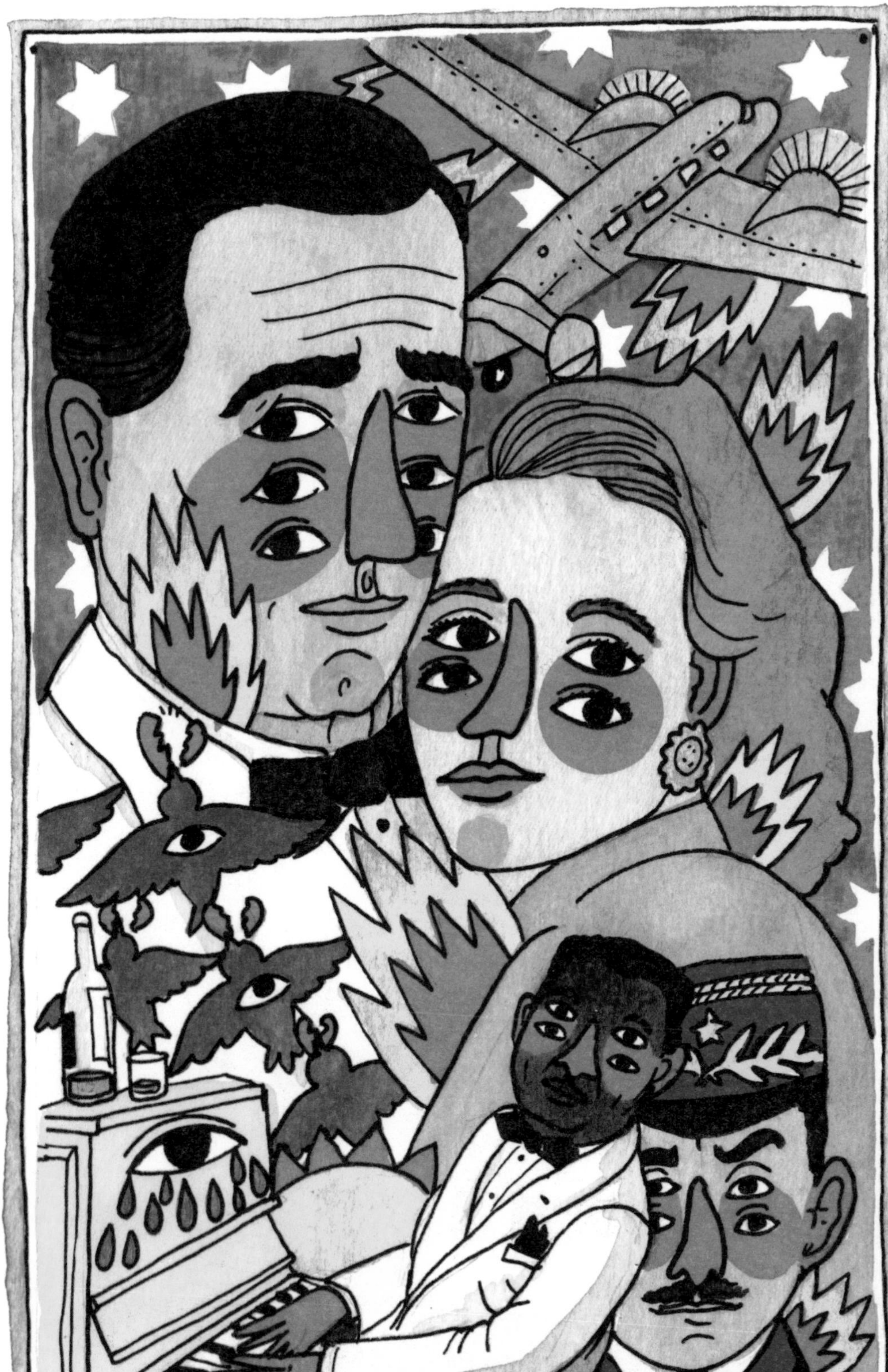

CASABLANCA

CITIZEN KANE

(1941)

THIS IS ONE HELL OF A MOVIE. ORSON WELLES NAILED IT. i LOVE PLOTS THAT COVER THE WHOLE LIFE OF ONE CHARACTER. AND iF THAT ~~CHARA~~ CHARACTER HAPPENS TO BE CHARLES FOSTER KANE, PLAYED BY WELLES HIMSELF. iT JUST DOESN'T GET ANY BETTER. YOU GET COMPLETELY CAUGHT UP IN WELLES'S WORLD OF LIGHTS AND SHADOWS. FOR THE ENTIRE TWO HOURS i'M GLUED TO THE SCREEN. i WISH CiTiZEN KANE WAS A WHOLE DAY LONG EVEN! AND ONCE iT'S OVER i'M COMPLETELY WHACKED, AS iF iT WERE ME WHO HAS JUST LIVED THAT INTENSE LIFE UNTIL MY LAST WORD, "ROSEBUD". iT'S ANOTHER CASE OF PERFECT CINEMA WHICH GIVES ME INFINITE PLEASURE TO RETURN TO TIME AND AGAIN. AND iT'S THE SAME THING THAT HAPPENS WITH SHAKESPEARE — iT FEELS INCREDIBLY MODERN TO ME. ~~████████████~~ iT'S FASCINATING HOW EVEN THOUGH 80 YEARS HAVE PASSED, THERE ARE SOME THINGS IN CINEMA THAT HAVEN'T BEEN IMPROVED UPON SINCE THEN.

i LOVE THAT.

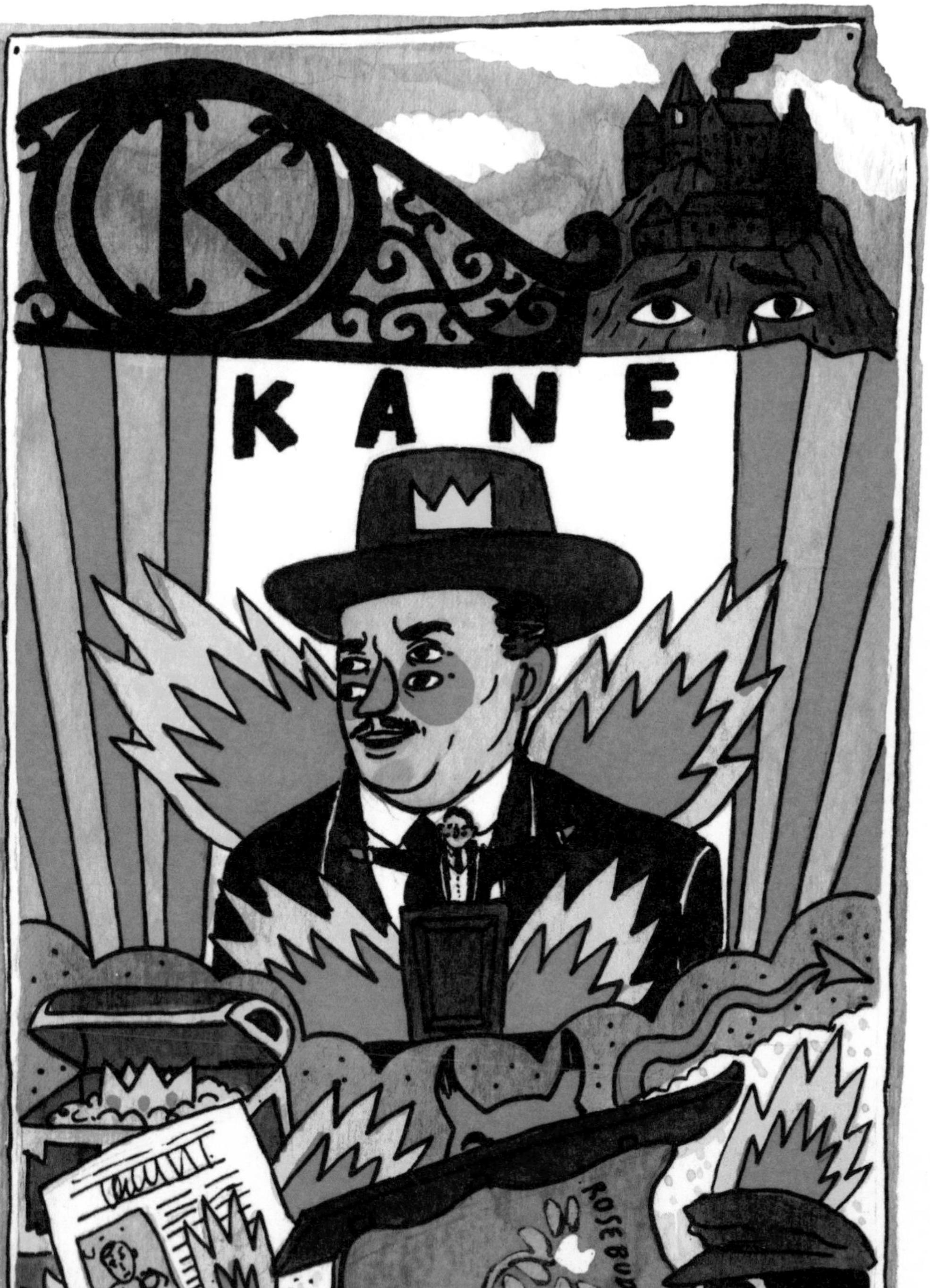
KANE
ROSEBUD

CITIZEN · KANE

REAR·WINDOW

(1954)

...AND ALONG CAME HITCHCOCK. WELL, IN CINEMA HISTORY HE CAME ALONG MUCH EARLIER, AND WAS ALWAYS MAKING IMPECCABLE MOVIES. BUT WITH REAR WINDOW HE FULLY CASTS ME UNDER HIS SPELL AND TURNS US ALL INTO FRONT ROW VOYEURS. IT MAKES ME LAUGH, IT ENTERTAINS ME, IT KEEPS ME ON THE EDGE OF MY SEAT. AND THIS MOVIE LOOKS BEAUTIFUL, WITH THOSE 50s COLOURS AND VOYEUR SHOTS THAT WES ANDERSON WOULD LATER USE IN HIS MOVIES. HITCHCOCK WAS A MAGICIAN, AND HE'S NEVER, EVER LET ME DOWN. I OWE HIM DOZENS OF HOURS OF HAVING BOTH A GOOD AND BAD TIME AT THE SAME TIME. JAMES STEWART IS FUNNIER THAN EVER, ESPECIALLY CONSIDERING THERE ARE MURDERS INVOLVED. THERE'S ONLY ONE THING THAT WOULD MAKE THIS MOVIE BETTER... I'D LIKE THINGS TO GET EVEN MORE TWISTED AND FOR ALFRED TO PUSH US TO THE LIMIT. HE KNOWS WE DON'T WANT TO LOOK AWAY.

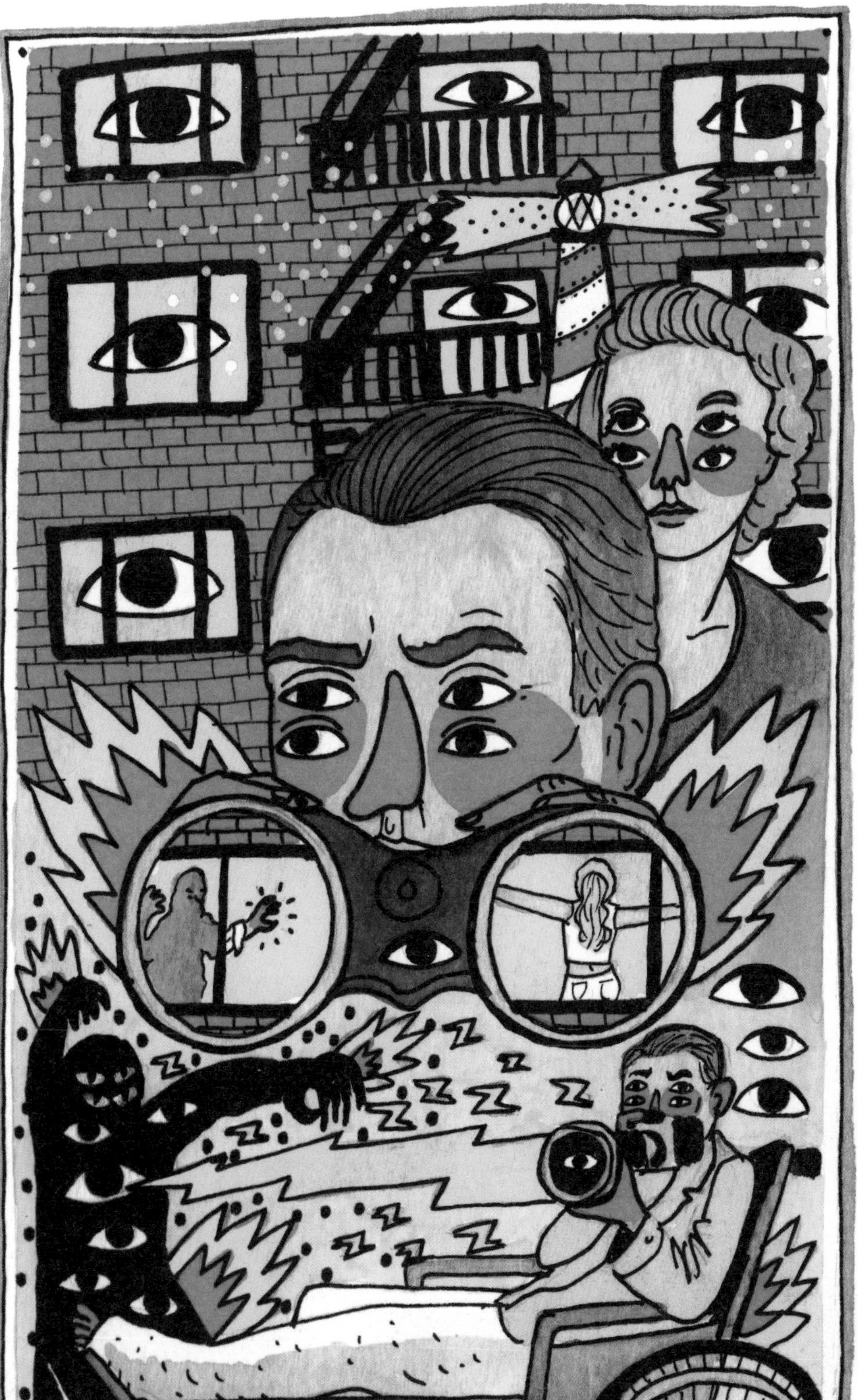

REAR · WINDOW

GIANT

(1956)

THIS BRILLIANT MOVIE SHARES AN ELEMENT WITH CITIZEN KANE, WHERE IT TELLS VARIOUS DECADES OF ONE CHARACTER'S LIFE. ~~YOU~~ YOU LIVE WITH THEM. IN THIS CASE, TOO, THERE ARE CERTAIN THINGS THAT MAKE IT REALLY GREAT VIEWING. FOR STARTERS, IT'S SET IN TEXAS IN THE 50s AND FOR A LOVER OF AMERICAN CULTURE LIKE ME, IT'S ANOTHER PART OF THE COUNTRY'S HISTORY TO LEARN ABOUT. THAT ALONE WOULD HAVE BEEN ENOUGH TO WIN ME OVER. BUT THIS STORY OF ONE MOMENT IN AMERICA RUNS ALONGSIDE THE PERSONAL STORY OF A FAMILY, WITH ALL ITS TWISTS AND TURNS, REALLY MAKING IT A COMPLETE MOVIE. OH, AND THEN THERE'S THE SMALL MATTER OF THE FACES WHO APPEAR IN IT - LIZ TAYLOR, JAMES DEAN AND ROCK HUDSON.

WHAT MORE COULD YOU WANT?

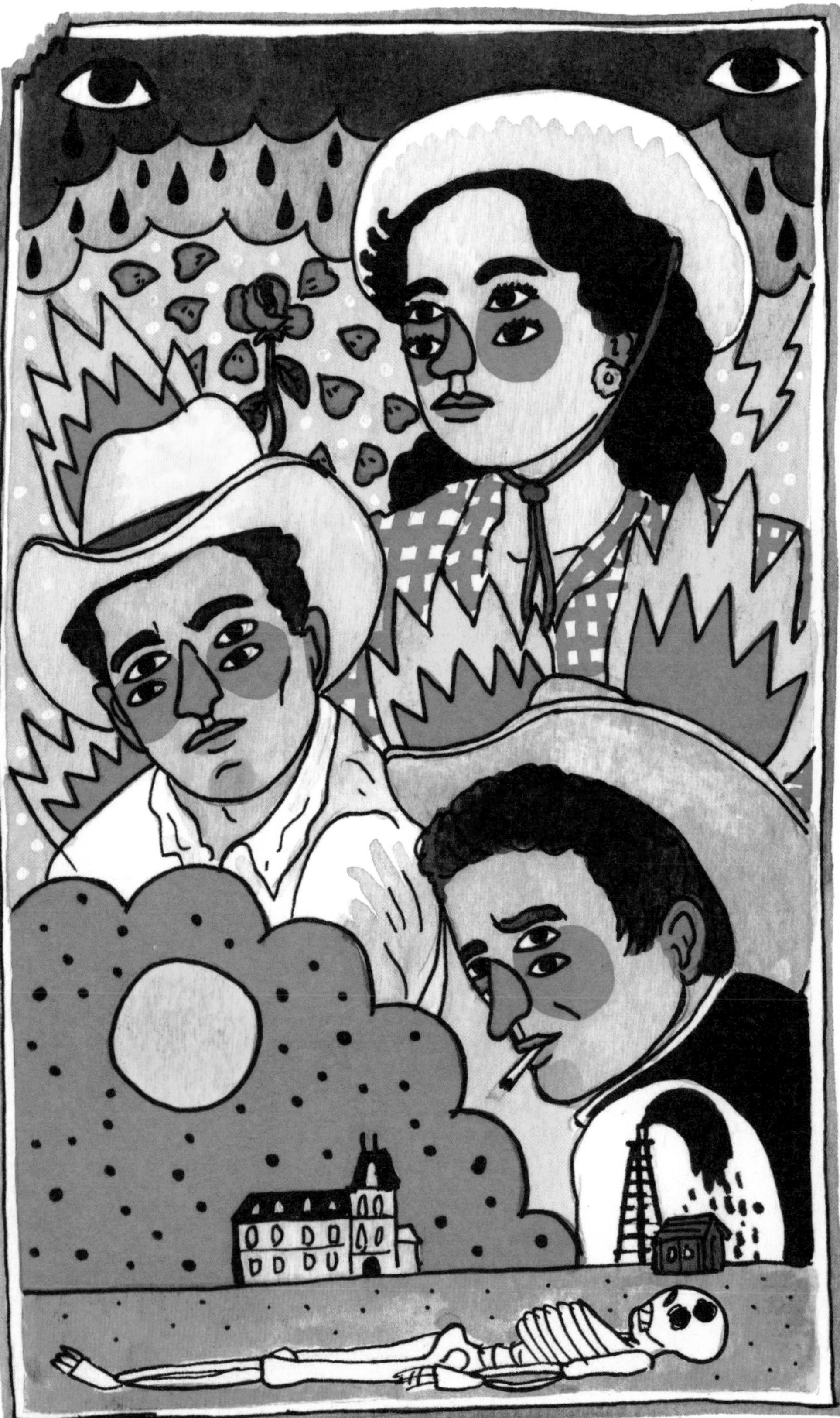

GIANT

THE · SEARCHERS

(1 9 5 6)

i LOVE WESTERNS. iVE ALREADY MENTIONED THAT i'M A FAN OF AMERICAN CULTURE, AND THIS GENRE OF CINEMA IS A MARVELLOUS EXALTATION OF IT. i LOVE ALL THE PARAPHERNALIA, THE MUSIC, THE PLOTS... BUT THERE IS ONE THING iVE NEVER LIKED, EVER SINCE i WAS A KID. i WAS ALWAYS ON THE SIDE OF THE INDIANS. ALWAYS. i HATED THAT IN 90% OF WESTERNS THEY KILLED THE INDIANS. OR THEY PAINTED THEM AS HEARTLESS ~~THE~~ ANIMALS. THAT MADE ME REALLY ANGRY, AND i ALWAYS HOPED THAT IN SOME STRANGE PLOT TWIST IT WOULD BE THE COMANCHES OR THE APACHES ~~WHO~~ WHO WIPED OUT ALL THOSE WHITE GUYS (HISTORICAL JUSTICE), AND RECLAIMED THEIR FREEDOM AND WAY OF LIFE.

i REMEMBER THOSE SHOTS WHERE YOU SEE HUNDREDS OF NATIVES MOUNTED ON HORSES AT THE TOP OF A HILL WAITING TO ATTACK THE DAMNED 7TH CAVALRY. THEN THOSE DRUMS WOULD ANNOUNCE THE START OF THE BATTLE AND i'D RUB MY HANDS TOGETHER, THINKING: "COME ON, LET'S SEE IF WE CAN TAKE 'EM DOWN THIS TIME".

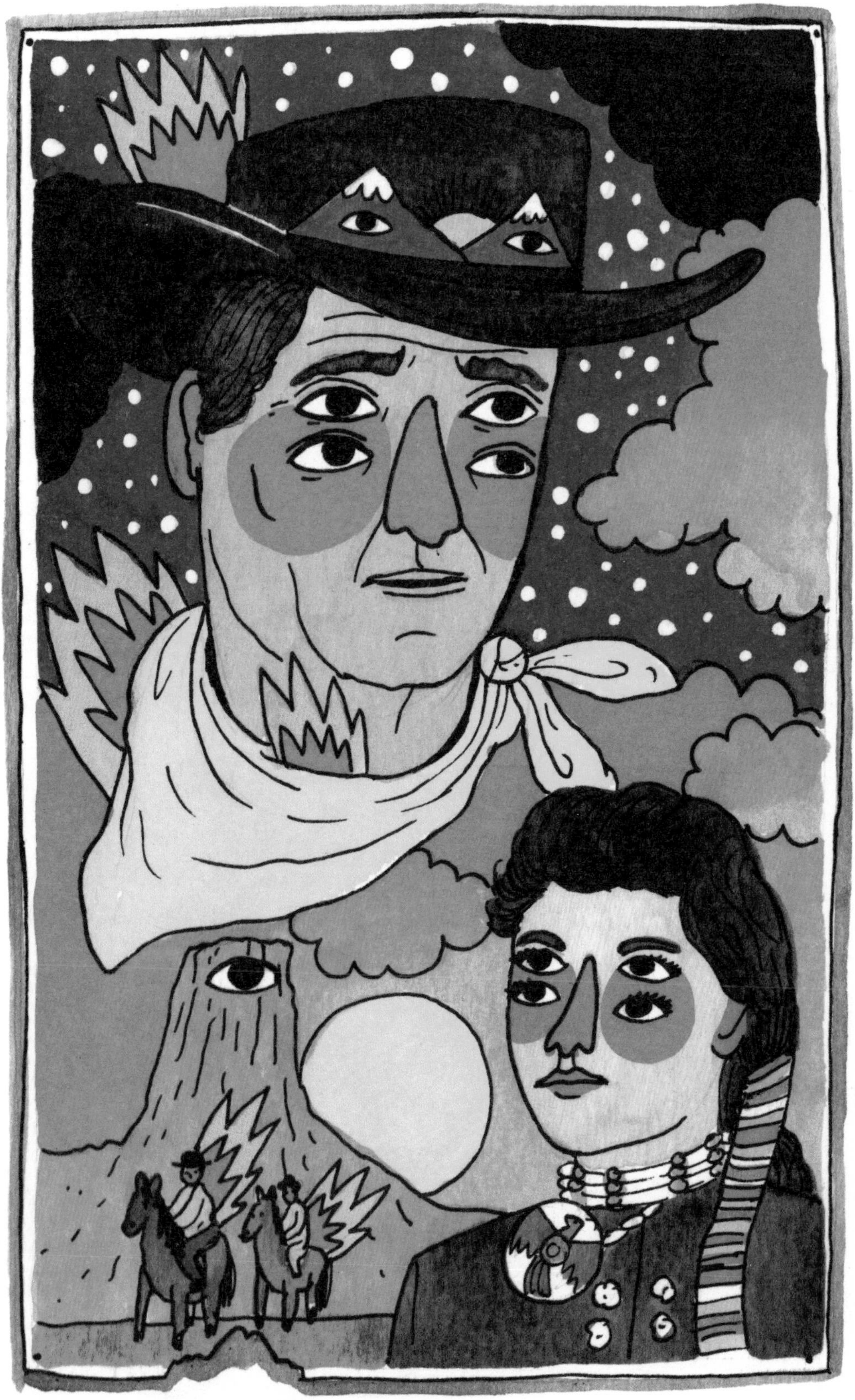

THE·SEARCHERS

Mon Oncle

(1958)

JACQUES TATI, THE DIRECTOR OF THIS MOVIE, WAS A TRUE MASTER.
WITH MON ONCLE, HE REWORKED CHAPLIN'S MAGIC IN THE
VERY BEST WAY, WHICH IS WHY IT NEVER FAILS TO UNLEASH
MY INNER CHAPLIN-LOVING CHILD. WHEN I WATCH THIS
MOVIE, I BEAM THROUGH MOST OF IT. AND I THINK SOMEHOW
TATI LAYS DOWN THE GROUND RULES THAT ALLOW MOVIES
LIKE AMELIE TO COME ABOUT YEARS LATER. BUT THE REAL
MAGIC LIES IN MONSIEUR HULOT, WHO, WITHOUT SAYING A
WORD, STEALS MY HEART AND MAKES ME WISH HE WERE
MY UNCLE. MON ONCLE SHOWS A MICROCOSM, BUT ONE THAT
GLEAMS AND DAZZLES LIKE THE GREATEST UNIVERSE.
I'VE ALWAYS THOUGHT THAT IF I MANAGE TO HOLD ON TO A
LITTLE BIT OF HULOT'S NAIVETY AND MAGIC, THEN LIFE CAN BE
A THOUSAND TIMES BETTER AND MORE BEAUTIFUL.

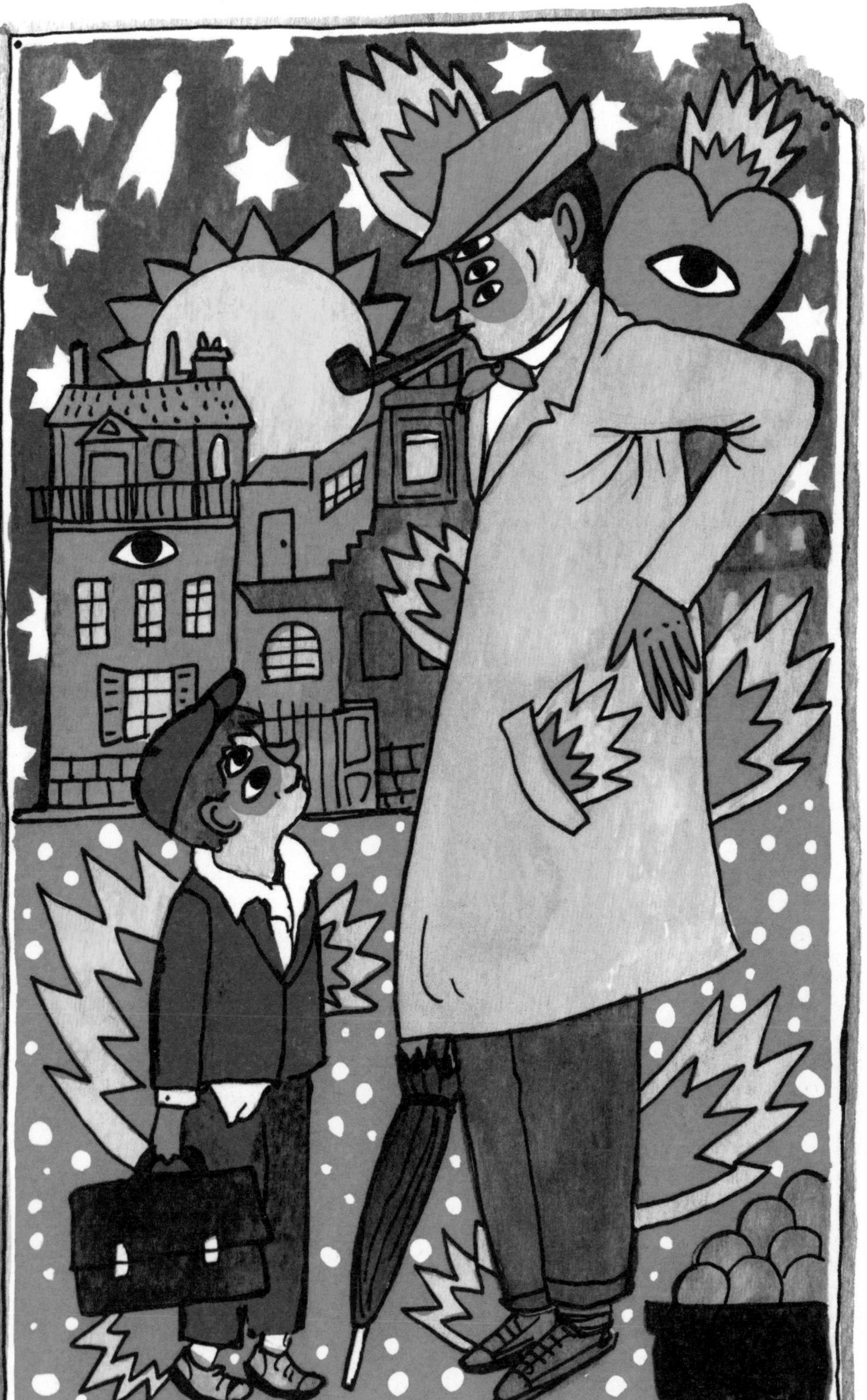

MON·ONCLE

"SOME·LIKE IT·HOT"

(1959)

BILLY WILDER IS THE BOSS. ONLY HE KNOWS HOW TO MAKE
THOSE CLASSIC COMEDIES YOU FALL IN LOVE WITH AND CHERISH
FOR THE REST OF TIME. IT'S ALWAYS THE RIGHT MOMENT TO
WATCH ONE OF HIS MOVIES. AND SOME LIKE IT HOT IS
POSSIBLY THE MOST HILARIOUS OF ALL. MARILYN
IS ALWAYS A DRAW, BUT IN THIS CASE IT'S JACK LEMMON
WHO REALLY HAS ME HOOKED. I'D HAPPILY BE HIS
SIDEKICK ~~OR~~ ON ANY OF HIS ADVENTURES. ~~OR~~
THE BEST NEW YEAR I CAN REMEMBER WAS WHEN I WAS TEN
YEARS OLD. EVERYONE HAD GONE TO BED AFTER THE USUAL TOASTS,
AND I COULDN'T SLEEP SO I WENT TO WATCH TV. SOME LIKE IT HOT
WAS JUST STARTING. I WATCHED IT FROM START TO FINISH,
EATING THE LEFTOVERS FROM OUR DINNER FEAST AND
CHOKING WITH LAUGHTER.
THE MOVIES AR
MAGIC.

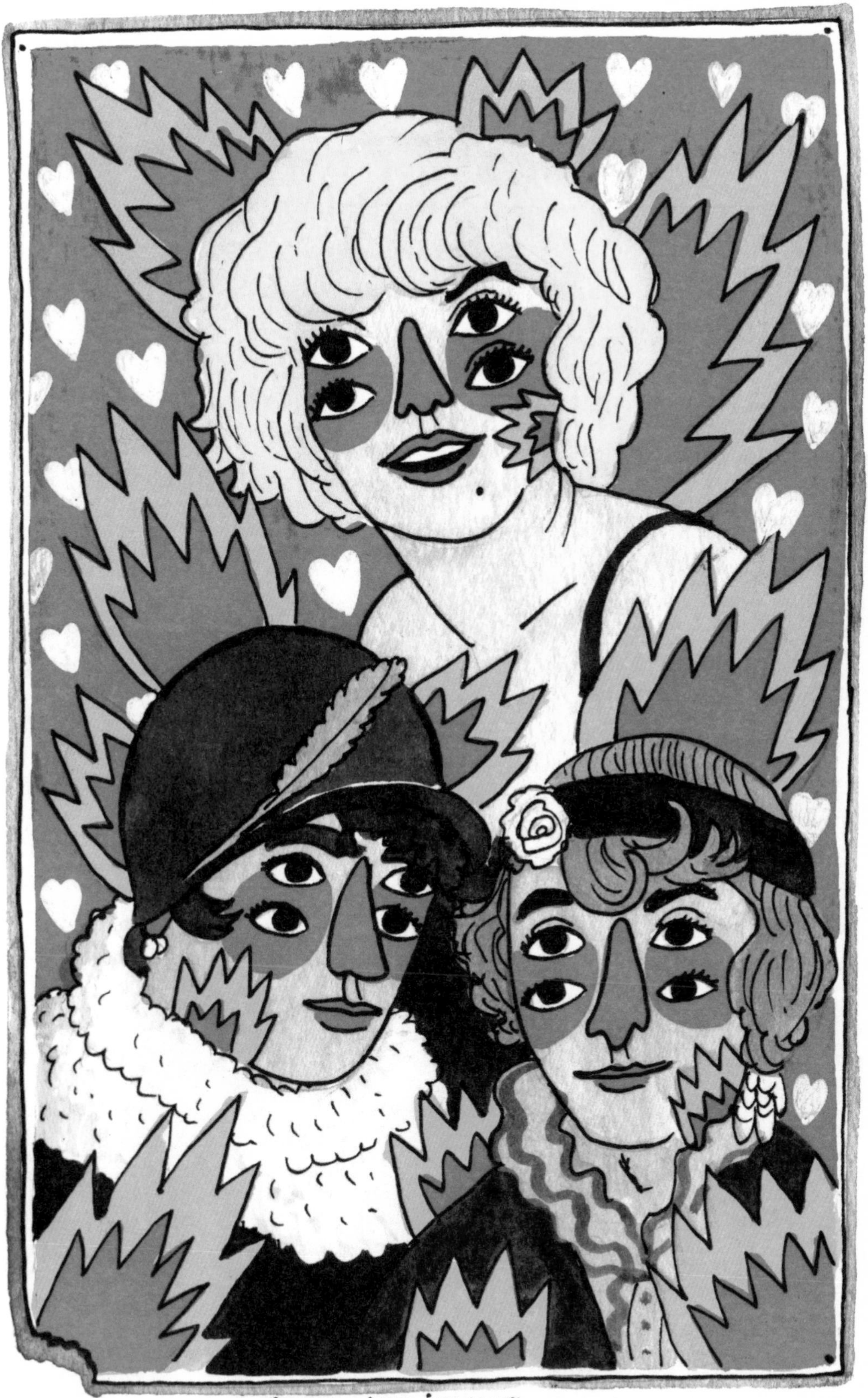

SOME · LIKE · IT · HOT

NORTH·BY·NORTHWEST

(1959)

IN MY OPINION, HITCHCOCK'S BEST MOVIE. IT'S GOT THE
JEOPARDY, THE SUSPENSE, AND THE TENSION OF THE
OTHERS, BUT IN THIS ONE WE GET CARY GRANT AT
HIS BEST. HE IS SIMPLY BRILLIANT. THE FIRST TIME
i WATCHED THIS MOVIE i DECIDED THAT IF i WERE BORN
AGAIN i'D COME BACK TO EARTH AS HANDSOME AS
GRANT. HE'S THE IDEAL ACTOR FOR ALL THOSE LOVE
TRIANGLES AND SHOOT-OUTS. HE'S JUST AS SMOOTH
WOOING A LADY AS FLEEING HIS ENEMIES, AND iN NORTH
BY NORTHWEST HE PERFORMS THIS ROLE TO ~~ROLE~~
PERFECTION. THE PLOT IS ONE CONFUSION AFTER THE
OTHER UNTIL YOU DON'T KNOW WHO TO TRUST. BY THE
END OF THE MOVIE YOU'RE DRIVEN HALF MAD WITH
SUSPENSE, NOT KNOWING WHAT WILL HAPPEN. AND THE
SEQUENCE ON MOUNT RUSHMORE IS THE STUFF OF THE
BEST JAMES BOND CHASES.
CARY GRANT IS ONE OF A KIND.

36

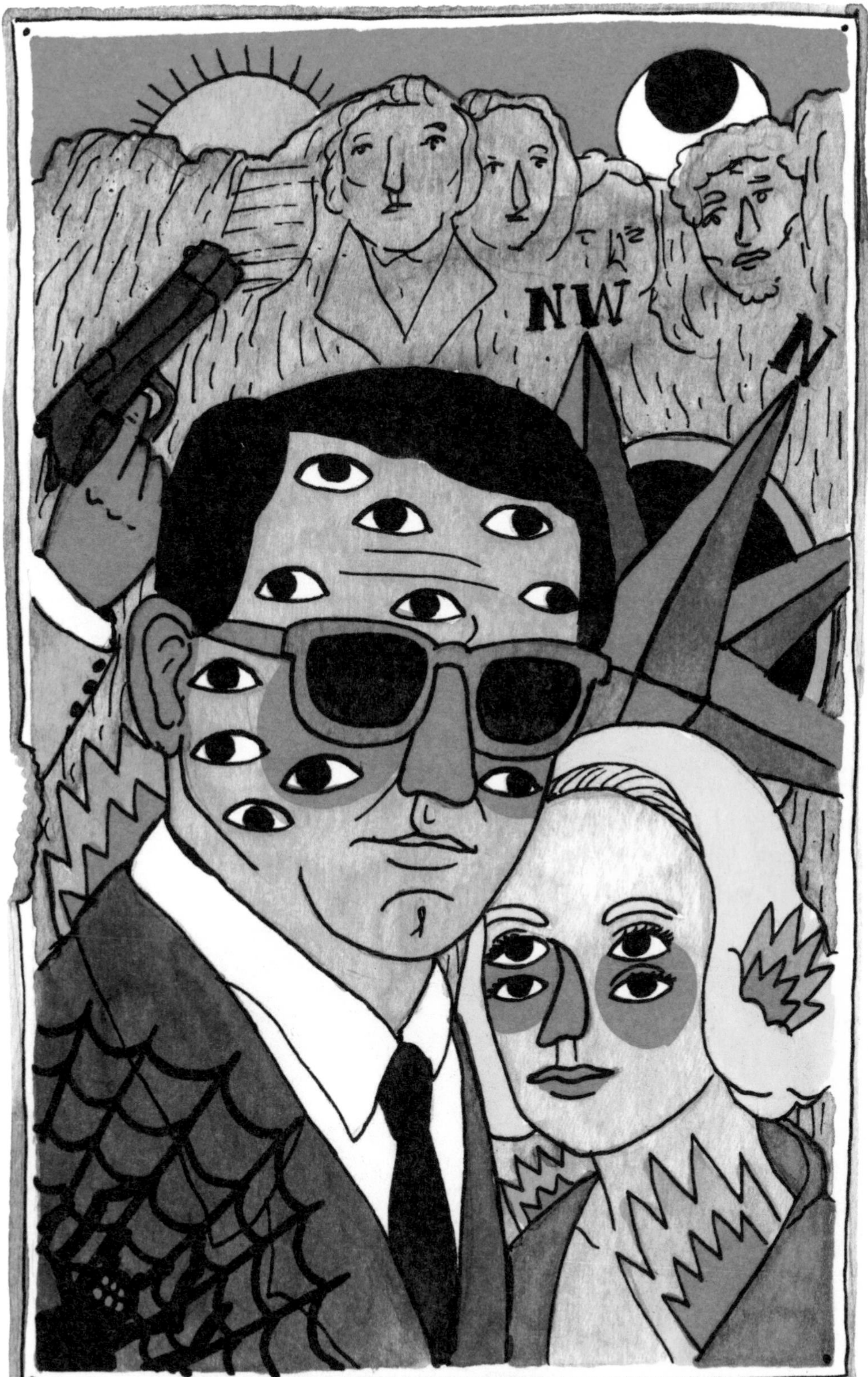
NW
N

NORTH·BY·NORTHWEST

THE·APARTMENT

(1960)

ANOTHER PEARL FROM BILLY WILDER, WITH THE LOVELY JACK LEMMON AND SHIRLEY MACLAINE (WHO I'VE HAD A SOFT SPOT FOR EVER SINCE). FROM THE OPENING SCENES, WITH BAXTER WORKING LATE IN HIS OVERAMBITIOUS INSURANCE OFFICE, WE'RE ON HIS SIDE. WE WANT TO SAVE HIM FROM ALL THAT. WE WANT HIM TO SHINE WITH THE BRILLIANCE WE SUSPECT HE HAS.

i DON'T THINK THERE'S EVER BEEN A LOVE STORY AS BEAUTIFUL AS THIS. THEY'VE TRIED EVERY POSSIBLE WAY TO MAKE ROMANTIC COMEDIES LIKE THIS, BUT IT'S JUST NOT POSSIBLE. AND i ALMOST PREFER IT THAT WAY, SO THIS ONE RETAINS ITS PLACE AS THE BEST LOVE STORY IN CINEMA HISTORY. ♥

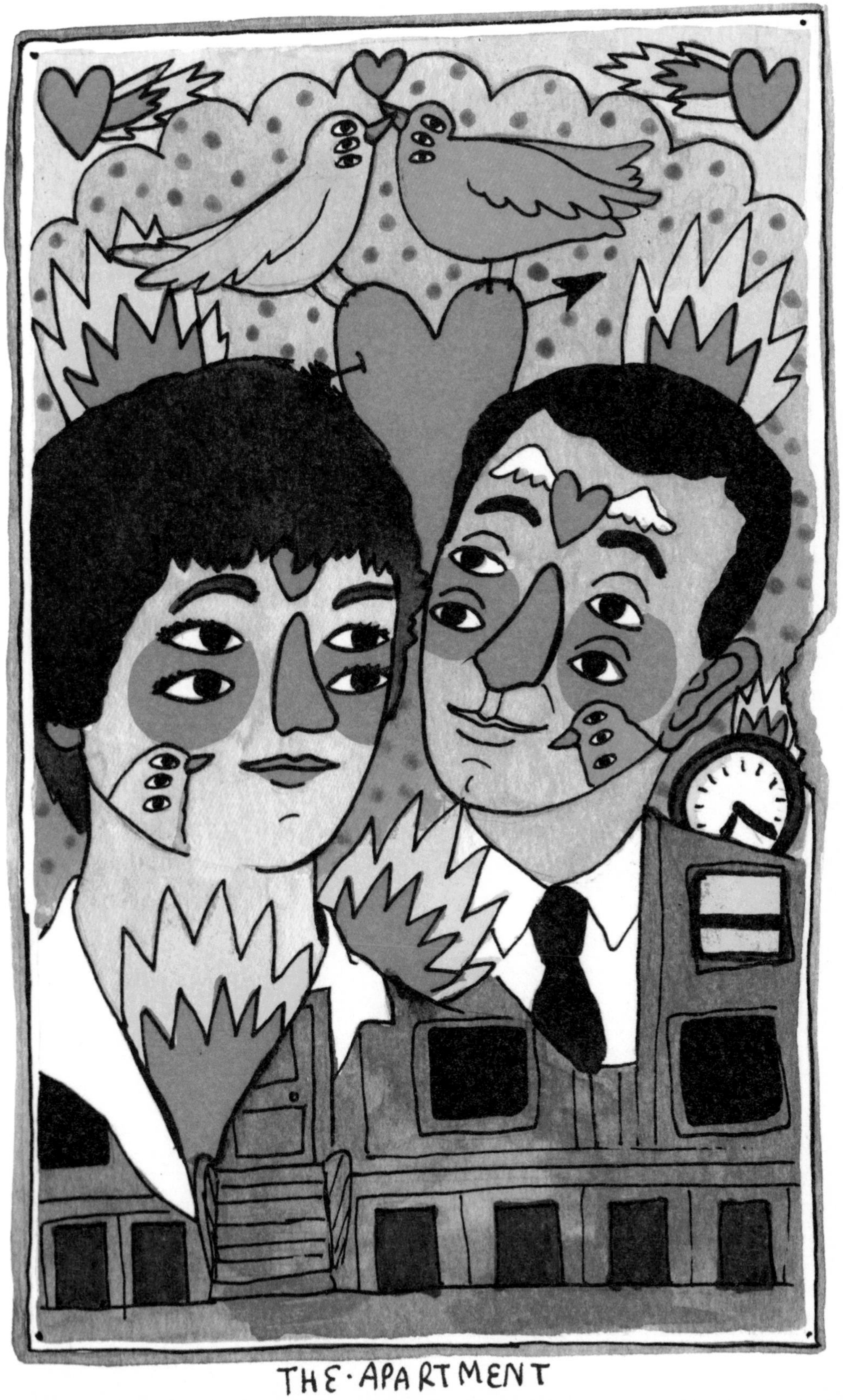

THE · APARTMENT

SPARTACUS

(1960)

I'LL ADMIT IT — I LOVE PEPLUM MOVIES (ALSO KNOWN AS SWORD-AND-SANDAL MOVIES... THOSE EPICS SET IN ANCIENT TIMES). I LIKE THEM ALL, BUT SPARTACUS IS MY FAVOURITE. EVERY TIME IT COMES ON TV I ~~WATCH IT~~ WATCH IT. I GRAB A BLANKET AND SOME SNACKS AND SETTLE DOWN FOR THE BEST THREE HOURS OF THE WEEK. I'M MAD ABOUT THE PEPLUM GENRE IN GENERAL, BUT IF KUBRICK MAKES IT, YOU JUST KNOW IT'S GOING TO BE THE CRÈME DE LA CRÈME. I'VE ALSO ALWAYS BEEN A FAN OF KIRK DOUGLAS. COULD I ASK FOR ANYTHING BETTER? WELL, HOW ABOUT A CLASS STRUGGLE STORY WHERE ONE SLAVE REBELS AGAINST ROME ITSELF. I'M SPELLBOUND BY THE BATTLE SCENE AT SILER RIVER, WHERE THE SLAVES GO TO WAR TO FIGHT FOR THEIR LIBERTY KNOWING THAT THIS IS IT — THERE'S NO GOING BACK. I'M A LEFTY, HOW COULD I NOT LOVE THIS STORY? AND AS THEY SAY AT THE START OF THE MOVIE, SPARTACUS' SACRIFICE BECAME THE TRIUMPH OF HUMANITY. "SPAR-TA-CUS! SPAR-TA-CUS! SPAR-TA-CUS!"

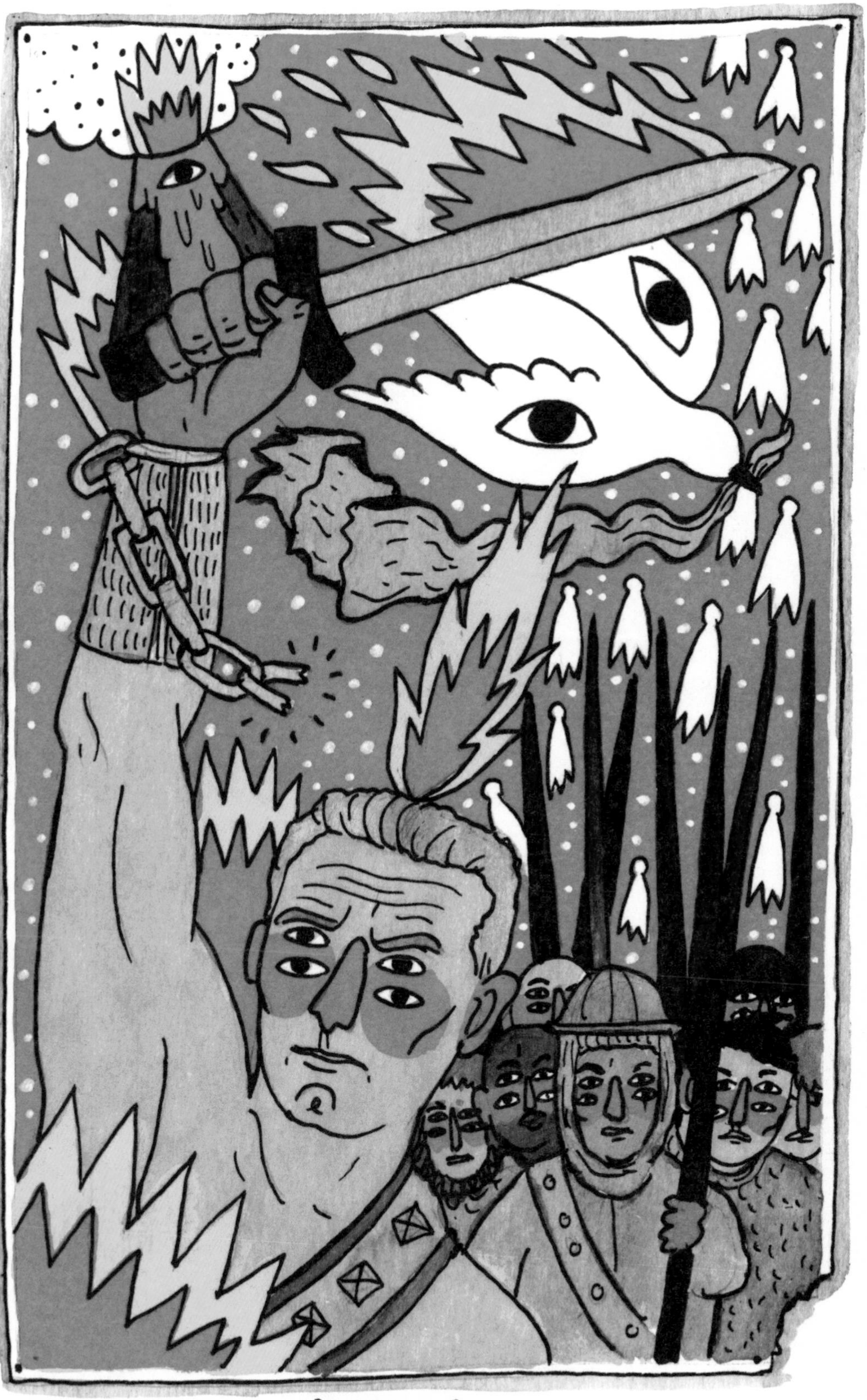

SPARTACUS

LA·DOLCE VITA

(1960)

i'M GOING TO TAKE THIS OPPORTUNITY TO MAKE A
CONFESSION: i'M REALLY AN ITALIAN BORN IN SPAIN.
SONO iTALIANO! AND THIS MOVIE IS ITALIANISSIMA.
iT'S A PERFECT EXERCISE IN HOW THE ITALIANS LOVE
AND RELISH LIFE—SOMEWHERE BETWEEN CONTROLLED
DECADENCE AND AN UNDERSTANDING OF HOW TO LIVE
LIKE GODS. EVEN THE STRUCTURE OF THE MOVIE IS CHAOTIC
AND ~~PLEASING~~ PLEASING AT THE SAME TIME! THROUGH
MASTROIANNI'S EYES WE GET A GLIMPSE OF THE NIGHT
LIFE IN THE ALWAYS-PERFECT STREETS OF ROME. EVERY
FRAME IS WORTHY OF BEING HUNG ON A WALL AS A LESSON
IN STYLE AND ENDURING ELEGANCE. i LOVE iTALY, AND iF
FELLINI IS THE ONE SHOWING IT TO ME, IT BECOMES A TANGIBLE
PARADISE.

VIVA ITALIA!

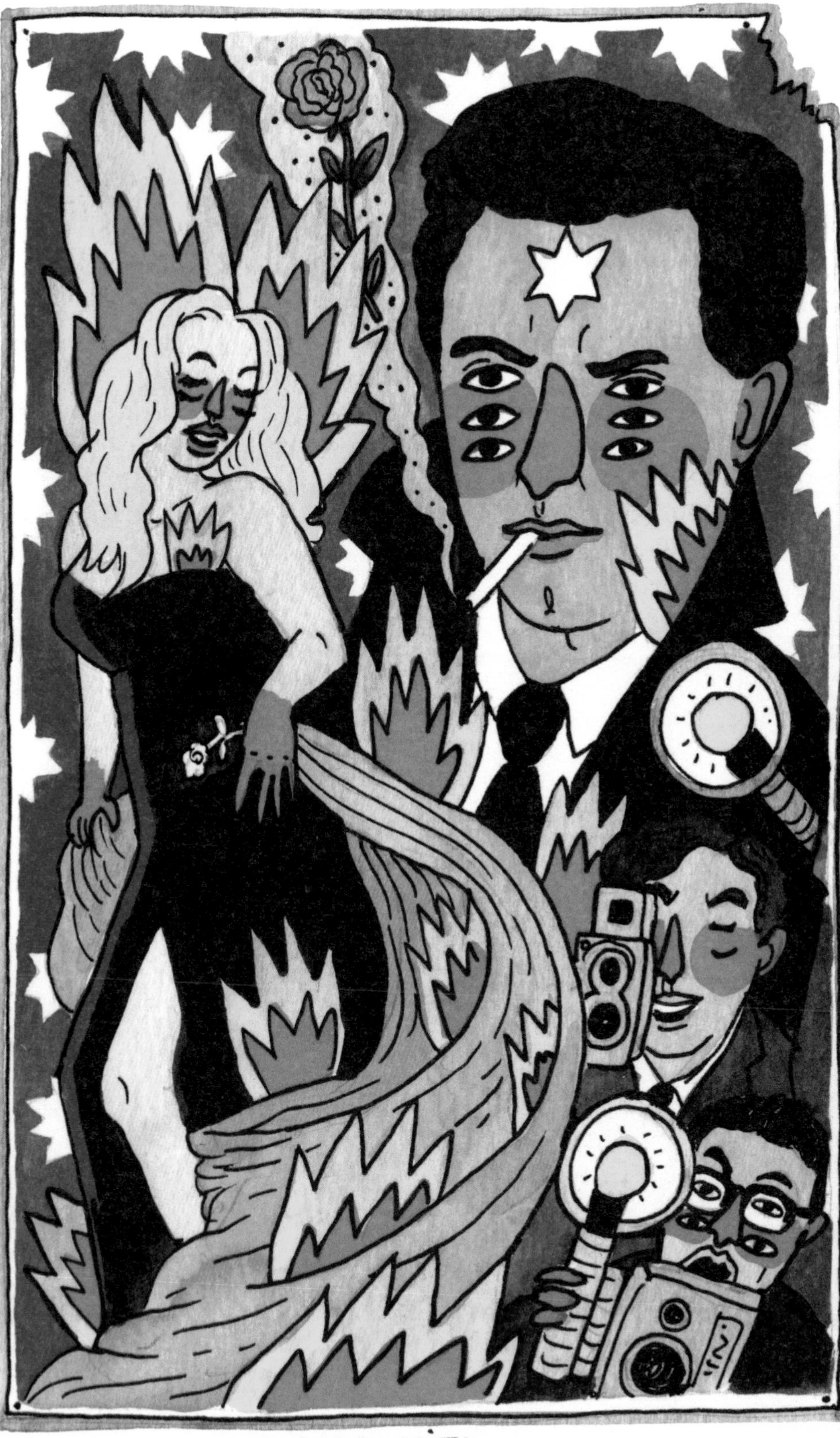

LA · DOLCE · VITA

IRMA · LA DOUCE

(1963)

BACK AGAIN WITH BILLY WILDER'S WINNING FORMULA: A BEAUTIFUL LOVE STORY STARRING JACK LEMMON AND SHIRLEY MACLAINE. YOU MIGHT THINK THAT ONCE YOU'VE WATCHED THE ~~ASS~~ APARTMENT, THERE'S NO NEED TO WATCH THIS. NO WAY! OUR LIVES ARE MADE MORE BEAUTIFUL FOR WATCHING THIS CHARMING, FUNNY STORY. NOW THE SETTING IS AN URBAN PARISIAN NEIGHBOURHOOD BUSTLING WITH PROSTITUTES, PIMPS, AND VEGETABLES LITTERED ALL OVER THE GROUND. AS IF IT WERE A MYTHOLOGICAL TALE, WILDER INTRODUCES US TO LEMMON, A GENDARME CHARGED WITH THE RESPONSIBILITY OF TACKLING AND ERADICATING PROSTITUTION; AND SHIRLEY MACLAINE, ONE OF THE MOST NOTORIOUS HARLOTS ON THE STREETS. IT'S OBVIOUS THEIR PATHS WILL CROSS, AND WE EVEN KNOW HOW IT'LL END — HAPPILY. LOVE IS ALWAYS MORE BEAUTIFUL WHEN BILLY WILDER'S INVOLVED.

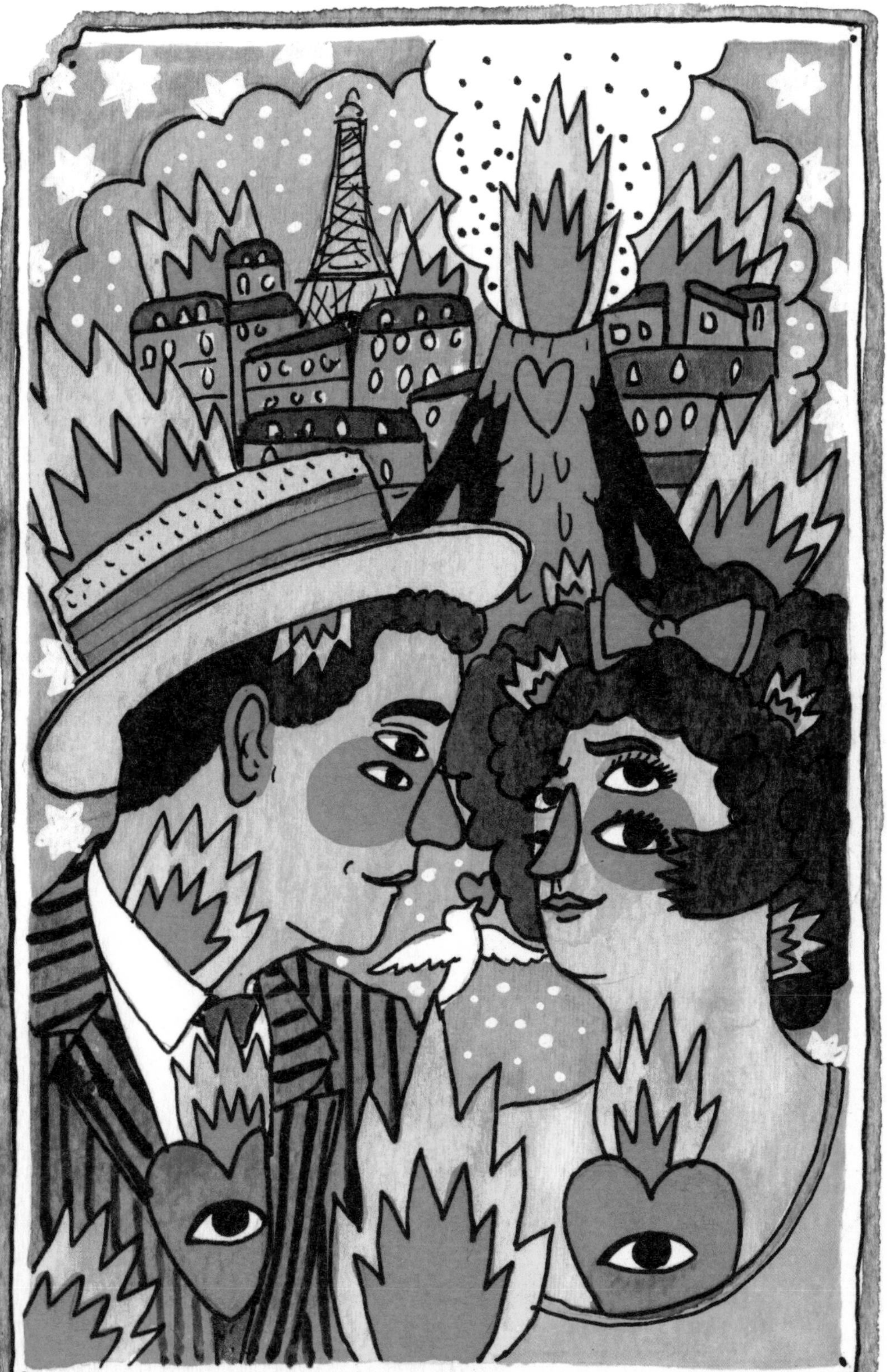

IRMA · LA · DOUCE

IL BUONO · IL BRUTTO · IL CATTIVO

(1966) (THE GOOD, THE BAD AND THE UGLY)

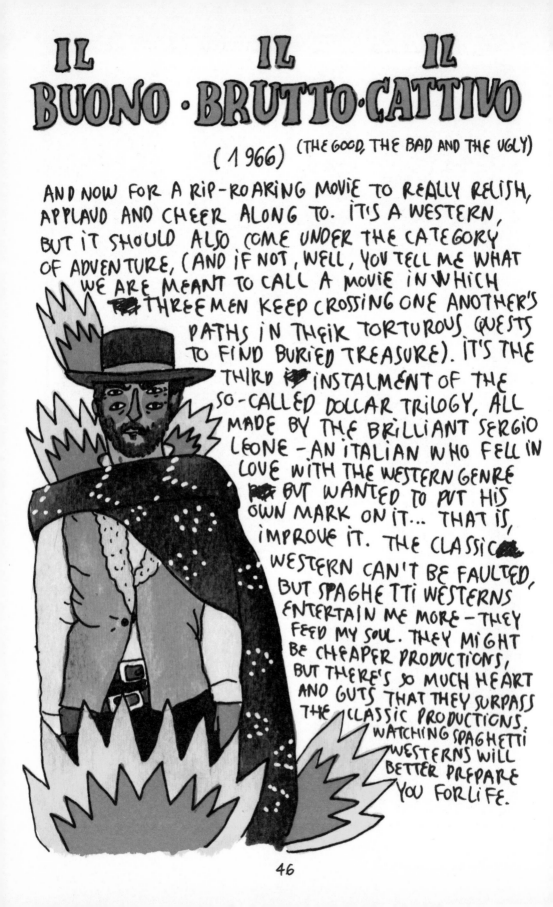

AND NOW FOR A RIP-ROARING MOVIE TO REALLY RELISH, APPLAUD AND CHEER ALONG TO. IT'S A WESTERN, BUT IT SHOULD ALSO COME UNDER THE CATEGORY OF ADVENTURE, (AND IF NOT, WELL, YOU TELL ME WHAT WE ARE MEANT TO CALL A MOVIE IN WHICH THREE MEN KEEP CROSSING ONE ANOTHER'S PATHS IN THEIR TORTUROUS QUESTS TO FIND BURIED TREASURE). IT'S THE THIRD INSTALMENT OF THE SO-CALLED DOLLAR TRILOGY, ALL MADE BY THE BRILLIANT SERGIO LEONE - AN ITALIAN WHO FELL IN LOVE WITH THE WESTERN GENRE BUT WANTED TO PUT HIS OWN MARK ON IT... THAT IS, IMPROVE IT. THE CLASSIC WESTERN CAN'T BE FAULTED, BUT SPAGHETTI WESTERNS ENTERTAIN ME MORE - THEY FEED MY SOUL. THEY MIGHT BE CHEAPER PRODUCTIONS, BUT THERE'S SO MUCH HEART AND GUTS THAT THEY SURPASS THE CLASSIC PRODUCTIONS. WATCHING SPAGHETTI WESTERNS WILL BETTER PREPARE YOU FOR LIFE.

46

IL·BUONO, IL·BRUTTO, IL·CATTIVO

THE·PARTY

(1968)

A COMIC GEM. i ONLY HAVE TO THINK ABOUT PETER SELLERS AND i'M ALREADY LAUGHING. AND IN THE PARTY ~~●~~ IT'S A LAUGH A SECOND. WHEN i WATCH THIS MOVIE, THE SAME FACE MADE BY THE LITTLE BOY WATCHING CHAPLIN OR THE MARX BROTHERS COMES BACK. i'D BE PETER SELLERS' SIDEKICK AT EVERY PARTY IN THE WORLD.

THIS MOVIE IS A RELENTLESS OFFERING OF CLASSIC SLAPSTICK HUMOUR, BUT WITH ADDED SELLERS ~~MAGIC~~.

– A MAN CAPABLE OF GATE CRASHING A PARTY WITH A FLOOD OF FOAM, A BABY ELEPHANT, A DRUNK WAITER, A FLYING CHICKEN AND EVEN A GROUP OF RUSSIAN MUSICIANS. THE MORE CHAOTIC THE PARTY BECOMES, THE BETTER IT GETS, AND THE MORE WE LAUGH. ADD TO THIS THE ORIGINAL SOUNDTRACK BY HENRI MANCINI AND YOU HAVE GOT THE BEST PARTY EVER.

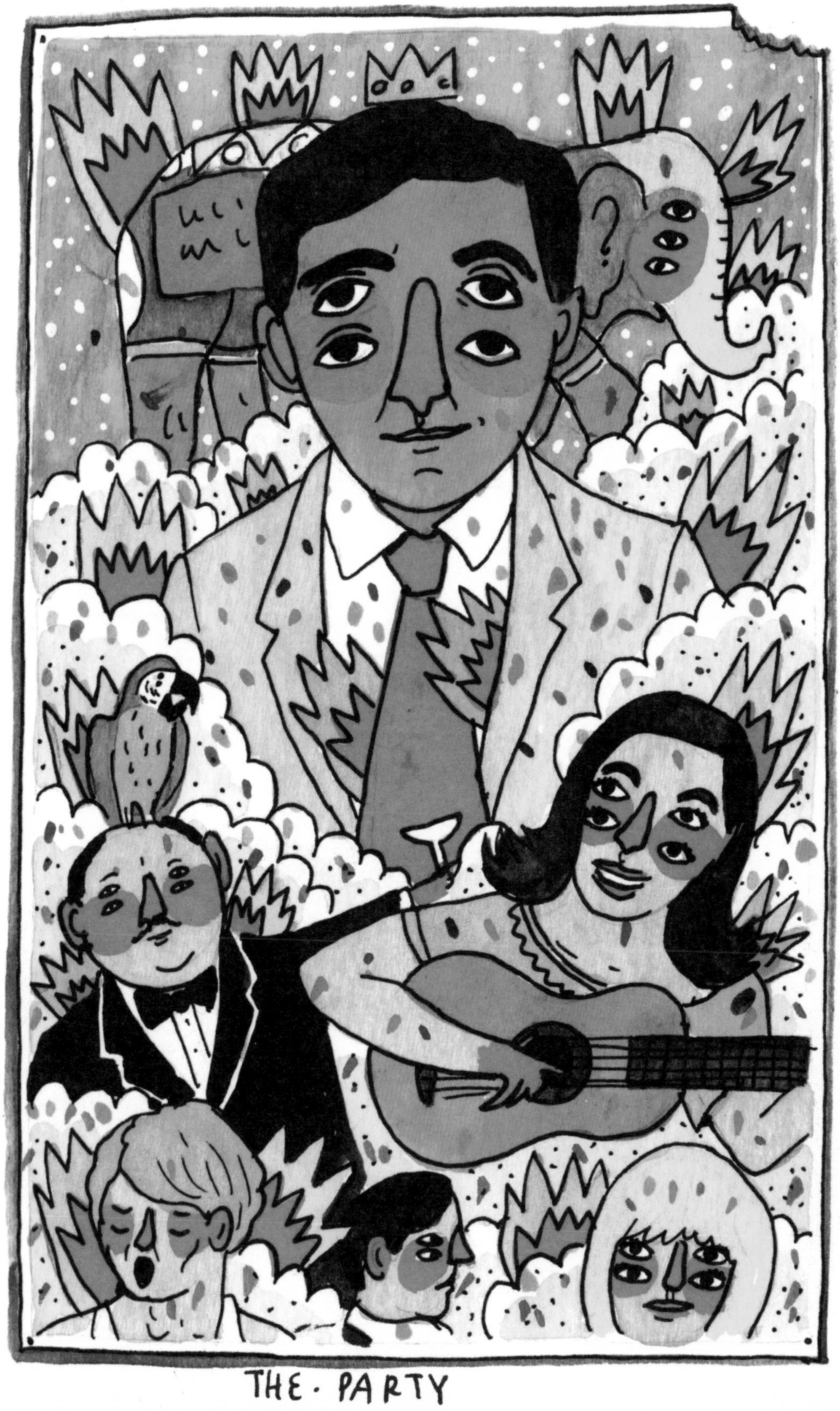

THE · PARTY

NIGHT·OF·THE LIVING·DEAD

(1968)

THEN ALONG CAME GEORGE ROMERO AND HIS ZOMBIES. AND HE BROUGHT THEM TO STAY. THEY'VE EVEN INVADED OUR TVS. ROMERO REALLY INVENTED THE HORROR GENRE, BECAUSE UP UNTIL THEN ZOMBIES WERE SERVILE CREATURES, LINKED WITH HAITI'S FOLKLORE TRADITION. ROMERO TRANSFORMED ~~xxxxxxxxxx~~ THOSE BEINGS INTO EVIL CREATURES THAT WANT TO EAT US ALIVE AND PROLONG THEIR TORMENTED EXISTENCE. HORROR MOVIES FROM BACK IN THE DAY ALWAYS HAVE A TOUCH OF COMEDY BECAUSE OF A LACK OF RESOURCES, AND ROMERO HAD SUCH A RIDICULOUSLY SMALL BUDGET THAT THEY HAD TO SHOOT ALMOST THE ENTIRE MOVIE IN A HOUSE AND ITS GROUNDS. ROMERO PLAYED THIS LIMITATION TO HIS ADVANTAGE, CREATING AN EVEN ~~xxxxx~~ GREATER SENSE OF CLAUSTROPHOBIA. THANKS, ROMERO, FOR BRINGING THE DEAD BACK TO LIFE FOR US.

NIGHT · OF · THE · LIVING · DEAD

The Godfather

(I, II, III / 1972-1990)

AND AT LAST WE GET TO THE MAIN EVENT.
I HAVE A REAL SOFT SPOT FOR ITALIAN-AMERICAN MAFIA
MOVIES. DESPITE HAVING BEEN BORN IN SPAIN, I'M ITALIAN,
AND WATCHING A MOVIE LIKE THE GODFATHER IS LIKE
READING MY OWN BIBLE. COPPOLA'S MASTERPIECE TURNS
ME INTO A CORLEONE, AND FRANKLY, I'M HONOURED TO
BE PART OF THE FAMIGLIA. GOD KNOWS HOW MANY
TIMES I'VE WATCHED THE FIRST TWO MOVIES IN THE
TRILOGY. AS I'VE SAID, I REALLY LIKE FAMILY SAGAS,
AND THIS IS THE QUEEN OF THEM ALL. EVERY
SINGLE CHARACTER IS RIPE FOR THEIR OWN
SPIN-OFF. THIS IS COPPOLA AT HIS BEST. AND THE
STORY ITSELF MAKES ME WANT TO CURSE THE
PLACE AND TIME I LIVE IN AND WISH I COULD BE
TELEPORTED TO CONNIE CORLEONE'S WEDDING ~~WHERE THE~~
WHERE THAT UNIVERSE BEGINS.
THANK YOU COPPOLA, FOR
MAKING ME FEEL LIKE
PART OF THE FAMILY.
        GRAZIE.

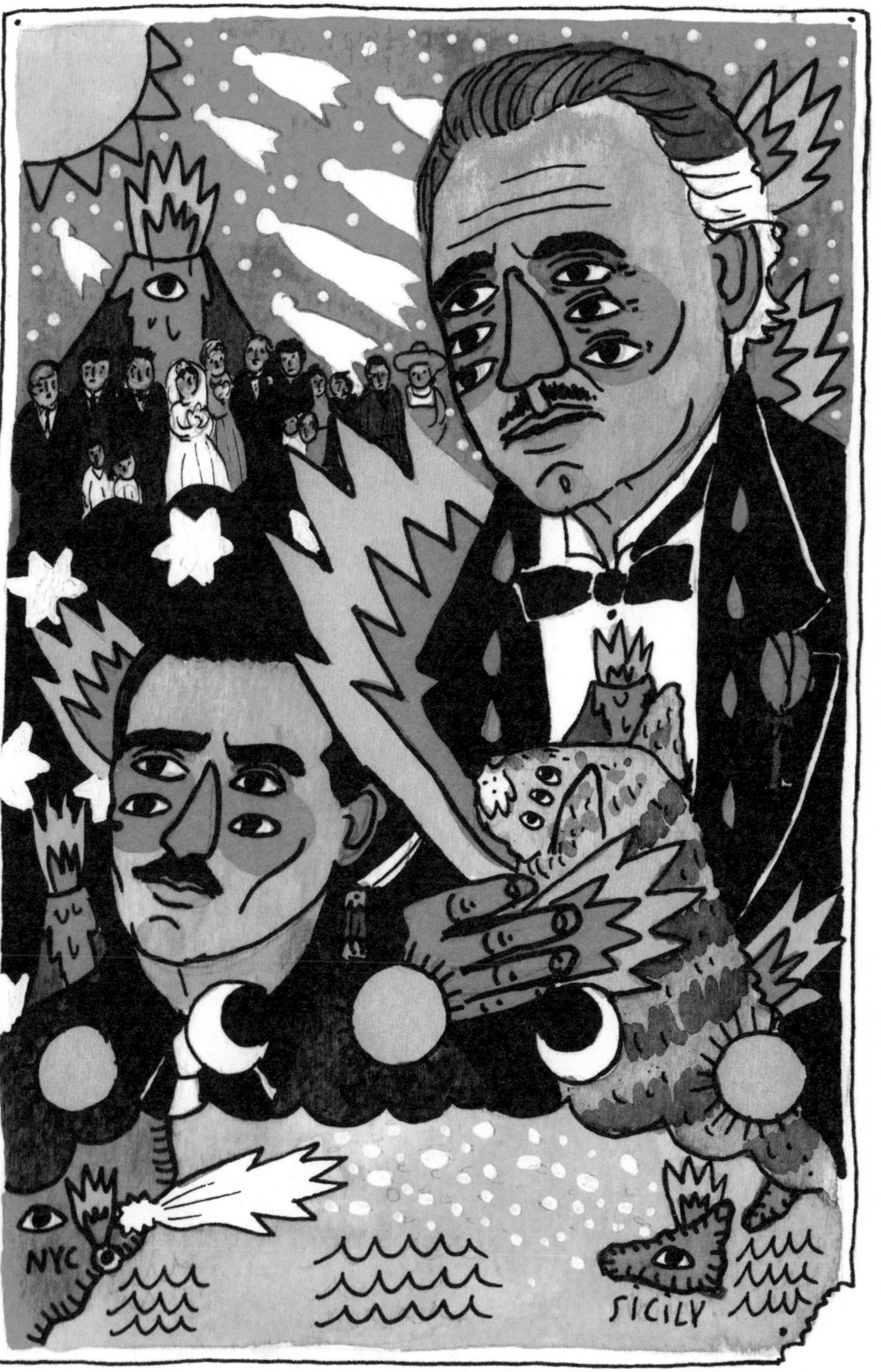
NYC
SICILY

THE · GODFATHER

THE·STING

(1973)

POSSIBLY ONE OF THE THREE MOST ENTERTAINING MOVIES OF ALL TIME.
THIS STORY OF FRAUDSTERS AND MOBSTERS DURING THE 1920s DEPRESSION DOESN'T LET UP FOR A SINGLE SECOND. THERE ARE SO MANY TWISTS AND TURNS AND DOUBLE DEALINGS IN EVERY SEQUENCE THAT YOU HAVE TO PAT YOUR POCKET TO MAKE SURE YOUR WALLET HASN'T BEEN LIFTED! THERE'S NO BETTER PAIR FOR THIS THAN PAUL NEWMAN AND ROBERT REDFORD. FROM THE FIRST SECOND, YOU FEEL DAZZLED BY THE EASY, SUPERIOR AURA THEY GIVE OFF. I STILL REMEMBER WHEN I SAW IT FOR THE FIRST TIME. I MUST HAVE BEEN ABOUT 11 OR 12 AND I WAS BOWLED OVER THAT A MOVIE FROM THIS GENRE COULD BE SO ENTERTAINING AND SO FUNNY. IN FACT, I EVEN FANTASIZED ABOUT FOLLOWING IN NEWMAN AND REDFORD'S FOOTSTEPS.

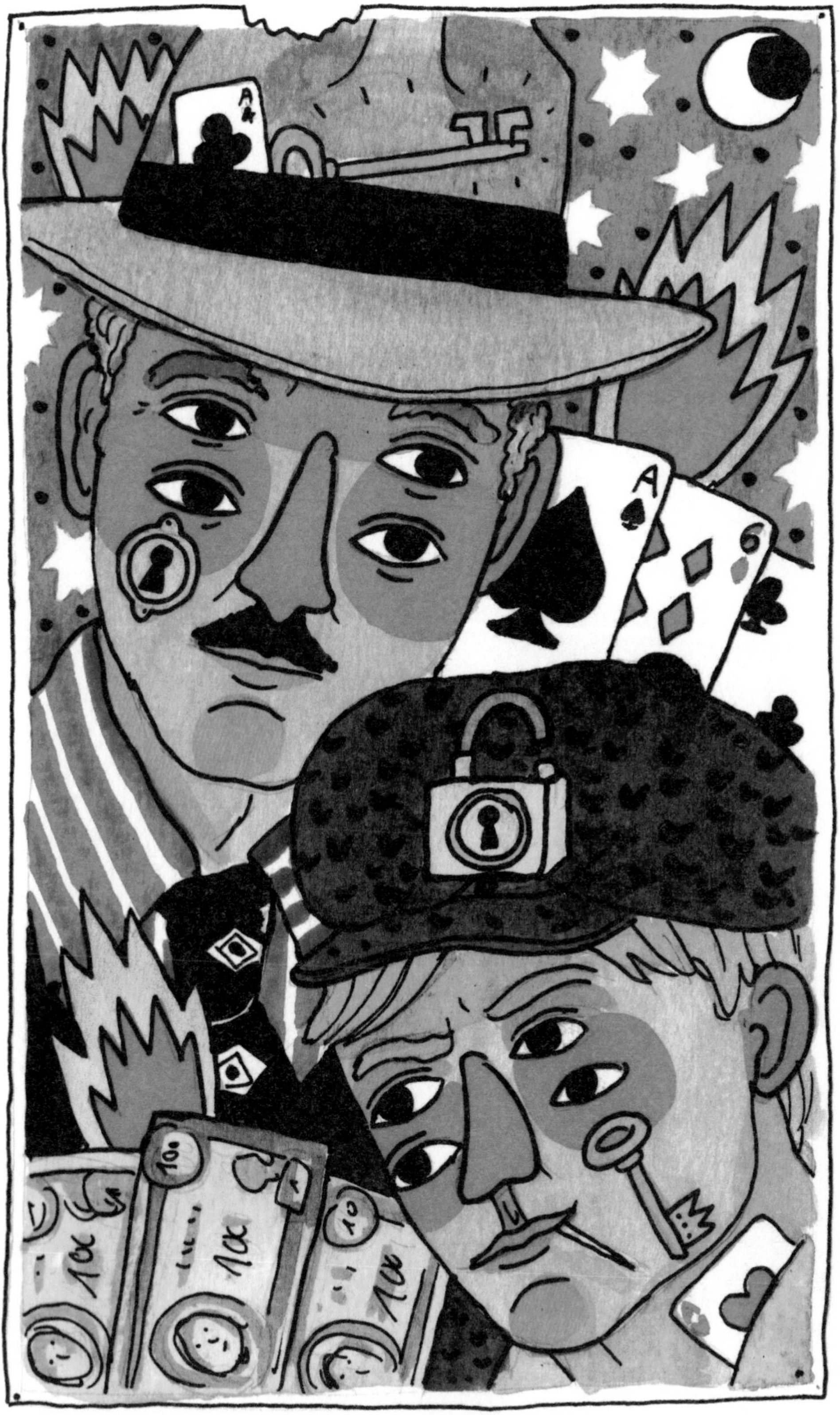

THE· STING

AMARCORD

(1973)

ANOTHER FROM MY PERSONAL BIBLE OF ITALIANISMO. I STILL WANT TO BE MORE ITALIAN AND LIVE IN BORGO, THE FICTIONAL TOWN WHERE THIS MOVIE IS SET. IT MIGHT BE MADE UP, BUT BORGO REFLECTS A VERY REAL AND TRULY DELIGHTFUL RURAL ITALY.

HERE, ON THE TOWN'S STREETS, FELLINI MAKES A SURREAL WORLD COLLIDE WITH PERFECT ITALIAN REALISM. HIS COMBINATION BRIMS WITH MAGIC, BUT AT THE SAME TIME IS BELIEVABLE AND TRUE TO LIFE. EVERY TIME I WATCH AMARCORD I SPEND THE FOLLOWING DAYS SEARCHING FOR MAGIC IN THE CITY WHERE I LIVE... AND I ALWAYS FIND IT! THIS MOVIE GIVES YOU A FRESH PAIR OF EYES. I SPENT A YEAR LIVING IN ITALY AND I REMEMBER THE FIRST MOVIE I SAW THERE WAS AMARCORD, AND I THOUGHT: "OH YES, I'M IN THE DREAM COUNTRY".

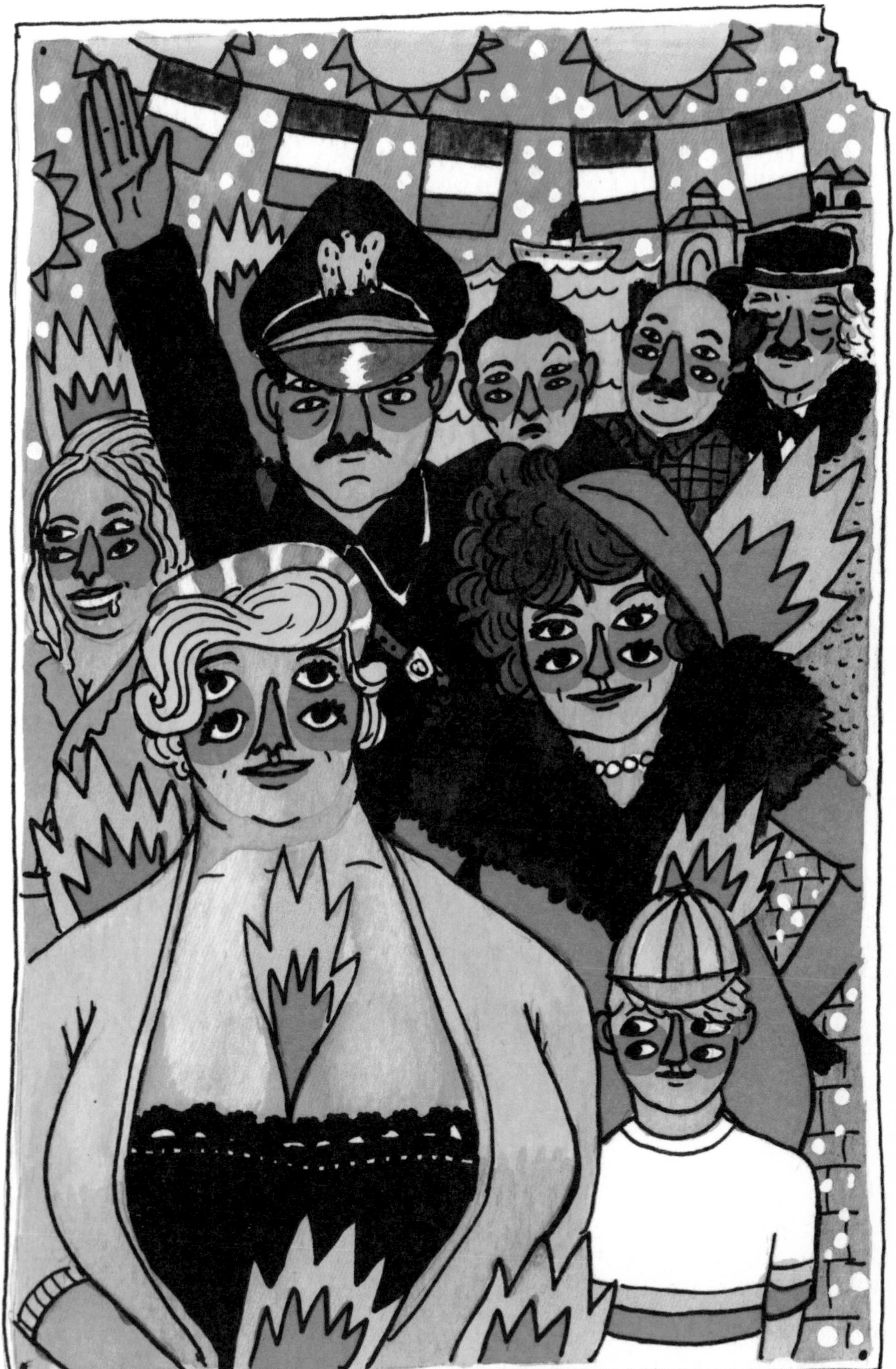

AMARCORD

GREY·GARDENS

(1975)

THIS DOCUMENTARY IS ABOUT ONE OF THE
THINGS THAT MOST INTERESTS ME IN THE WORLD
— EXTRAORDINARY PEOPLE WHO DON'T FIT INTO
SOCIETY. THEY ARE REJECTED BY OTHERS, BUT HOLD
A GREAT TREASURE INSIDE OF THEMSELVES. THIS
~~WE~~ DOCUMENTARY FOLLOWS THE LIVES OF A ~~A~~
MOTHER AND ~~A~~ DAUGHTER (THE AUNT AND
COUSIN OF JACKIE KENNEDY), USED TO LIVING
FROM PARTY TO PARTY IN NEW YORK'S HIGH
SOCIETY. BUT THEY'VE ENDED UP COOPED UP
IN A MANSION IN THE HAMPTONS. NEVER
LEAVING THE GROUNDS, LIVING IN THEIR OWN
CELEBRITY UNIVERSE SURROUNDED BY RUBBISH,
THOUSANDS OF MAGAZINES, RACCOONS AND
FANCY DRESSES THAT THEY SPEND ALL DAY TRYING
ON. THIS DOCUMENTARY IS A DOOR TO AN
INCREDIBLE WORLD THAT COMPLETELY ~~DOOR~~
DUMBFOUNDS ME. COME WITH ME INTO GREY
GARDENS AND DISCOVER A WHOLE NEW DIMENSION.

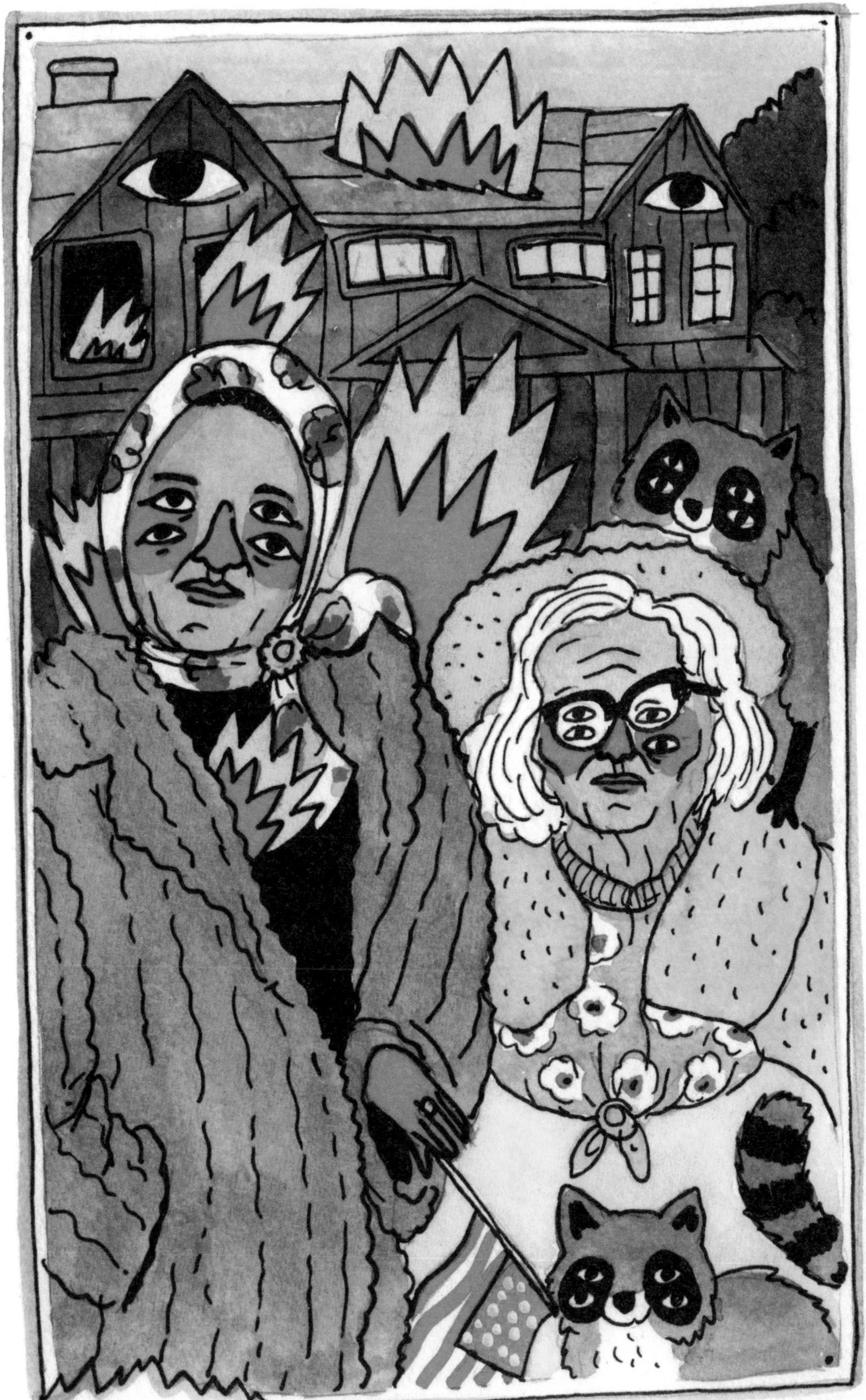

GREY · GARDENS

STAR WARS

(IV, V, VI / 1977-1983)

FINALLY, WE GET TO ONE OF THE HIGHLIGHTS OF MY CINEMATOGRAPHIC LOVE FEST. THERE'S SO MUCH TO SAY ABOUT THIS ONE i MIGHT TRIP OVER MY OWN TONGUE. i CAN ONLY SAY THAT i FEEL HAPPY EVERY TIME i WATCH EPISODES 4, 5, AND 6 OF THE SAGA. GEORGE LUCAS KNEW HOW TO CREATE A WORLD THAT YOU NEVER GROW TIRED OF, AND WHOSE EVERY INHABITANT ON EACH PLANET, YOU'D LIKE TO GET TO KNOW. AND THEN OF COURSE iT'S A FANTASY STORY WHICH ALSO TALKS ABOUT MORE PROFOUND AND SERIOUS THINGS. iT'S AN UNBEATABLE COMBINATION AND i KNOW i'LL LOVE iT TILL MY LAST WAKING MOMENT. THE OPENING THEME TUNE COMES ON WITH THAT SCROLLING TEXT ABOUT THE REBELLION AND THE EMPIRE AND i LITERALLY START JUMPING IN MY SEAT. i TURN INTO AN 8-YEAR-OLD BOY SEEING THE MOVIE FOR THE FIRST TIME, COMPLETELY AGOG. i LOVE ALL THE CHARACTERS—THE GOODIES, THE BADDIES, AND THE NEUTRAL ONES. AND i LOVE THE SPECIAL EFFECTS FROM THAT TIME. THE SOUND FROM THE X-WING STARFIGHTERS' LASERS MAKES MY HAIR STAND ON END. VIVA THE REBELLION!

BUT VIVA THE EMPIRE, TOO!

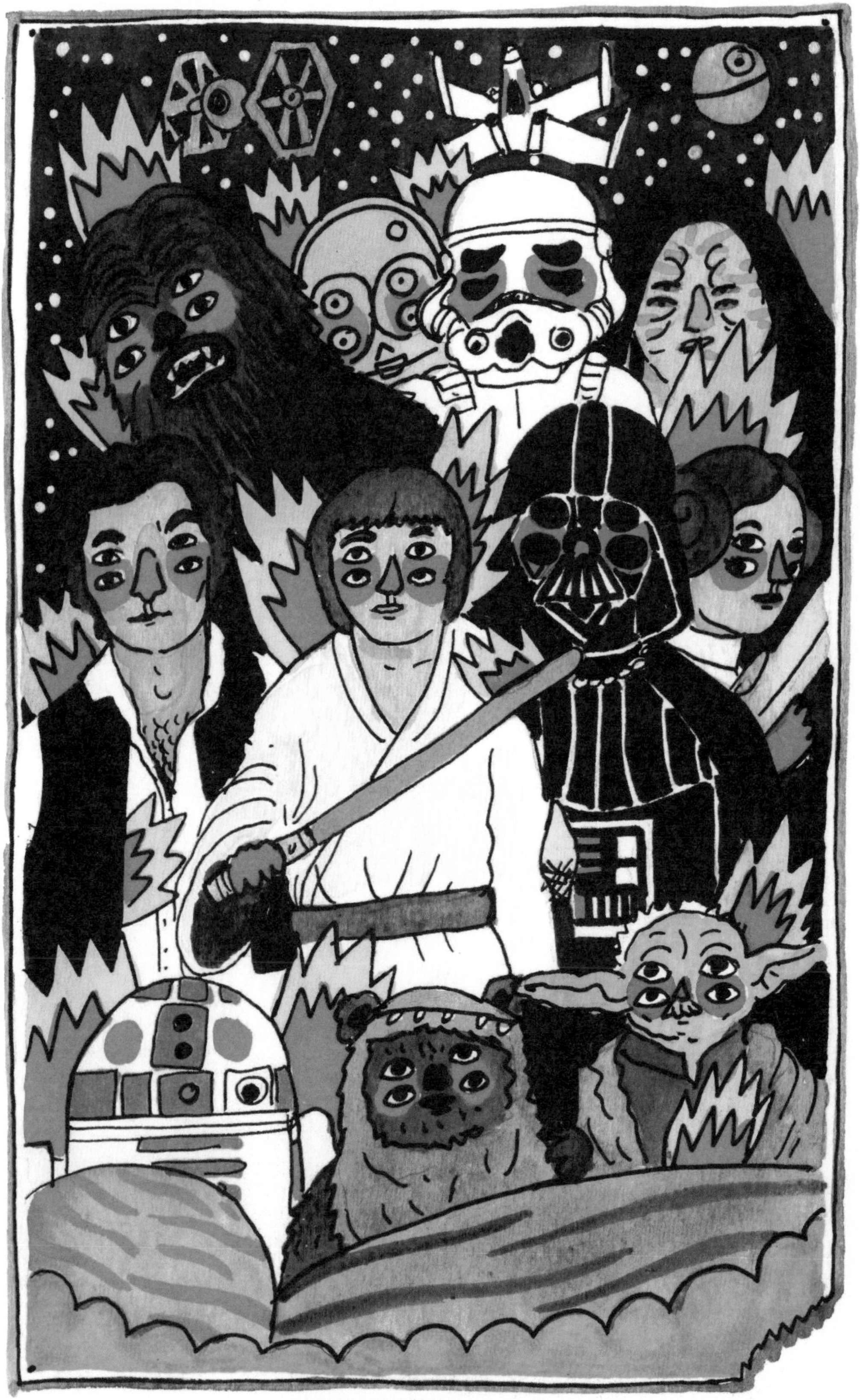

STAR-WARS.

GREASE

(1978)

WHAT I'M ABOUT TO TELL YOU IS TRUE. AS A CHILD I TOOK PART IN ONE OR TWO CHILDREN'S FASHION SHOWS. AND I REMEMBER ONE IN PARTICULAR WHERE ALL THE BOYS HAD TO DRESS UP AS JOHN TRAVOLTA IN GREASE. I HAD TO WALK LIKE DANNY ZUKO, STRUTTING MY STUFF AND TOUCHING UP MY WIG WITH MY POCKET COMB. FROM THAT DAY ON, I'VE ALWAYS HAD A SPECIAL AFFINITY FOR DANNY AND GREASE. AND ASIDE FROM THAT, I LOVE THIS MOVIE BECAUSE IT'S SUCH A FUN DEPICTION OF 1950s AMERICAN HIGH SCHOOL. I WANTED TO BE THERE AND BE ONE OF THE T-BIRDS, ~~XXXXX~~ DAMN IT! I'M NOT A GREAT LOVER OF MUSICALS, BUT IN THIS CASE I COULDN'T CARE LESS. QUITE THE CONTRARY, IT ADDS SOMETHING TO THIS IDYLLIC SETTING. IN FACT, I KNOW ALMOST ALL THE SONGS WORD FOR WORD. "DO A SPLIT, GIVE A YELL, SHAKE A TIT FOR OL' RYDELL!"

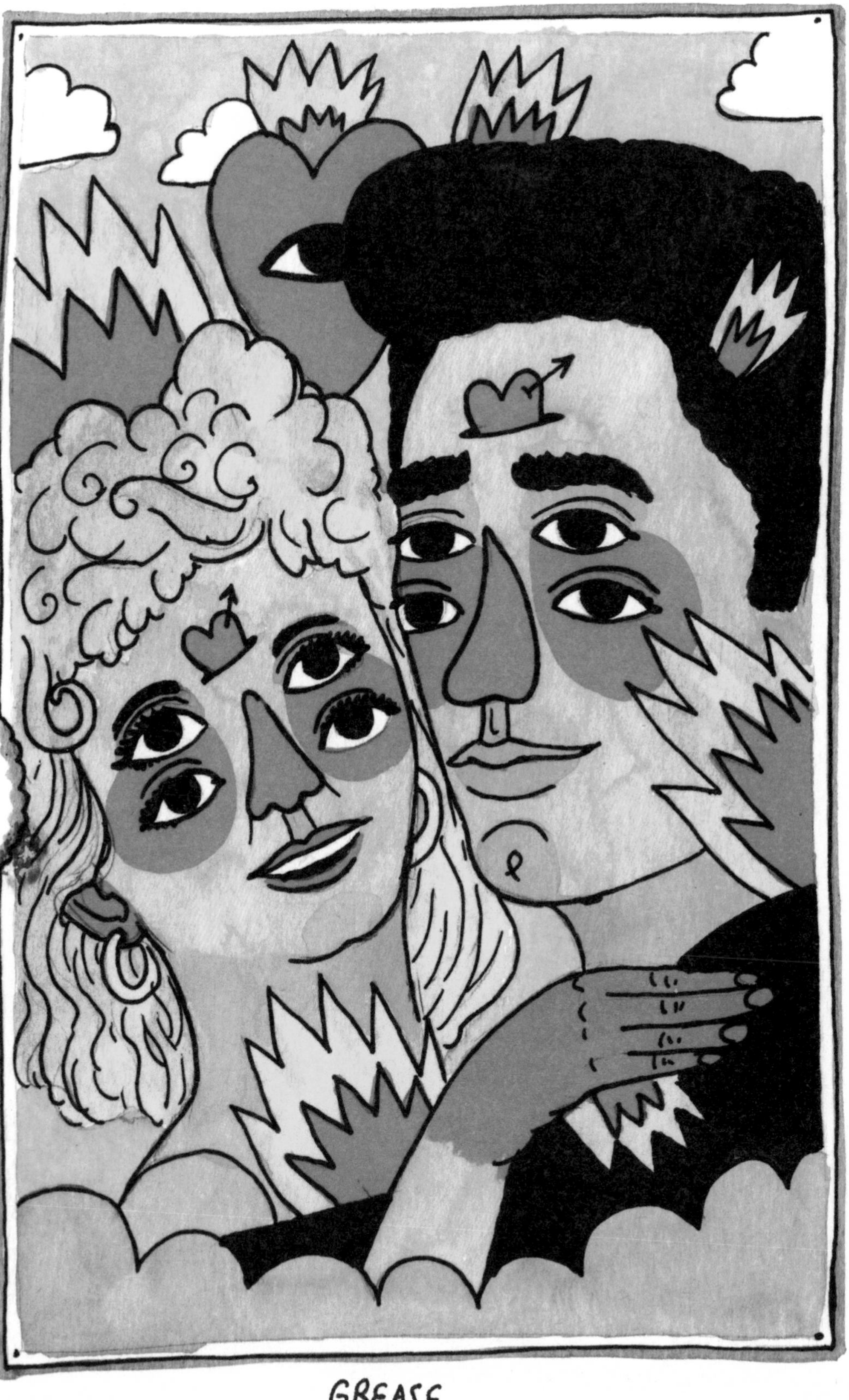

GREASE

Apocalypse Now

(1 9 7 9)

i THINK THE FIRST THING i THOUGHT AFTER SEEING COPPOLA'S MASTERPIECE FOR THE FIRST TIME WAS: "WELL, NOW i'M A BIT MORE GROWN-UP THAN i WAS." COPPOLA THROWS US iNTO THE VIETNAM WAR. iT'S A NIGHTMARE OF NON-STOP SHOCKING, TERRIBLE SiGHTS. BUT AT THE SAME TIME, YOU DON'T WANT TO GET OUT OF THERE.

AFTER SEEING APOCALYPSE NOW YOU'RE NOT JUST OLDER — YOU'RE WISER TOO. iT MAKES YOU CONFRONT THE SAME DEMONS THAT MARTIN SHEEN AND MARLON BRANDO BATTLE WITH, AND EVEN IF YOU DON'T KILL THEM, YOU LEARN HOW TO GET IN AND OUT OF THAT DARKNESS.

i DON'T THINK ANYONE OTHER THAN COPPOLA HAS BEEN ABLE TO PRODUCE THE SAME FEELING OF BEING iN THE MiDST OF THAT TORTUROUS WAR AND SIMULTANEOUSLY COMBINE iT WiTH THAT DARK, SYMBOLiC MAGiC AS SHEEN ENTERS THE JUNGLE. iN THE END iT'S A TIMELESS FEAT.

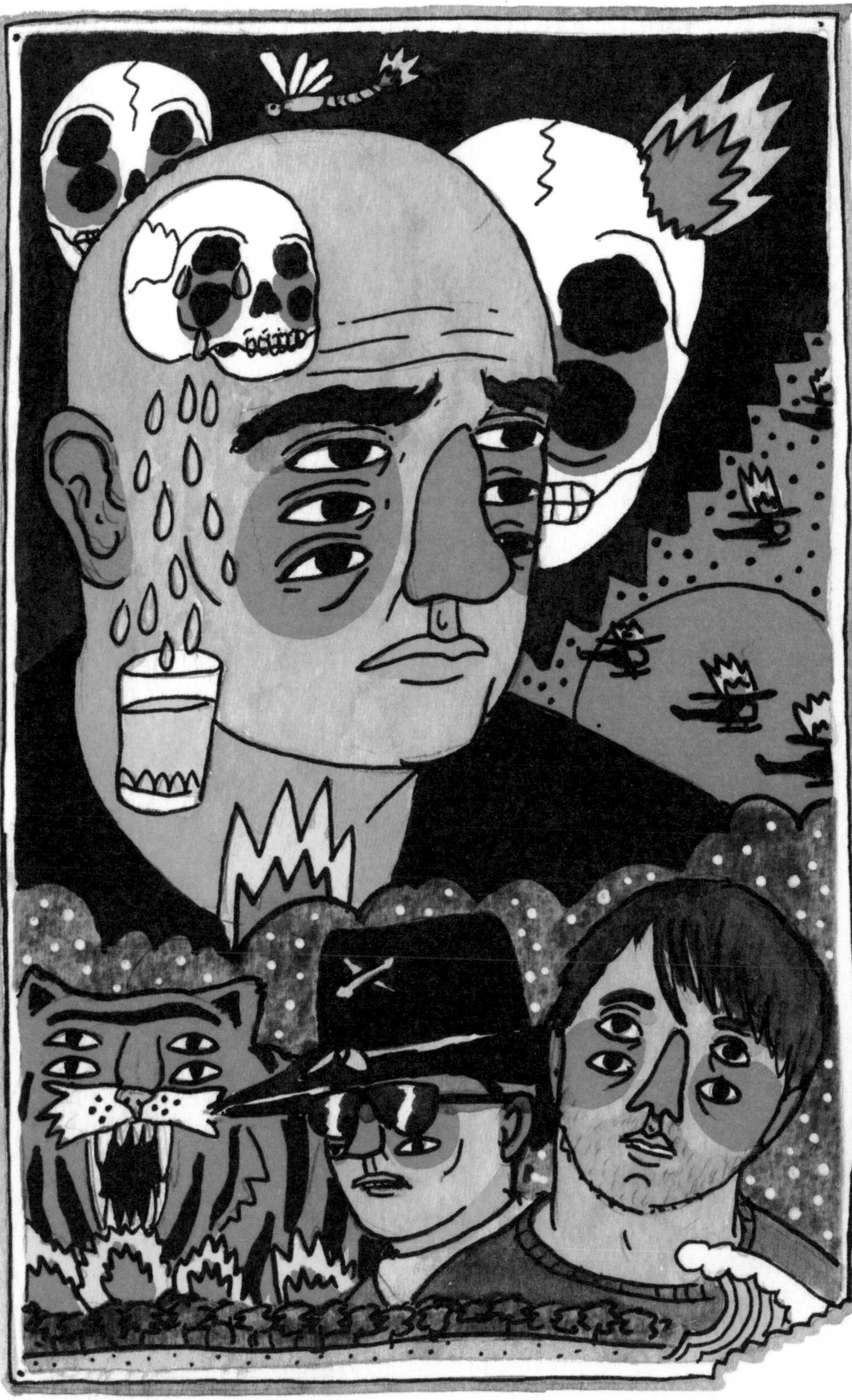

APOCALYPSE NOW

RAGING·BULL

(1980)

AT LAST WE GET TO MY FAVOURITE DIRECTOR.
MARTIN SCORSESE IS SO INTEGRAL TO MY LIFE THAT i
CALL HIM UNCLE MARTIN. HE'S FAMILY, WHETHER HE
KNOWS ~~IT~~ IT OR NOT. i LOVE EVERYTHING HE DOES, AND
SOME OF HIS MOVIES HAVE GENUINELY CHANGED MY LIFE.
i THINK MY MATURITY IN CERTAIN THINGS WAS THANKS
TO SCORSESE. WITH RAGING BULL, HE TAKES DE NIRO BY
THE HAND AND CREATES A BLACK AND WHITE BLOCKBUSTER
ABOUT THE LIFE OF THE BOXER JAKE LAMOTTA. THIS IS
ANOTHER MOVIE THAT NARRATES ONE PERSON'S LIFE
OVER SEVERAL DECADES, IN THIS CASE TRACING THE
UPS AND MOST OF ALL THE DOWNS OF THIS CHARACTER.
AND LEST WE FORGET JOE PESCI'S MAGNIFICENT
STARRING ROLE.
SCORSESE SAID HE PUT EVERYTHING HE KNEW AND
FELT INTO THE MOVIE, AND HE WAS SURE THAT THIS ~~WOULD~~
WOULD BE THE END OF HIS CAREER. A KAMIKAZE
MOVIE: YOU GIVE IT ALL YOU'VE GOT, FORGET ABOUT IT,
AND THEN TRY TO FIND ANOTHER WAY TO LIVE.
i THINK THAT'S THE BEST WAY TO MAKE ART.
HOW COULD i NOT ADORE UNCLE MARTIN?

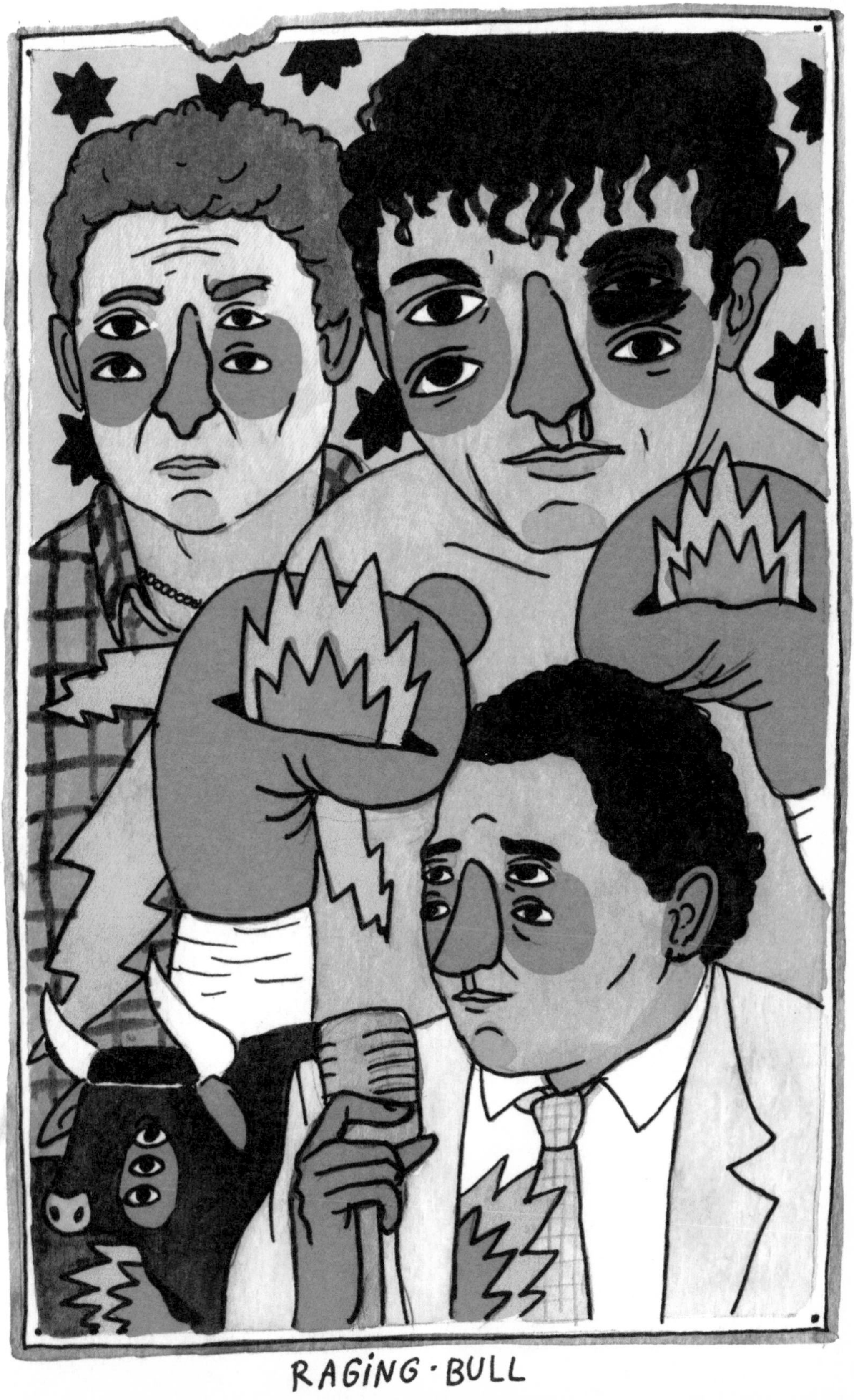

RAGING · BULL

INDIANA·JONES

(I, II, III / 1981-1989)

HALF OF MY CHILDHOOD FANTASIES ~~WERE~~ CAME FROM THE INDIANA JONES MOVIES. i WAS SO OBSESSED WITH THE ARCHAEOLOGIST'S ADVENTURES THAT i EVEN MADE MY OWN NOTEBOOK LIKE THE ONE HIS FATHER WENT AROUND WITH AND WHICH CONTAINED CLUES ABOUT HOW TO REACH THE HOLY GRAIL ALIVE. i COPIED ALL THE MAPS AND TEXTS i COULD MAKE OUT FROM@ FREEZE FRAMES. MAN, WHAT i WOULD HAVE GIVEN TO BE INDIANA JONES. i FELT LIKE I WAS MADE FOR ADVENTURES LIKE THOSE. i'D GUESS EVERYTHING THAT WOULD HAPPEN IN THE MOVIE A SECOND BEFORE iT ACTUALLY DiD. BEHIND MY FATHER'S HOUSE THERE WAS A CLEARING WITH TREES, DUMPED RUBBISH AND WEEDS AND i WOULD SPEND ENTIRE AFTERNOONS THERE PLAYING AT BEING INDIANA JONES AND DISCOVERING TREASURE. BUT IN MY ~~OWN~~ ADVENTURES THERE WERE NEVER ENEMY NATIVE TRIBES. NO, THEY WERE ALWAYS ~~on~~ ON MY SIDE (i NEVER LIKED HOW THEY WERE REPRESENTED, THE SAME AS IN WESTERNS).

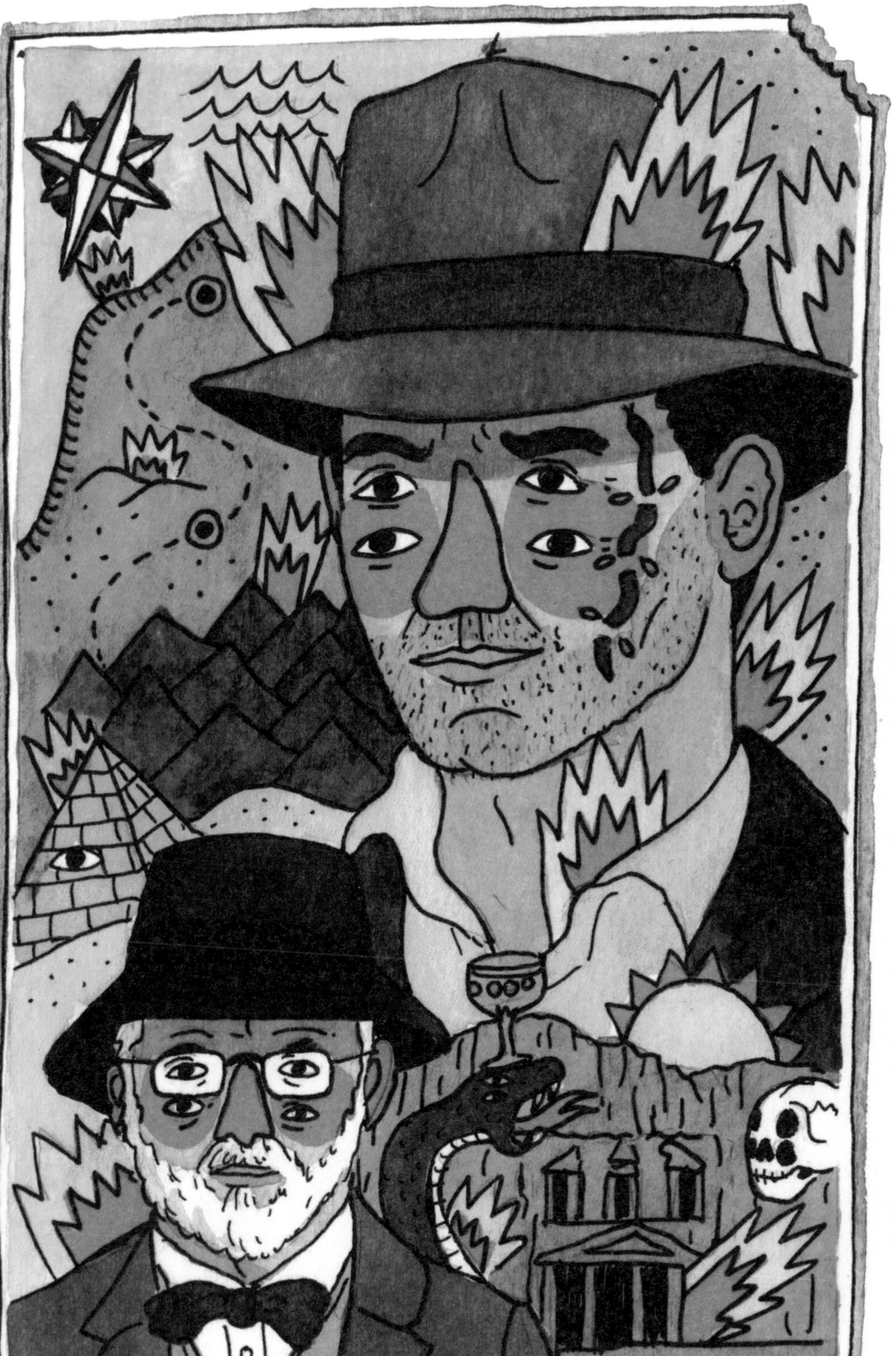

INDIANA JONES

CONAN

THE·BARBARIAN

(1982)

CONAN IS ANOTHER CHARACTER IN MY LIFE WHO'S LIKE FAMILY. MY FATHER HAD DOZENS OF COMICS OF THE BARBARIAN HERO, WHICH I WOULD DEVOUR BEFORE I EVEN KNEW HOW TO READ. ALSO, MY FIRST DOG, AN ENORMOUS GERMAN SHEPHERD, WAS CALLED CONAN. AND TO TOP IT ALL OFF, I DISCOVERED THAT THE CONAN MOVIE STARRED ARNOLD SCHWARZENEGGER. MY HEAD BURST. I THINK IT WAS MY FIRST CONTACT WITH THE SWORD AND SORCERY GENRE, WHICH WOULD DEVELOP INTO AN INORDINATE LOVE OF ROLE-PLAYING GAMES. THIS MOVIE PUT MY FIRST HERO IN MOTION. CONAN THE BARBARIAN WAS MY ORIGINAL IDOL, AND SEEING HIM WAS LIKE AN APPARITION OF THE VIRGIN MARY. I SOAKED UP EVERY SECOND OF EVERY DETAIL ON THE SCREEN. I'M PRETTY SURE THAT I DRAW THE THINGS I DRAW TODAY BECAUSE ~~THEY~~ THEY RELATE SOMEHOW TO EVERYTHING I STORED IN MY HEAD FROM CONAN. CROM!!!

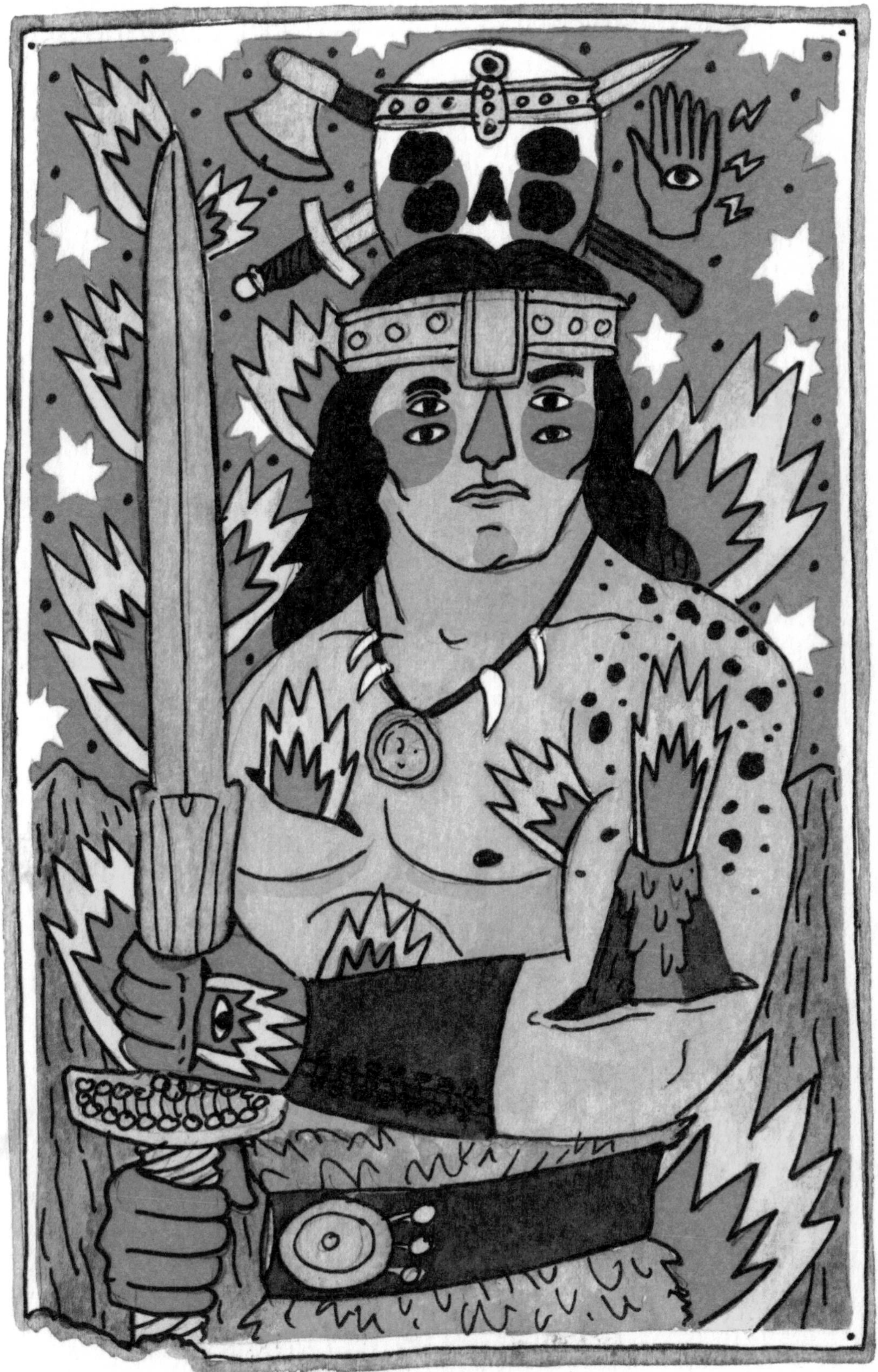

CONAN · THE · BARBARIAN

ONCE·UPON·A·TIME IN AMERICA

(1984)

AND WE ARE BACK WITH THE ● HISTORY OF THE ITALIAN-AMERICANS AND THEIR "AFFAIRS" IN ● NEW YORK, NOW AT THE HANDS OF SERGIO LEONE.

HE DID A ● BEAUTIFUL JOB HIGHLIGHTING, THROUGH THE EYES OF AN EUROPEAN, WHAT WAS HAPPENING IN THE U.S. IN THE EARLY TWENTIETH CENTURY — THE ARRIVAL OF THE EUROPEAN IMMIGRANTS AND THEIR ADAPTATION TO THIS NEW COUNTRY (SOMETIMES WITH UNORTHODOX JOBS AND PROFESSIONS).

THE VERY TITLE EVOKES A CHILDHOOD TALE, ● WHERE ASPECTS BEFITTING THAT AGE ARE COMBINED WITH THE DISCOVERIES PEOPLE MAKE AS THEY TRY TO EARN A LIVING IN A THOUSAND DIFFERENT WAYS, ALWAYS DODGING THE POLICE. FOR ME, THERE'S A DICKENSIAN ELEMENT TO THIS MOVIE WITH ITS STREET URCHINS, POVERTY, AND CLASS CLASHES ON EVERY CORNER.

ONCE·UPON·A·TIME·IN·AMERICA

GH👻STBUSTERS

(1984)

I'VE ALWAYS BEEN REALLY INTO ANYTHING TO DO WITH GHOSTS, PARANORMAL ACTIVITY, THE OCCULT, ETC. AND IT'S TRUE THAT ⬛ THESE GHOSTBUSTERS ARE FAR FROM DARK, AND EVEN PRETTY SILLY. BUT THEY ARE BRILLIANT. THEY STOLE MY HEART FROM THE VERY FIRST MOMENT. BUT I HAVE TO MAKE A CONFESSION: WHAT I REALLY LOVED WERE THE GHOSTS. IN MY HEAD I WAS CONVINCED THAT THIS MOVIE WAS MADE FOR OUR DIMENSION —THE HUMAN ONE— AND THAT IN A ~~██████~~ PARALLEL WORLD THERE WAS A DARK, GHOSTLY VERSION, WHERE THE MAIN CHARACTERS ARE THE GHOSTS AND THE ENEMY IS BILL MURRAY AND CO.

AND I WOULD DREAM ABOUT THIS PARALLEL MOVIE, WHERE EACH SCENE WOULD BE BURSTING WITH THOSE CHEESY BUT LOVABLE GHOSTS. IN MOVIES ABOUT THE WILD ⬛ WEST I SIDED WITH THE NATIVES, AND IN GHOSTBUSTERS I SIDED WITH THE GHOSTS.

WHAT CAN YOU DO ?

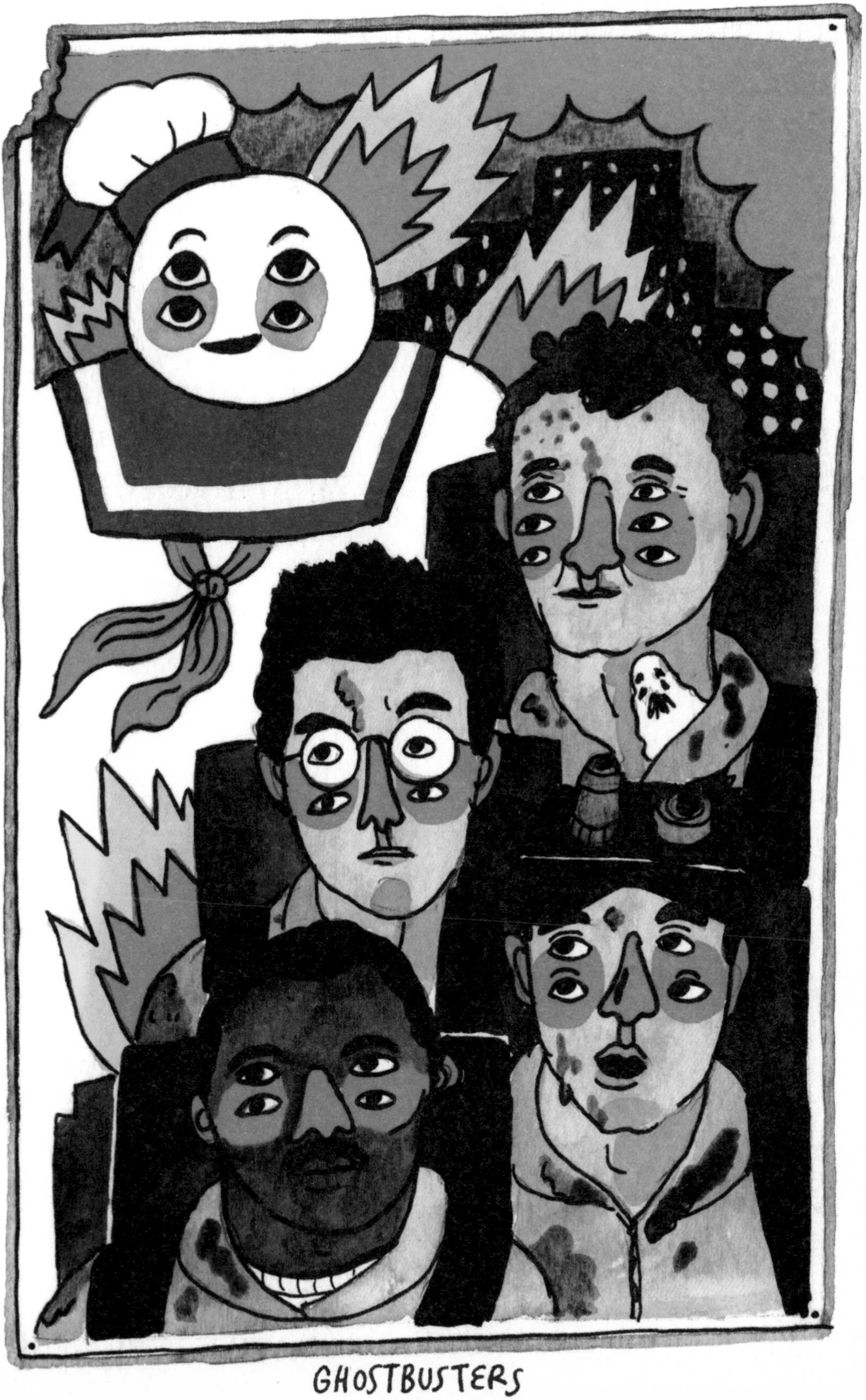

GHOSTBUSTERS

THE·NEVERENDING STORY

(1984)

ALL OF US WHO ~~WERE~~ WERE KIDS IN THE 80s
HAVE A SPECIAL MEMORY OF THIS MOVIE. WE HOLD
IT, DEAR. I'M SURE LOTS OF PEOPLE WOULD SAY THE
SAME THING, BUT I FELT THAT BASTIAN WAS A
FAITHFUL REPRESENTATION OF ME. I, TOO, WAS A
CHUBBY LITTLE KID, AND AT SCHOOL THE OTHER KIDS
WEREN'T TOO FRIENDLY TO ME. AND I LOVED READING.
ANY MOVIE WITH AN OPENING LIKE THAT GETS MY
VOTE, BUT THE NEVERENDING STORY THEN GOES ON
TO REVEAL ALL ITS MAGIC AND I GIVE MYSELF IN
TO THE FANTASY — MIND, BODY AND SOUL.
BESIDES THE STORY, I GENUINELY LOVE ALL THOSE
MODELS THEY MADE TO REPRESENT THE
CREATURES, BEFORE THE SPECIAL EFFECTS OF
TODAY. IT WASN'T HARD TO SPOT THE THREADS
AND CARDBOARD, BUT FOR ME THERE WAS
NOTHING MORE REAL AND MORE FANTASTIC AT
THE SAME TIME. FANTASIA FOREVER.

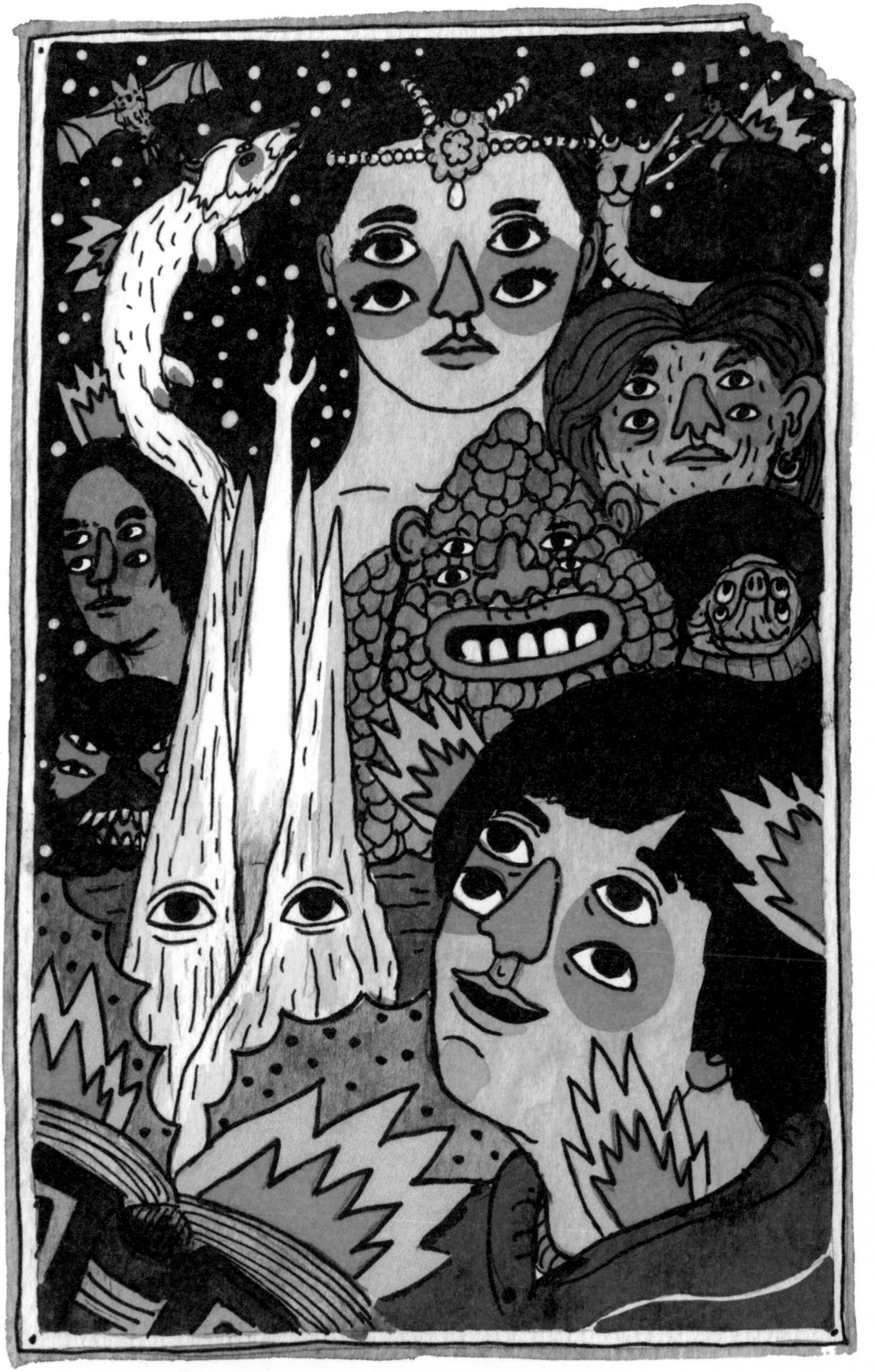

THE·NEVERENDING·STORY

BACK←!!!! TO THE FUTURE

(I, II, III / 1985-1990)

THIS IS ANOTHER MOVIE THAT'S ON THIS LIST
~~BORN~~ BECAUSE I WAS BORN IN THE 80s. AND IN ONE WAY
OR ANOTHER, WE ALL DREAMED ABOUT BEING McFLY.
SPIELBERG AND ZEMECKIS KNEW EXACTLY WHAT
THEY WERE DOING — THEY'RE MASTERS AT ~~ENTERTAINMENT~~
ENTERTAINMENT AND FILLING OUR HEADS TO THE BRIM
WITH WONDER AND FUN. THIS IS A SWEET, NAÏVE STORY
WITH ALL THE RIGHT COMPONENTS FOR US TO TRAVEL
LIKE LITTLE KIDS FROM THE MID-80s TO THE 1950s,
PASSING THROUGH A HILARIOUS "FUTURE" 2015 AND
ENDING UP IN THE AGE OF THE CLASSIC WILD WEST.
ZEMECKIS HAS THE ABILITY TO MAKE YOU FEEL LIKE
A TEN-YEAR-OLD KID (EVEN IF YOU'RE THIRTY-FIVE)
WHO WANTS TO GROW UP TO BE A TEENAGER LIKE
MICHAEL J. FOX AND EXPERIENCE ALL THOSE
PHENOMENAL ADVENTURES FOR YOURSELF.
AND OF COURSE, THANKS TO THE TRILOGY WE KNOW
WE HAVE TO BE CAREFUL WITH WHAT WE DO IN THE
PAST, BECAUSE IT CAN UPSET THE COURSE OF THE FUTURE
AND EVEN ERASE ENTIRE MOMENTS THAT ARE REALLY...

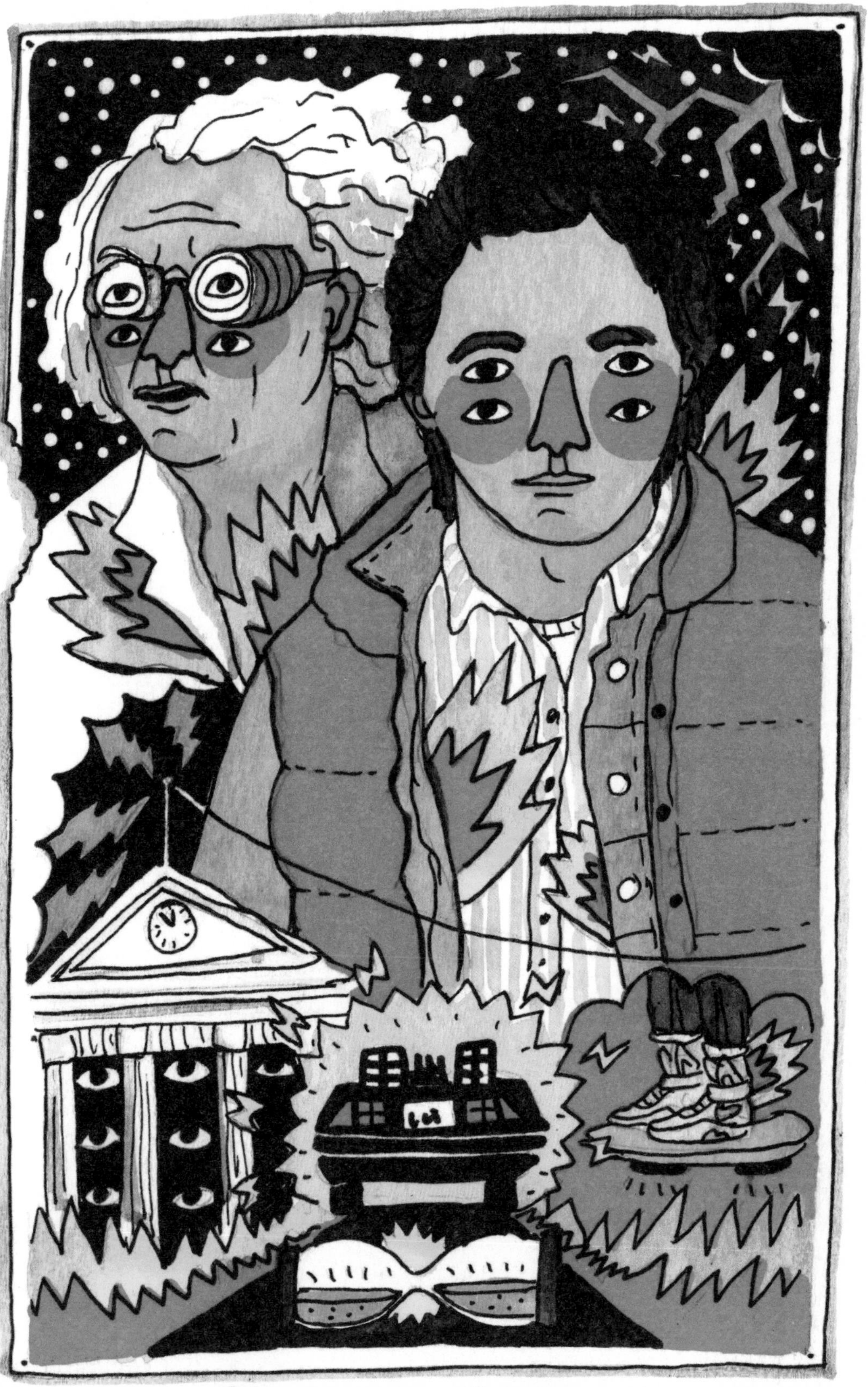

BACK·TO·THE·FUTURE

THE GOONIES

(1985)

NOW WE REACH THE CORNERSTONE OF THE ADVENTURE GENRE (TREASURE QUESTS AND ~~DEATH~~ DANGER LURKING AROUND EVERY CORNER) WHICH MADE ME THE ARTIST i AM TODAY. i DREAMED OF HAVING A GANG LIKE THE GOONIES AND GOING ON ADVENTURES. EVEN TODAY, WHEN i WATCH THE GOONIES' ESCAPADES AS THEY SEARCH FOR "ONE EYED" WILLY'S TREASURE, i'M ONE OF THEM — A GOONIE MYSELF. i CHUCKLE AT CHUCK'S ANTICS (HE WAS THE ONE i MOST RESEMBLED AS A BOY), TREMBLE DURING FRATELLI'S AMBUSHES, AND AM ON TENTERHOOKS AS WE INCH CLOSER AND CLOSER TO THE TREASURE.

WE'RE TALKING ABOUT THE MOST BASIC OF PLOTS, BUT i NEVER WANTED THE MOVIE TO END. i STILL REMEMBER HOW, AS A BOY, i MADE A MENTAL EFFORT TO MAKE THE PLOT TWIST AND TURN SO iT WOULD LAST TEN HOURS. i WOULD LIVE WITH MY GANG OF GOONIES iN GOON DOCKS FOR THE REST OF TIME.

AND A SPECIAL, ~~HEARTFELT~~ HEARTFELT SHOUT-OUT TO SLOTH, WHO NEVER SCARED ME AND WHO i ALWAYS WANTED AS A BUDDY, SO THAT WE COULD HAVE EACH OTHER'S BACK. **LOVE YOU, SLOTH !!!**

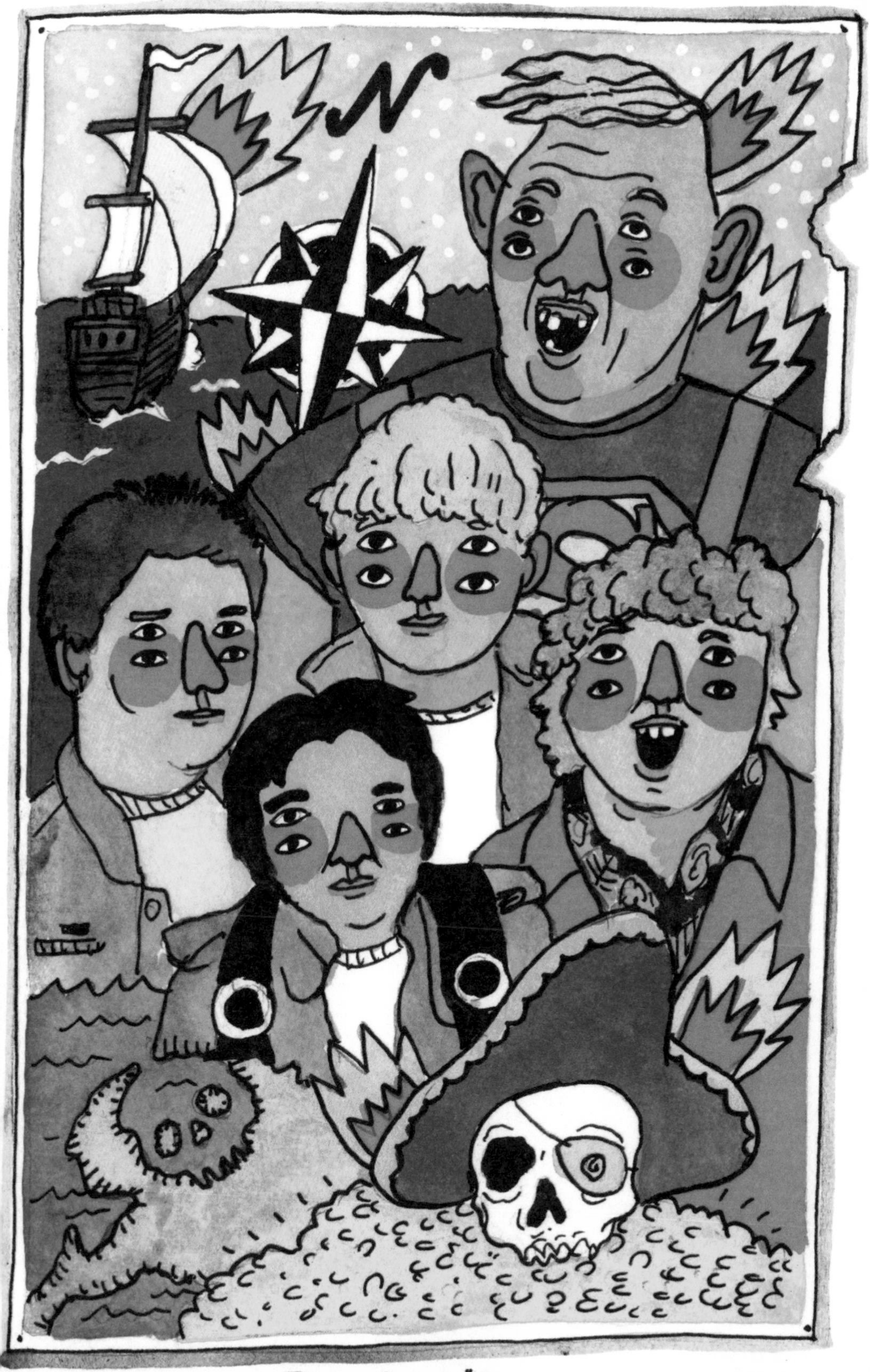
N

THE. GOONIES

THE PRINCESS BRIDE

(1987)

HERE'S ANOTHER SPECTACULAR ADVENTURE MOVIE THAT WAS FUNDAMENTAL IN DEVELOPING MY PASSION FOR SWORD AND SORCERY. IT IS IDEAL FOR THOSE YEARS WHEN YOU STILL COMPLETELY GIVE YOURSELF OVER TO THE ADVENTURES IN A MOVIE AS IF YOU WERE THE HERO OR HEROINE YOURSELF. I KNOW WHEN I WATCH IT AT 80, I'LL STILL HOLD ONTO THAT ADVENTURER'S SPIRIT.

I REMEMBER WHEN THE VIDEO CLUB WHERE MY FRIEND MIGUEL WOULD RENT MOVIES FOR US CLOSED DOWN — THAT WAS A REAL BLOW. BUT NOT LONG AFTER THAT I FOUND OUT THAT THE PRINCESS BRIDE WAS A BOOK BEFORE IT WAS A MOVIE...I GOT HOLD OF A COPY AND WOULD OPEN IT AND FLICK THROUGH THE PAGES TO SEE IF SCENES I REMEMBERED FROM THE MOVIE WOULD APPEAR IN THE FORM OF A MAGIC CLOUD BEFORE ME. THIS IS ANOTHER ADVENTURE I WOULD HAVE LIKED TO HAVE EXPERIENCED FIRST-HAND. BUT I WOULD HAVE GONE ON IT WITH ÍNIGO MONTOYA, RATHER THAN THE MORE OBVIOUS WESTLEY.

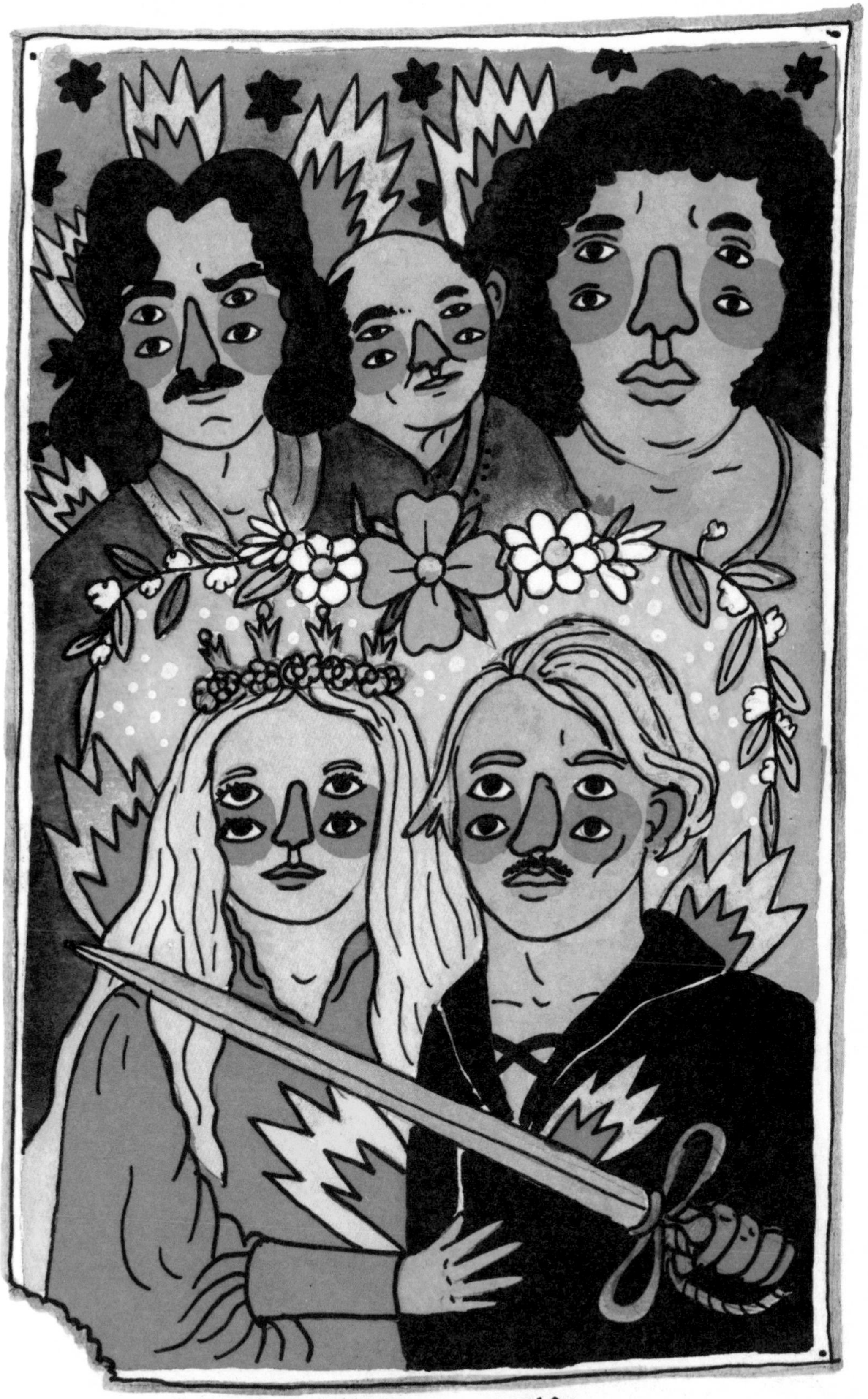

THE · PRINCESS · BRIDE

who framed ROGER RABBIT

(1988)

i WATCHED THIS IN THE CINEMA WHEN IT FIRST CAME OUT. i REMEMBER BEING SO COMPLETELY CAPTIVATED BY SEEING CARTOONS INTERACT WITH REAL HUMANS THAT i BARELY KNEW WHAT WAS GOING ON WITH THE PLOT. THAT'S WHAT THE WORLD SHOULD BE LIKE - CARTOONS AND REAL LIFE ALL CONSTANTLY MIXED UP TOGETHER.

i LEFT THE CINEMA SO EXCITED THAT i SPENT THE FOLLOWING YEAR LOOKING IN CORNERS AND DARK SPACES HOPING TO FIND CARTOONS RUNNING AROUND. THEN i RE-WATCHED THE MOVIE AND FOUND MYSELF ONCE AGAIN GOBSMACKED BY THOSE CARTOONS IN THE REAL WORLD, HA! BUT NOW i CAN FOLLOW THE PLOT AT LEAST, AND ● i'M PLEASED TO SAY THAT THIS MOVIE IS STILL A MASTERPIECE. NEARLY TWENTY YEARS HAVE PASSED SINCE IT CAME OUT BUT IT'S● SO MODERN AND SO GOOD THAT THEY COULD RELEASE IT NOW AND IT'D STILL BE A HIT.

SECRETLY, i STILL HARBOUR THE HOPE OF ONE DAY COMING ACROSS A CARTOON ON THE STREET.

WHO·FRAMED·ROGER·RABBIT

TIME·OF· THE·GYPSIES

(1989)

i HAD A ROMANi FAMILY FOR TEN YEARS, AND SiNCE
THEN i'VE ALWAYS CONSIDERED MYSELF A LiTTLE
BiT ROMANi. THAT'S WHY ~~*****~~ KUSTURICA iS
AN ESSENTiAL DiRECTOR FOR ME. THiS MOViE ~~*****~~
DOESN'T HAVE THE ~~*****~~ JOKEY, FUNNY ELEMENT
OF HiS OTHER ONES, BUT iT DOES BRiM WiTH ALL
THE SAME ADMiRATiON AND LOVE FOR ROMANi CULTURE.
THE STORY iSN'T ALL THAT CHEERFUL, BUT iT'S A
MASTERCLASS OF MAGiC AND TRADiTiON MiXED WiTH
THE COLD BALKANS OF THE 80S. GORAN BREGOViĆ'S
SOUNDTRACK iS THE CROWNiNG JEWEL OF THiS
ROMANi ATLAS. KUSTURICA KNOWS JUST HOW
TO SHOW US THAT THiN LiNE BETWEEN THE
REAL AND THE MAGiCAL WiTHiN ROMANi
CULTURE, AND HE DOES iT UP TO HiS KNEES iN
QUAGMiRES. AND iN COLD, GREY STREETS WiTH
MUD-SOAKED SHOES.
THiS MOViE PERFECTLY CAPTURES THE WORLD
i ALWAYS REFER TO iN MY WORK. THAT WORLD
iS MY UNiVERSE.

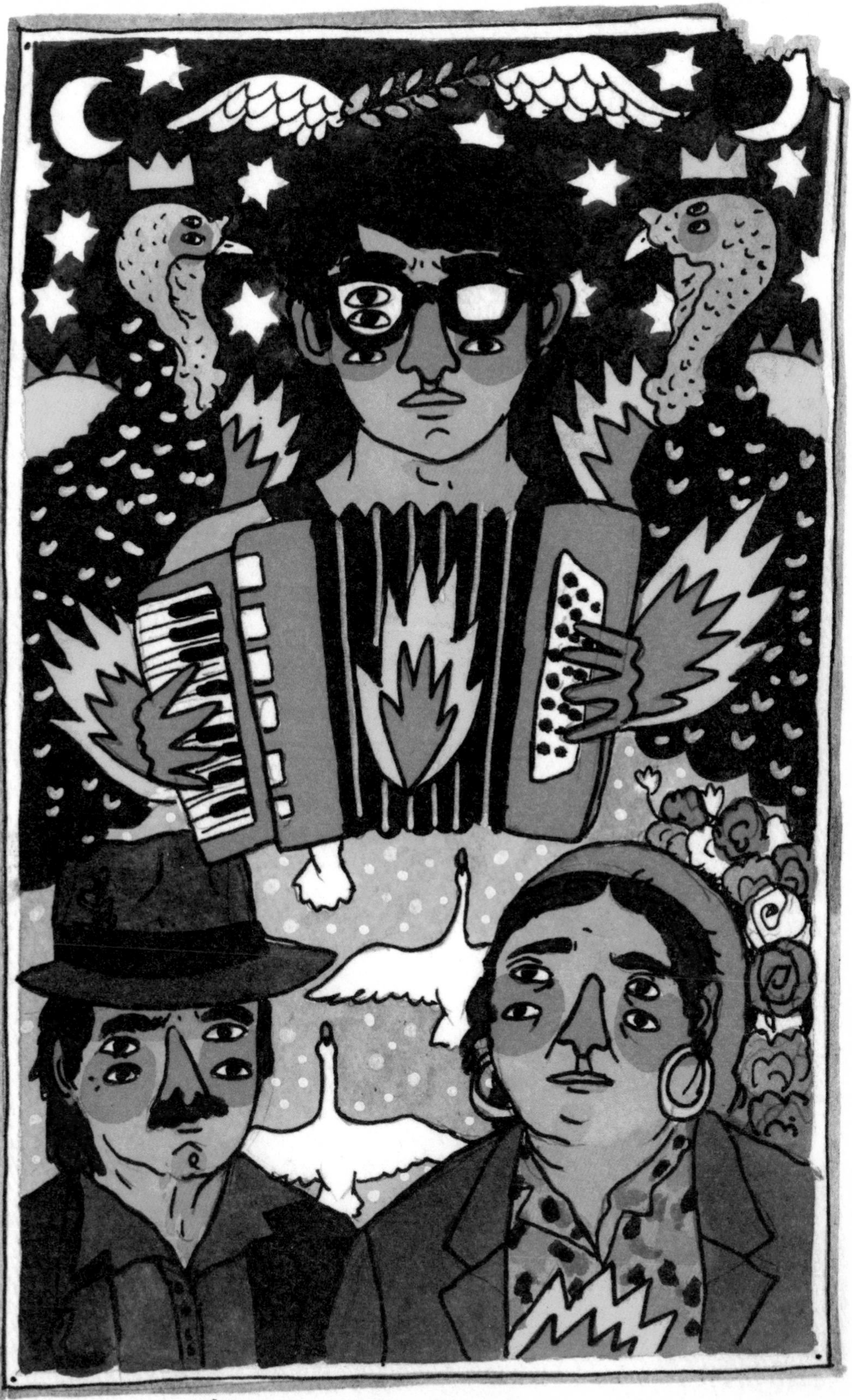

TIME · OF · THE · GYPSIES

BATMAN

(1989)

I'M A BATMAN FAN, END OF STORY. I WAS A BATMAN FAN EVEN BEFORE SEEING TIM BURTON'S MOVIE, BUT AS I LEFT THE CINEMA, I WOULD BE ON THE DARK KNIGHT'S SIDE FOR THE REST OF TIME. I REMEMBER THAT BURTON'S GOTHAM CITY BLEW ME ~~AWAY~~ AWAY SO INTENSELY THAT THE SECOND I GOT HOME I WENT LOOKING FOR A MAP OF THE USA AND SPENT AN ENTIRE DAY TRYING TO FIND THAT CITY. I HAD MY HEART SET ON IT BEING MY FIRST TRIP OUTSIDE OF EUROPE. I REMEMBER MY DAD'S FACE AS HE TRIED TO EXPLAIN TO ME (AS GENTLY AS POSSIBLE) THAT GOTHAM CITY DIDN'T EXIST. PARENTS KNOW A LOT OF THINGS, BUT I'M TELLING YOU ALL THAT GOTHAM CITY REALLY DOES EXIST.

KEATON'S BATMAN WAS GOOD, BUT JACK NICHOLSON'S JOKER WAS A WORK OF ART. I THINK THAT, BEING SO YOUNG, I CAUGHT A GLIMPSE OF A NEW KIND OF BAD IN THIS MOVIE — EXCITING, TERRIFYING, AND ONE THAT I COULDN'T TAKE MY EYES OFF.

HOW COOL THAT IN THE NEVER-ENDING BATTLE BETWEEN SUPERHERO AND VILLAIN, I LIKE AND ADMIRE BOTH. BATMAN COMES UP AGAIN IN THIS BOOK LATER. LIKE I TOLD YOU... I'M A BATMAN FANATIC!

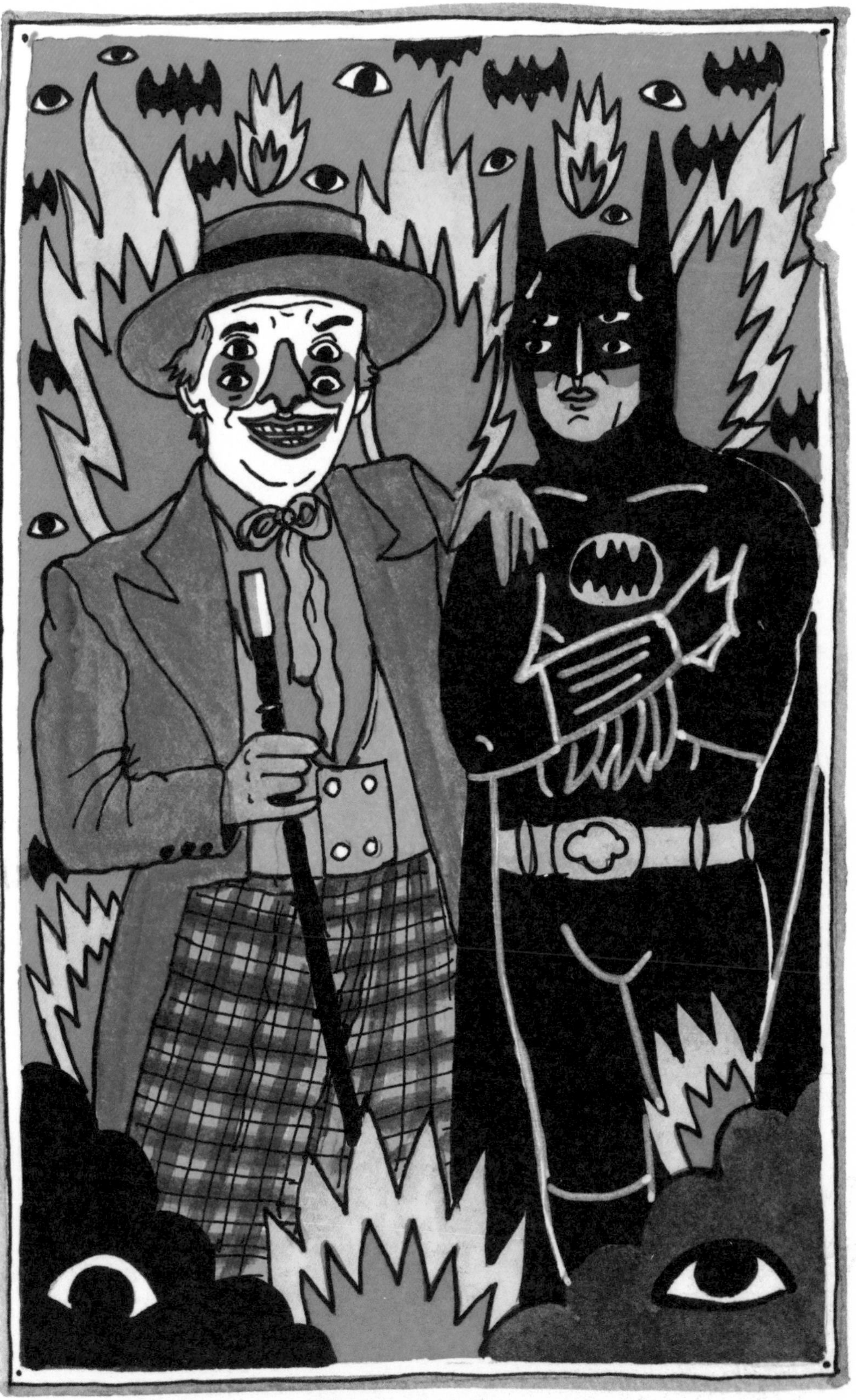

BATMAN

AMANECE, QUE·NO·ES·POCO

(1989)

A SPANISH MASTERPIECE. THIS MOVIE IS SO CRAZY, SO SURREAL AND SO SPANISH THAT, IN MY OPINION, IT'S THE PERFECT ~~XXXX~~ DEPICTION OF MY COUNTRY. MONTY PYTHON HAVE NOTHING ON JOSÉ LUIS CUERDA. EVERY SQUARE METRE OF THE TOWN IN THIS MOVIE CONTAINS A LITTLE BOX OF SURPRISES WITH ITS OWN INTERNAL LOGIC, FIREWORKS, AND WHIRLWIND OF GIGGLES AND WONDER. IF THIS TOWN EXISTED IN REAL LIFE, I'D SPEND EVERY SUMMER THERE. ALL OF IT TAKES ME BY SURPRISE BUT IS FAMILIAR AT THE SAME TIME – A TOTALLY UNIQUE FEELING. EVERY TIME I WATCH IT I THINK ABOUT WHO I'D BE FROM THAT TOWN. AND THE NICE THING IS THAT EVERY TIME, I COME UP WITH A DIFFERENT CHARACTER.

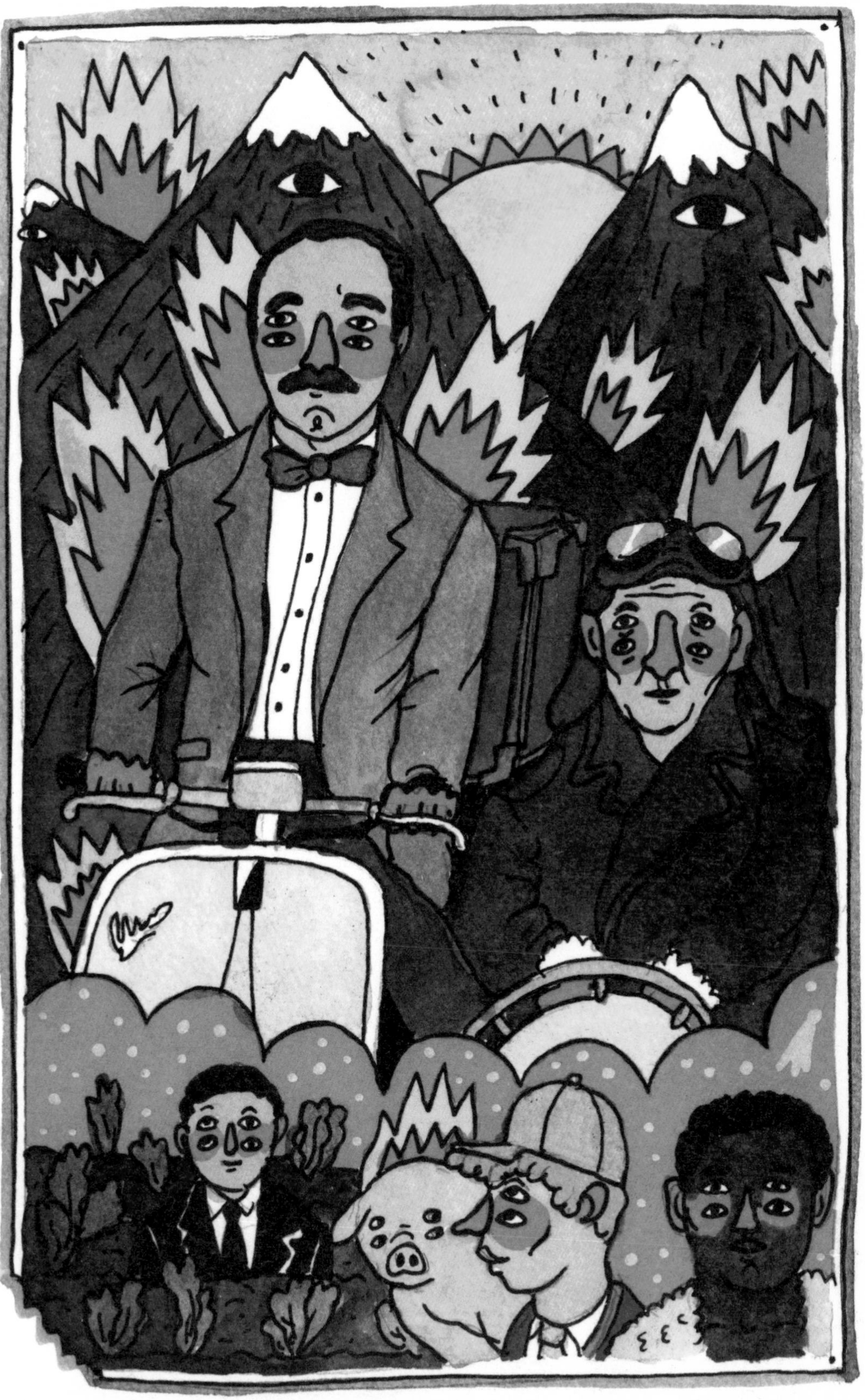

AMANECE · QUE · NO · ES · POCO

DO THE RIGHT THING

(1989)

MY PARENTS EDUCATED ME IN ALL KINDS OF DIFFERENT CULTURAL AND SOCIAL BACKGROUNDS FROM AN EARLY AGE, WHICH IS BRILLIANT. BUT WATCHING SPIKE LEE'S DO THE RIGHT THING WAS LIKE ENTERING A MOUNTAIN AND FINDING IT BRIMMING WITH GOLD. THIS MOVIE WAS BASICALLY MY FIRST ENCOUNTER WITH AFRICAN-AMERICAN CULTURE AND ITS CONTEXTS IN THOSE YEARS. IT OPENED MY EYES. UNTIL THEN, THE ONLY THING I'D HAD ACCESS TO WERE PUBLIC ENEMY LYRICS. THIS MOVIE MADE ME WANT TO DIG DEEPER. EVEN TODAY I LISTEN TO RAP MORE THAN ANY OTHER MUSIC — IT COMPLETELY ENTHRALLS ME.

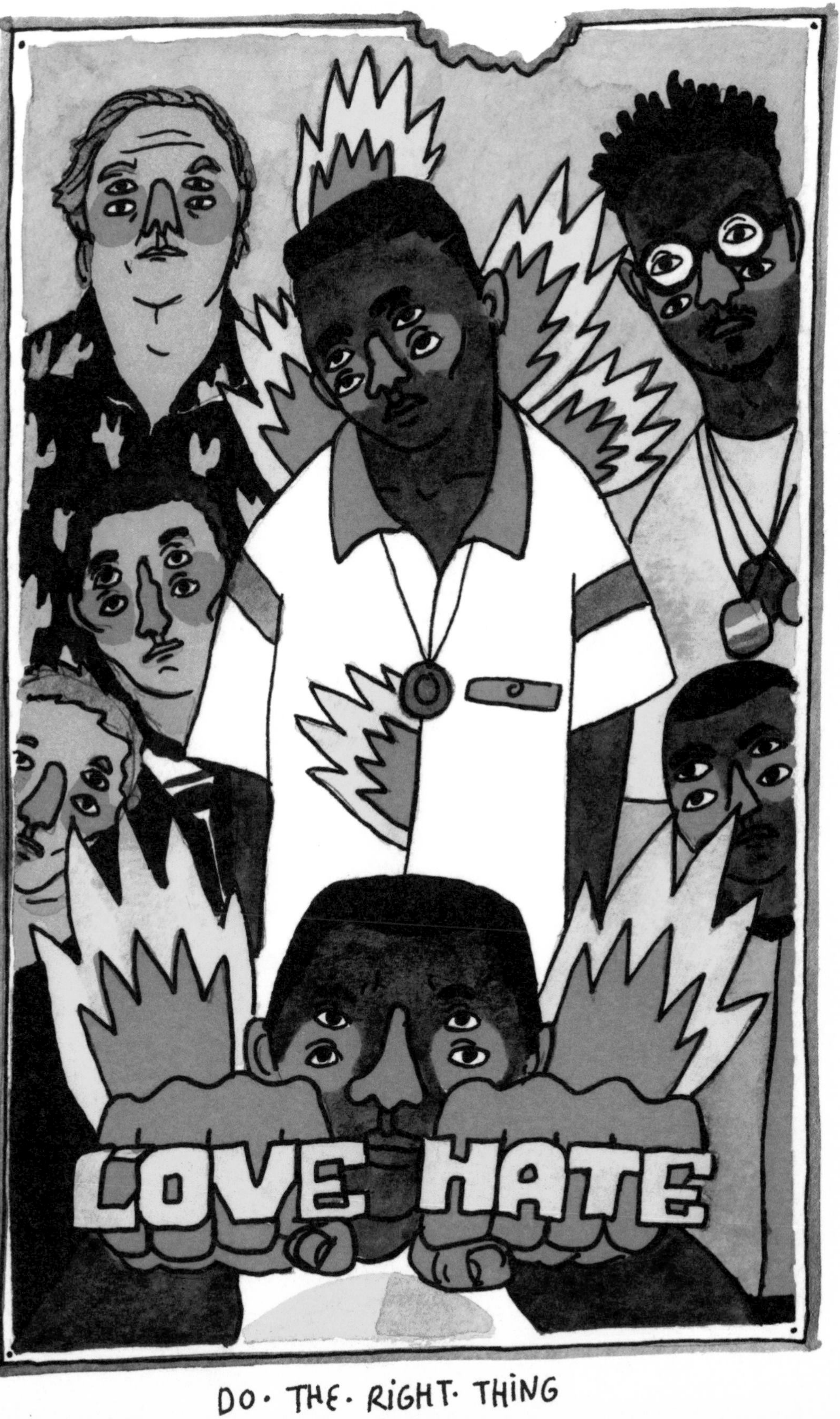
LOVE HATE

DO· THE· RIGHT· THING

GoodFellas

(1990)

i DON'T THINK i'VE EVER HAD A FAVOURITE MOVIE
PER SE. BUT iF SOMEONE ASKS ME i USUALLY SAY
GOODFELLAS. THIS MOVIE BRINGS TOGETHER ALL THE
ELEMENTS THAT DRIVE ME CRAZY — iTALIAN-AMERICAN
MAFIA, VIOLENT AND CONVOLUTED PLOTS, A COMPLETE
BIOGRAPHY OF A CHARACTER (OR iN THIS CASE
THREE CHARACTERS) AND MY DEAR SCORSESE.
AND YES, i SAVOUR iT AS iF iT WERE THE FIRST TIME.
AND iT HAS MY FAVOURITE SCENE iN CiNEMA HISTORY
— THAT TRACKING SHOT iN WHICH HENRY AND KAREN
PARK AT THE DOOR OF COPACABANA NIGHTCLUB AND
WIND THEIR WAY THROUGH ALL THE HALLWAYS AND
BACKROOMS AND KiTCHEN UNTIL THEY REACH A
TABLE LAID SPECIALLY FOR THEM DIRECTLY iN FRONT
OF THE STAGE. iT'S ~~scorsese~~ OUTSTANDING, AND
WITH THE CRYSTALS SINGING iN THE BACKGROUND.
PLEASE, ■ iF YOU DON'T KNOW THIS SCENE, CHECK iT
OUT ON YOUTUBE, AND THE THIRD OR FOURTH TIME
iN A ROW THAT YOU WATCH iT REMEMBER THAT iT'S
A SINGLE SEQUENCE, THE SAME SHOT FROM START
TO FiNiSH.   BRAVO, SCORSESE.

94

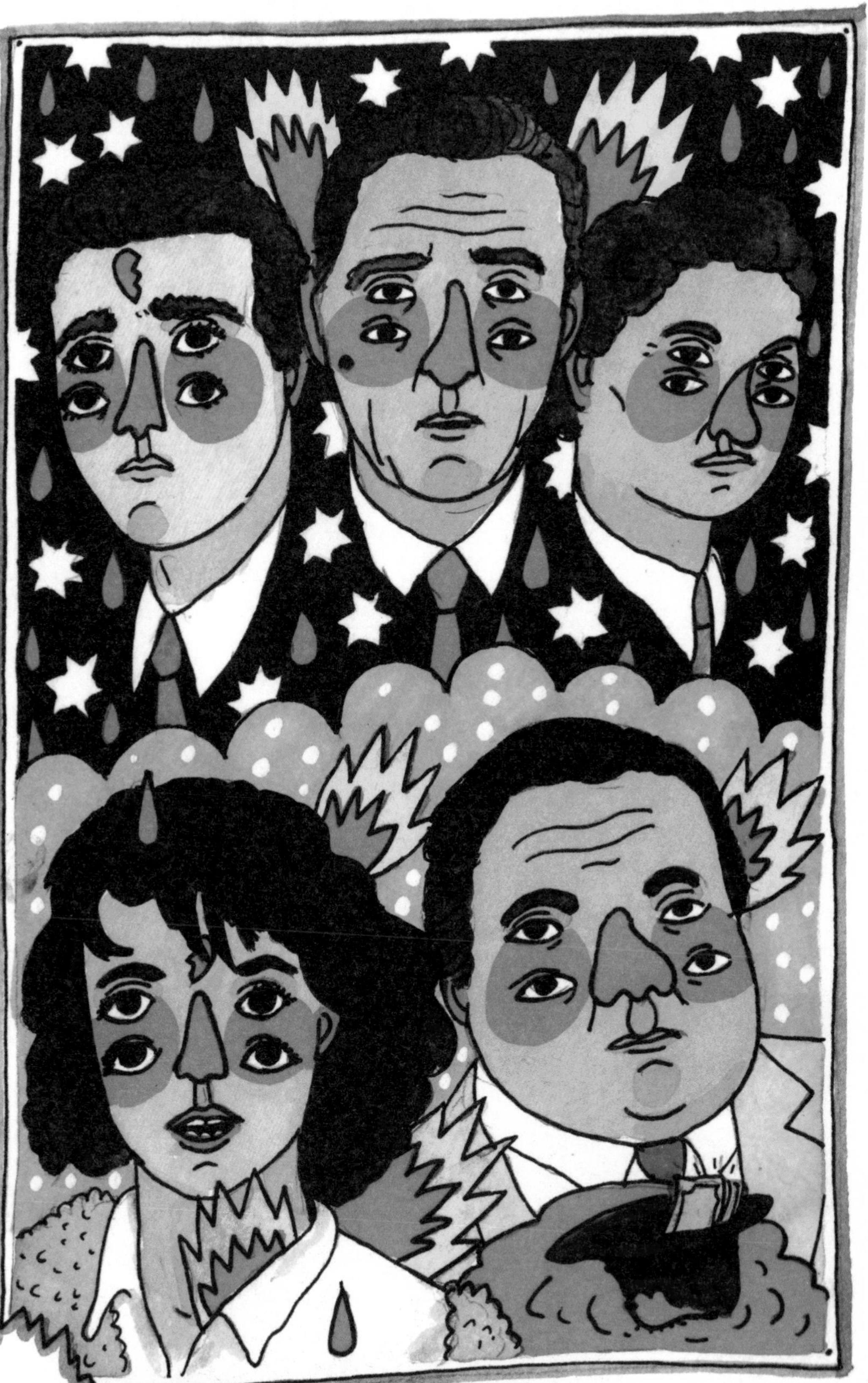

GOODFELLAS

The Addams Family

(1991)

AS A BOY, i WAS REALLY INTERESTED iN THE MURKY WORLD OF GHOSTS, VAMPIRES AND OTHER CREATURES FROM BEYOND THE GRAVE. AND THiS MACABRE AND SiNiSTER FAMiLY COMPLETELY STOLE MY HEART. i DREAMED OF HAVING A PET LiKE THING. AND i ADMiT THAT MY FiRST MOVIE LOVE WAS CHRISTINA RiCCi AS WEDNESDAY. THE FiRST PiCTURE OF A GiRL i STUCK ON MY BEDROOM WALL WAS OF HER. i WOULD'VE DONE ANYTHING FOR AN UNCLE LiKE FESTER. EVERY DETAiL OF THE ADDAMS FAMiLY MANSION LEFT ME iN AWE. i FANTASiZED ABOUT FINDING SOMETHING LiKE THAT iN REAL LiFE. CAN i BE AN ADDAMS— PLEASE, PLEASE, PLEEEEEASE?

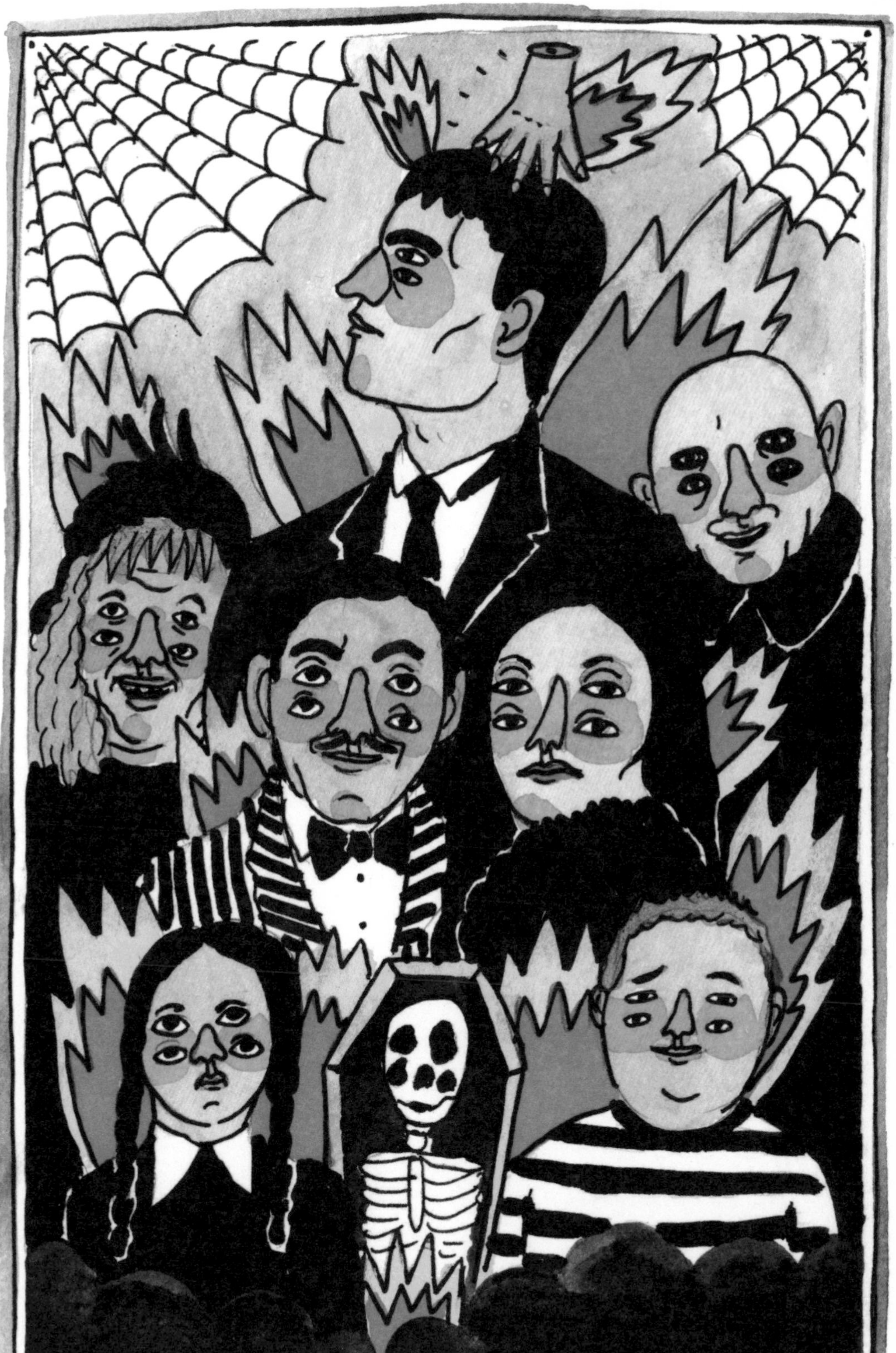

THE · ADDAMS · FAMILY

UNFORGIVEN

(1992)

~~strikethrough~~

WHAT. A. MOVIE. CLINT EASTWOOD HAD PLAYED THE LEADING ROLES IN MAJOR WESTERNS BEFORE, BUT NOW HE WAS STRUTTING HIS STUFF AS A DIRECTOR. HE MADE A TRULY COMPLETE WILD WEST MOVIE, AND FROM WHERE I'M STANDING, IT IS THE EPILOGUE TO THE GOLDEN AGE OF THE WESTERN.

IT MAKES SENSE THAT AFTER ALL THAT ACTING WITH A PISTOL ON EITHER SIDE OF HIS BELT, HE WAS THE BEST PERSON TO DIRECT THIS MOVIE. ONE OF THE BRILLIANT THINGS ABOUT FORGIVEN IS THAT THE PEOPLE ARE REAL, NOT JUST FLAT, NARROW STEREOTYPES LIKE YOU GET IN OTHER ~~other~~ EXAMPLES OF THIS GENRE. IT'S TRUE THAT THERE'S FUN TO BE HAD FROM WATCHING THOSE ~~stereo~~ STEREOTYPES, BUT WHAT EASTWOOD DID BY GIVING DEPTH TO HIS CHARACTERS WAS TURN THIS INTO A MASTERPIECE. THE CASTING IS ALSO FIRST CLASS. I'LL NEVER GROW TIRED OF WATCHING THIS MOVIE. LONG LIVE THE WESTERN!

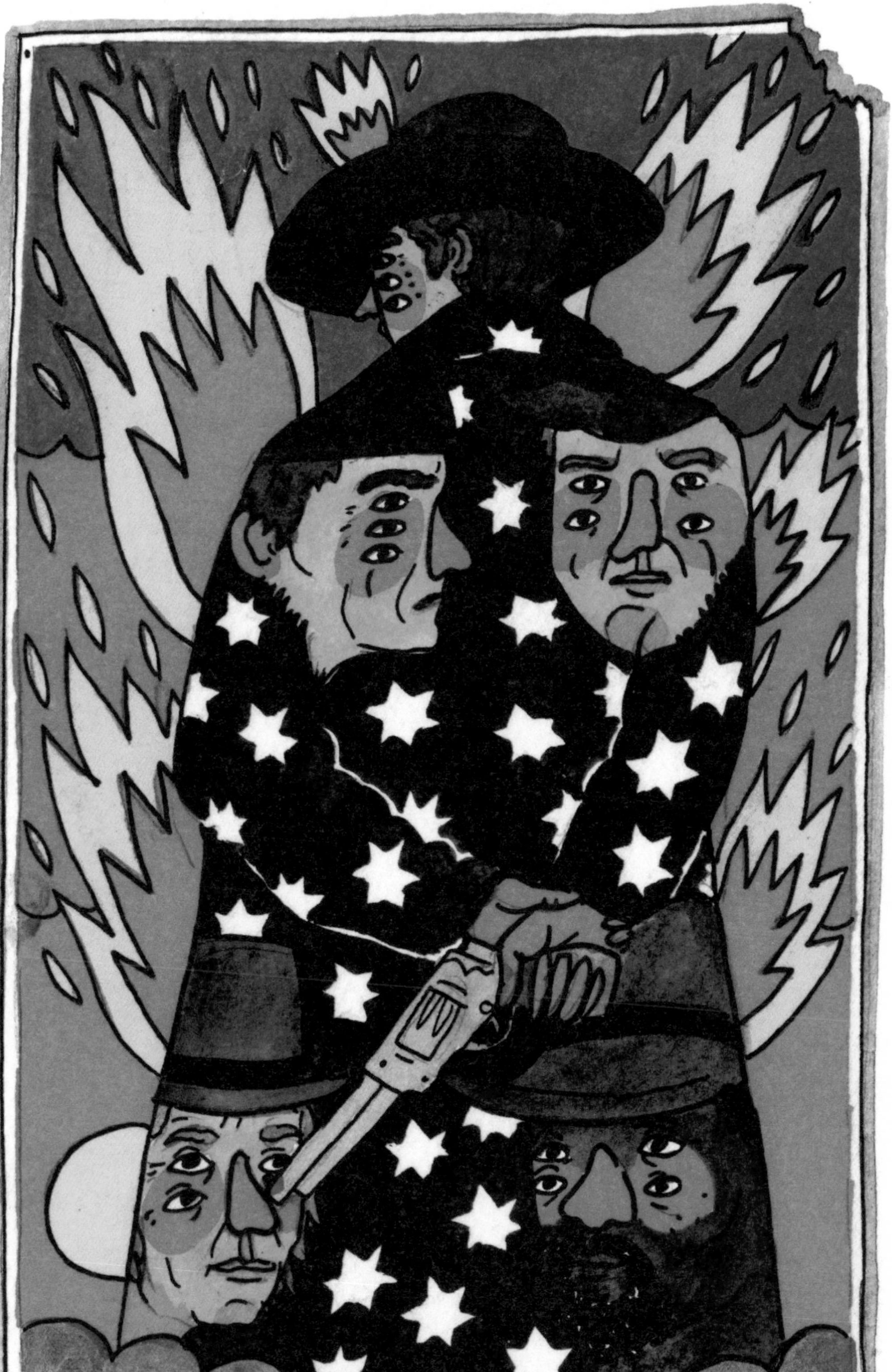

UNFORGIVEN

BRAM · STOKER'S Dracula

(1992)

i THINK i READ STOKER'S BOOK ABOUT FIVE TIMES AS A KID. VAMPIRES COMPLETELY ENGROSSED ME, SO WHAT ~~BE~~ BETTER BOOK TO READ THAN THE BIBLE ABOUT THE LORD OF DARKNESS. i WAS A LITTLE HESITANT ABOUT GOING TO SEE THIS AT THE CINEMA, BECAUSE i WAS WORRIED IT'D SPOIL THE MAGIC OF THE BOOK. BUT i HAVE TO SAY THAT COPPOLA DID AN ~~A~~ AMAZING JOB. GARY OLDMAN'S DRACULA SURPASSED ALL MY EXPECTATIONS. HE WAS TRULY TERRIFYING, BUT i COULDN'T LOOK AWAY! i THINK i SPENT HALF THE MOVIE WITH MY MOUTH WIDE OPEN, TAKING IN AND APPRECIATING EVERY DETAIL OF EACH SHOT. SO MUCH SO THAT i ASKED FOR IT ON VHS DESPITE THE FACT THAT WE DIDN'T EVEN HAVE A TAPE PLAYER AT HOME. i REMEMBER DRAWING THAT HORRIFYING DRACULA OVER AND OVER AGAIN... COPPOLA'S CREATION, MADE TO LEAVE ANY LOVER OF THE BLOODTHIRSTY TRANSYLVANIAN COUNT OPEN - MOUTHED.

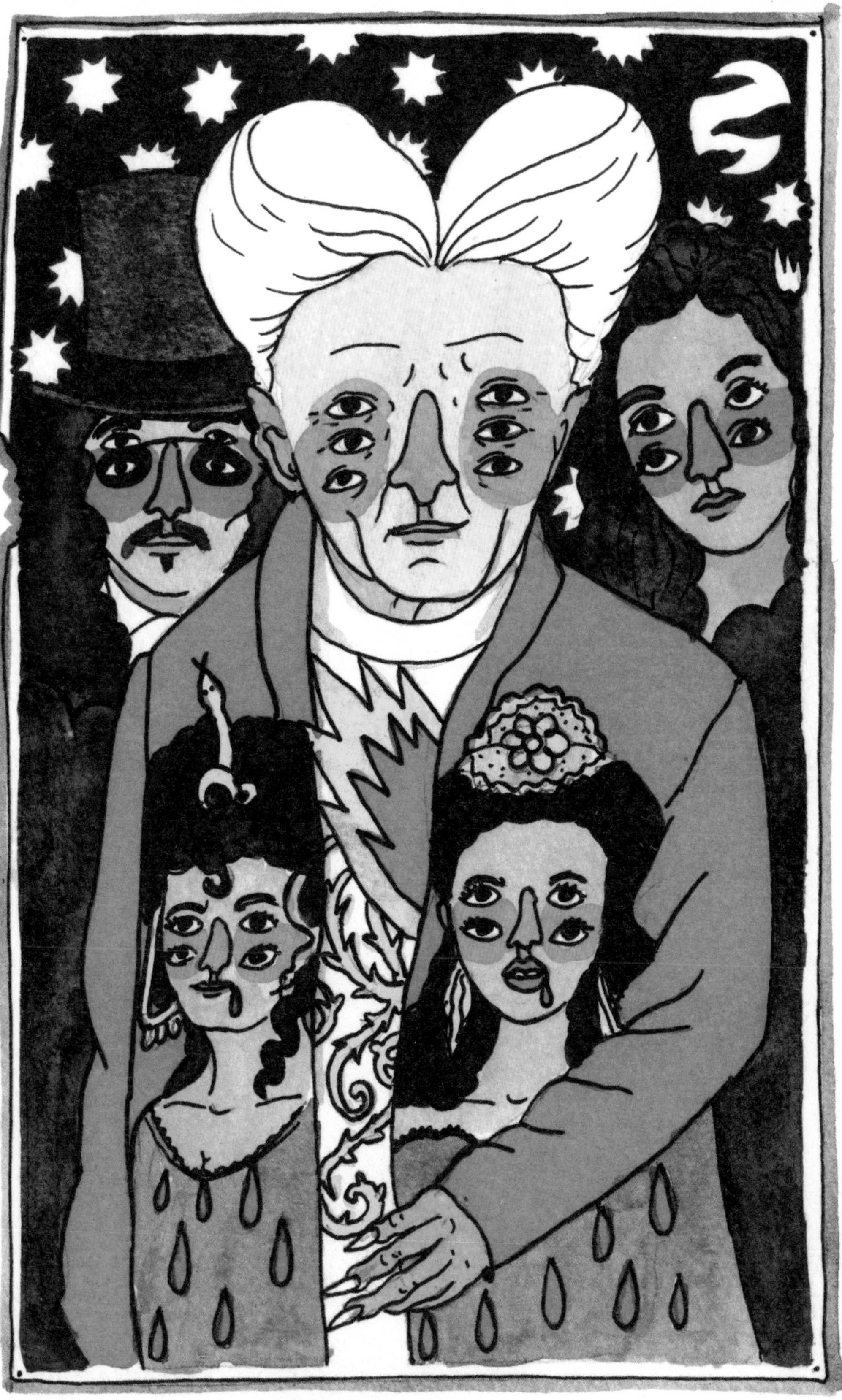

DRACULA

THE·NIGHTMARE BEFORE·CHRISTMAS

(1993)

OH, THE WONDERFUL WORLD OF TIM BURTON.
WHEN i WATCHED THiS MOViE AT THE CiNEMA
i FELT LiKE i ALREADY KNEW AND LOVED HiS
WHOLE SURREAL WORLD. iT WAS 100% THE KIND OF
CiNEMA i WOULD HAVE MADE iF i COULD HAVE MADE
MOViES AGED 11. ALL OF THAT HAD BEEN INSIDE ME
WITHOUT ME EVEN KNOWING iT. i THINK THAT'S
ONE OF BURTON'S MAJOR ViRTUES... HE CAN EXPRESS
THE EMOTIONS AND iNTERESTS OF A CHILD BUT iN THE
WAY THAT ONLY AN ADULT COULD. WHEN YOU'RE A KID
YOU WATCH THE MOViE AS iF iT SOMEHOW BELONGED
TO YOU, YOUR iDENTiTY.
AND WHEN YOU'RE AN
ADULT, TiM BURTON
TAKES YOU BY THE HAND
AND LEADS YOU TO THAT
YOUTH YOU HANKER AFTER,
AND FOR AN ENTIRE
HOUR AND A HALF
BRINGS YOU BACK iNTO
YOUR 11-YEAR-OLD
WORLD. YOU ARE
A MAD GENiUS,
TiM BURTON.

THE·NIGHTMARE·BEFORE·CHRISTMAS

INTERVIEW WITH · THE · VAMPIRE

(1994)

MORE VAMPIRES. i DID TELL YOU THEY WERE ONE OF THE MAIN THEMES OF MY CHILDHOOD. THIS MOVIE TOOK MY LOVE FOR ALL THINGS VAMPIRE TO A WHOLE NEW LEVEL. iT HAD THE STEREOTYPICAL VAMPIRES FROM LEGENDS, BUT WITH BRAND NEW ELEMENTS INTRODUCED iNTO THE CLASSIC VAMPIRE UNIVERSE.

i LOVE THE FEELING WHEN i REALIZE iT'S GOING TO BE SHOWN ON THE TV - i'LL SPEND THE ENTIRE DAY THINKING ABOUT THE MOVIE UNTIL THE EVENING, THE MOMENT OF TRUTH. AND THEN WHEN i WATCH IT, A MILLION SENSATIONS FROM MY TEENAGE YEARS COME BACK TO ME.

EVEN MEMORIES AND THINGS THAT i HAD FORGOTTEN POP INTO MY HEAD. i MIGHT NOT BE A VAMPIRE (OR AM i?), BUT THIS MOVIE MAKES ME IMMORTAL.

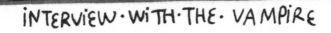
INTERVIEW · WITH · THE · VAMPIRE

CLERKS

(1994)

i SAW THIS MOVIE WHEN iT FIRST CAME OUT. i HEARD ABOUT iT BECAUSE i ALREADY FOLLOWED AND READ A LOT OF STUFF BY DIRECTOR KEVIN SMITH, AND THEN A LITTLE LATER i FOUND OUT ABOUT THIS GEM. BY THAT POINT i'D ALREADY ~~FIRST~~ BECOME A TOTAL COMICS NERD AND LOVER OF CULT MOVIES LIKE STAR WARS, AND i WAS SUFFICIENTLY TEENAGERY TO HAVE HAD MY FAIR SHARE OF DEEP CONVERSATIONS ABOUT LIFE. i WAS PERFECTLY PREPARED TO DIVE HEAD FIRST INTO CLERKS AND MAKE iT THE MOST VITAL, ESSENTIAL MOVIE OF MY TEENAGE LIFE. i'VE ALWAYS THOUGHT THAT THE ~~ONE~~ GREATEST GIFT i COULD EVER HOPE TO RECEIVE WOULD BE iF SMITH DECIDED TO PRODUCE A TV SERIES WITH DOZENS OF SEASONS BASED ON CLERKS. AND i'M STILL HOLDING OUT FOR MY WISH TO COME TRUE.

IF YOU PLAN TO SHOPLIFT LET US KNOW

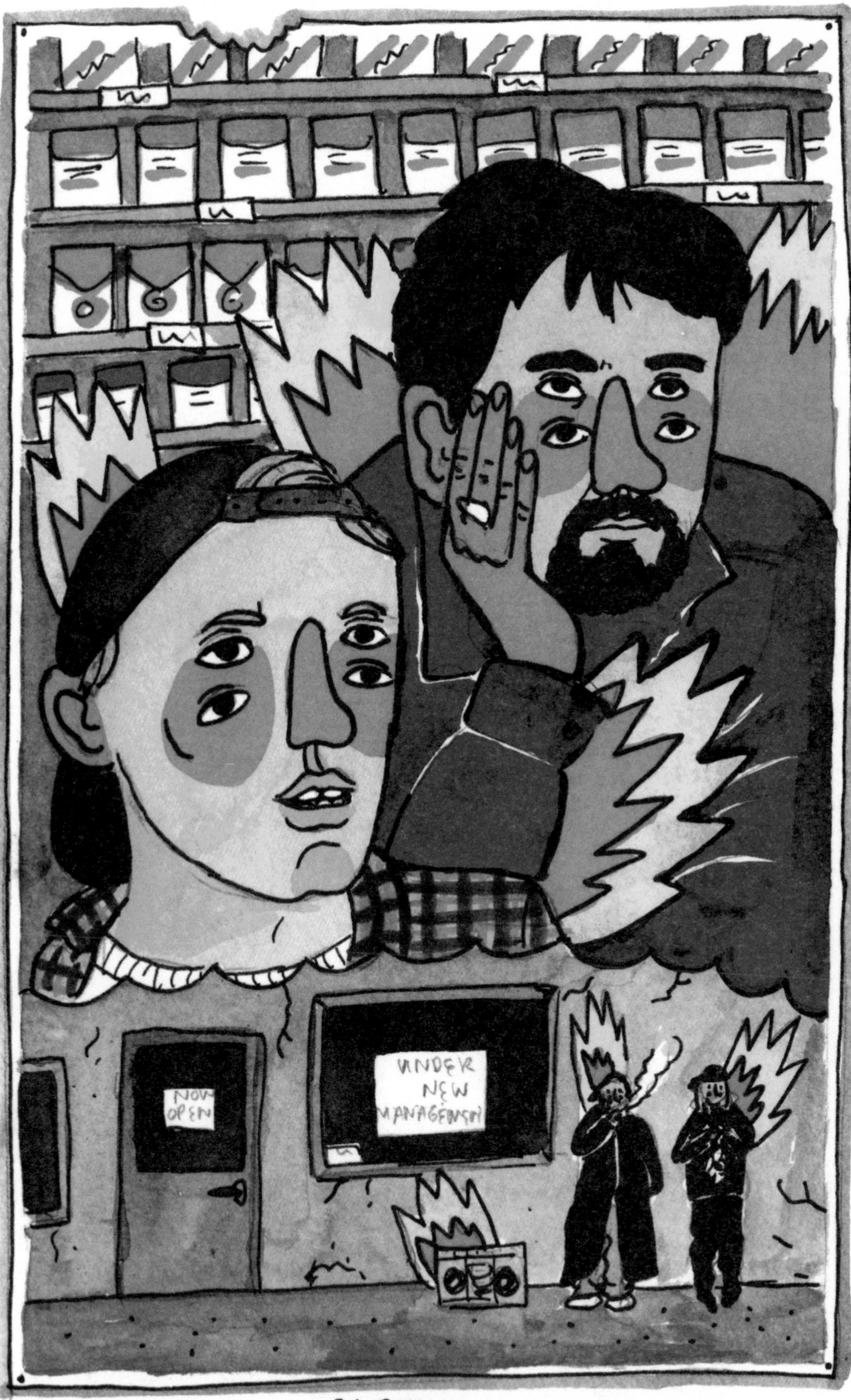
NOW
OPEN
UNDER
NEW
MANAGEMENT

CLERKS

PULP FICTION

(1994)

WATCHING PULP FICTION IN THE CINEMA HAS TO BE ONE OF THE ~~ENTIRELY~~ GREATEST MOMENTS OF MY LIFE. TARANTINO MADE ME TREMBLE IN MY SEAT LIKE NO OTHER. i LIKE <u>EVERYTHING</u> ABOUT PULP FICTION, AND WIHOUT A DOUBT IT'S ONE OF THE MOST IMPORTANT MOVIES OF MY LIFE. TARANTINO OPENED UP A WHOLE NEW DIMENSION IN MY CINEMATIC WORLD: THE DIALOGUES, THE VIOLENCE, <u>EVERYTHING.</u> EVERY~~ONE~~ ONE OF THESE CHARACTERS IS WORTHY OF A SPIN-OFF, AND EACH INTERWEAVING STORY IN THE PLOT IS WORTHY OF ITS OWN MOVIE. THE REVIVAL OF TRAVOLTA WAS A STROKE OF GENIUS AND IN FACT SET THE PRECEDENT FOR MANY MORE TO COME. i HAD A PULP FICTION POSTER ON MY WALL FOR ALMOST 10 YEARS. TARANTINO KNEW EXACTLY HOW TO BRING US ALL THE ENTERTAINMENT OF B-MOVIES, AND THE RESULT IS A MASTERPIECE LIKE FEW OTHERS. EVEN NOW i JUST GAWP AT EVERY SHOT, INCAPABLE OF LOOKING AWAY — NOT EVEN AT MY PHONE! TARANTINO, I'M UNDER YOUR SPELL.

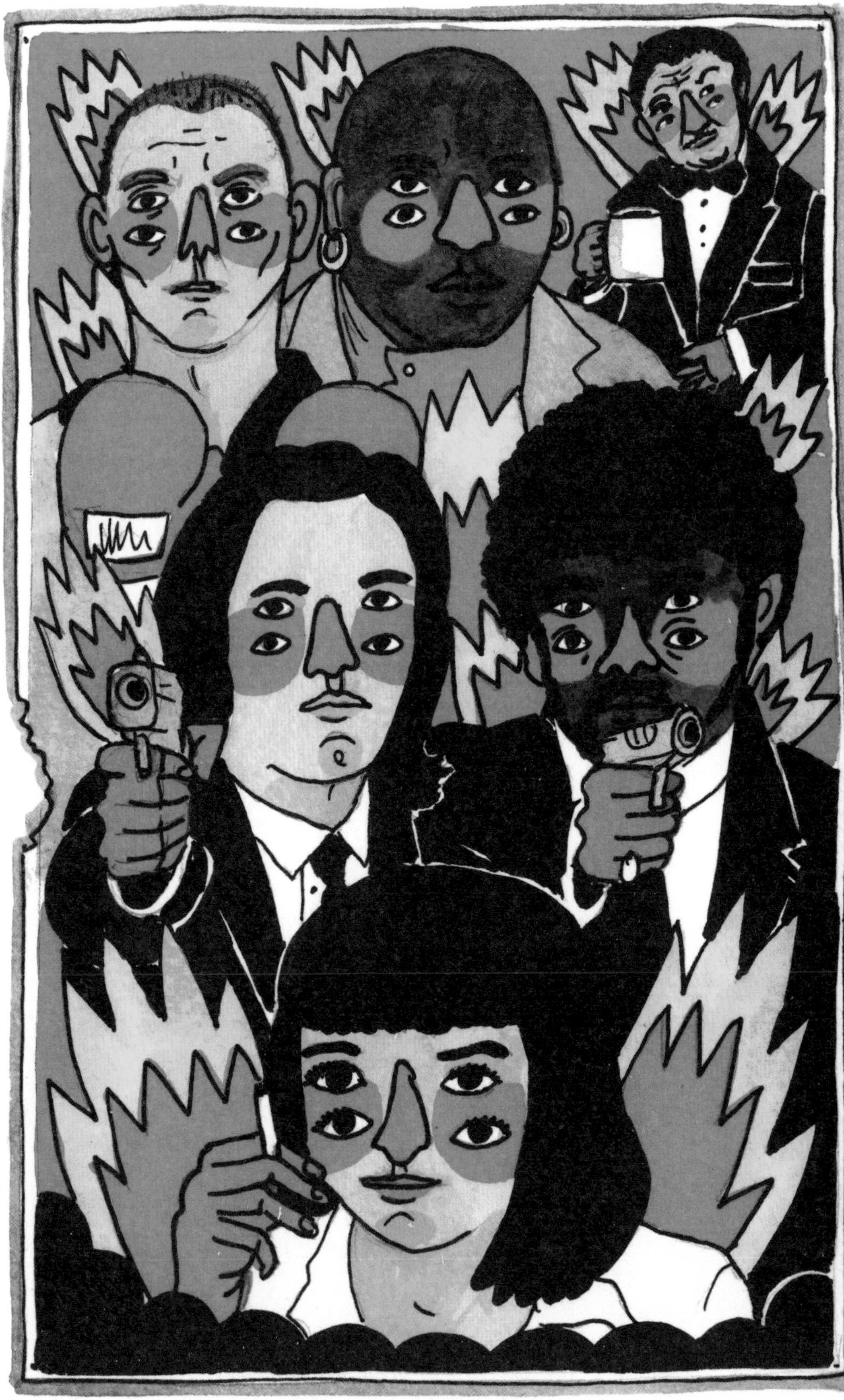

PULP · FICTION

THE CROW

(1994)

THIS MOVIE REALLY BLEW ME AWAY. MAYBE BECAUSE IT SORT OF CHIMED WITH THAT DARK SIDE I ALWAYS DEFEND, THE CROW SLOTTED SEAMLESSLY INTO MY LIFE. LADIES AND GENTS, I WAS RIGHT IN THE MIDDLE OF MY TEENS — WAS IT EVER GOING TO BE ANY OTHER WAY?

I REMEMBER DOODLING THE CROW MAKEUP OVER ALL THE PICTURES IN MY TEXTBOOKS AT SCHOOL. I EVEN PAINTED MY OWN FACE LIKE THE LEAD CHARACTER A COUPLE OF TIMES. I THINK IT WAS THE PERFECT PRODUCT FOR A TEENAGER IN THE MID-90S. I RE-WATCHED IT RECENTLY AND IT WAS LIKE PROUST'S MADELEINE CAKE: I WAS A TEENAGER AGAIN FOR A MINUTE, AND IT WAS GLORIOUS. TRY IT WITH A MOVIE THAT MARKED YOUR ADOLESCENCE AND I SWEAR YOU'LL SEE — IT'S LIKE TIME TRAVELLING.

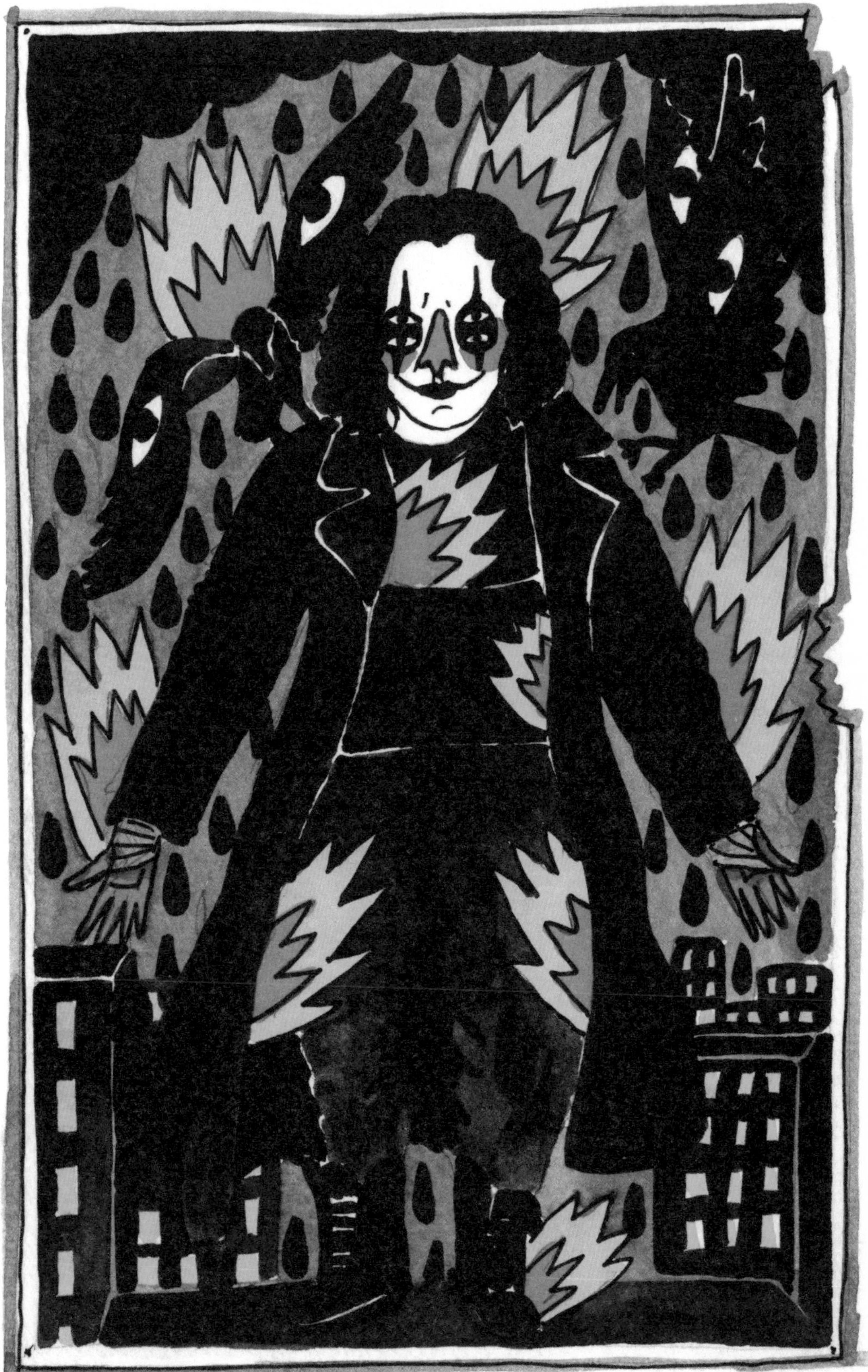

THE · CROW

TOY STORY

(I, II, III / 1995-2010)

I'D SAY THIS TRILOGY CHANGED THE COURSE OF MAINSTREAM ANIMATED MOVIES. EVERY SINGLE ONE IS PRICELESS. AND I'M NOT JUST REFERRING TO THE SPECIAL EFFECTS, BUT TO THEIR HUMAN QUALITY. WRITING AND DRAWING THIS BOOK I REALIZED THAT LOTS OF THE MOVIES THAT APPEAL TO ME DO SO BECAUSE THEY TAKE ME BACK TO MY CHILDHOOD. AND TOY STORY IS A PERFECT EXAMPLE OF THAT. AND YET, THERE'S ONE ADDED, AWESOME DETAIL: EACH MOVIE MATURES WITH US, AND IN ● EVERY NEW INSTALMENT● THERE ARE MORE GREY AREAS AND GROWN-UP SITUATIONS. ON TOP OF THAT, THE MAKERS MANAGED TO CREATE A CAST OF CHARACTERS WHO WE CHERISH AS IF THEY WERE FAMILY. AND THROUGH COMPUTER CODE ALONE THEY MAKE US FEEL JUST AS MUCH AS ANY REAL ACTOR OR ACTRESS COULD. FAULTLESS FILMMAKING.

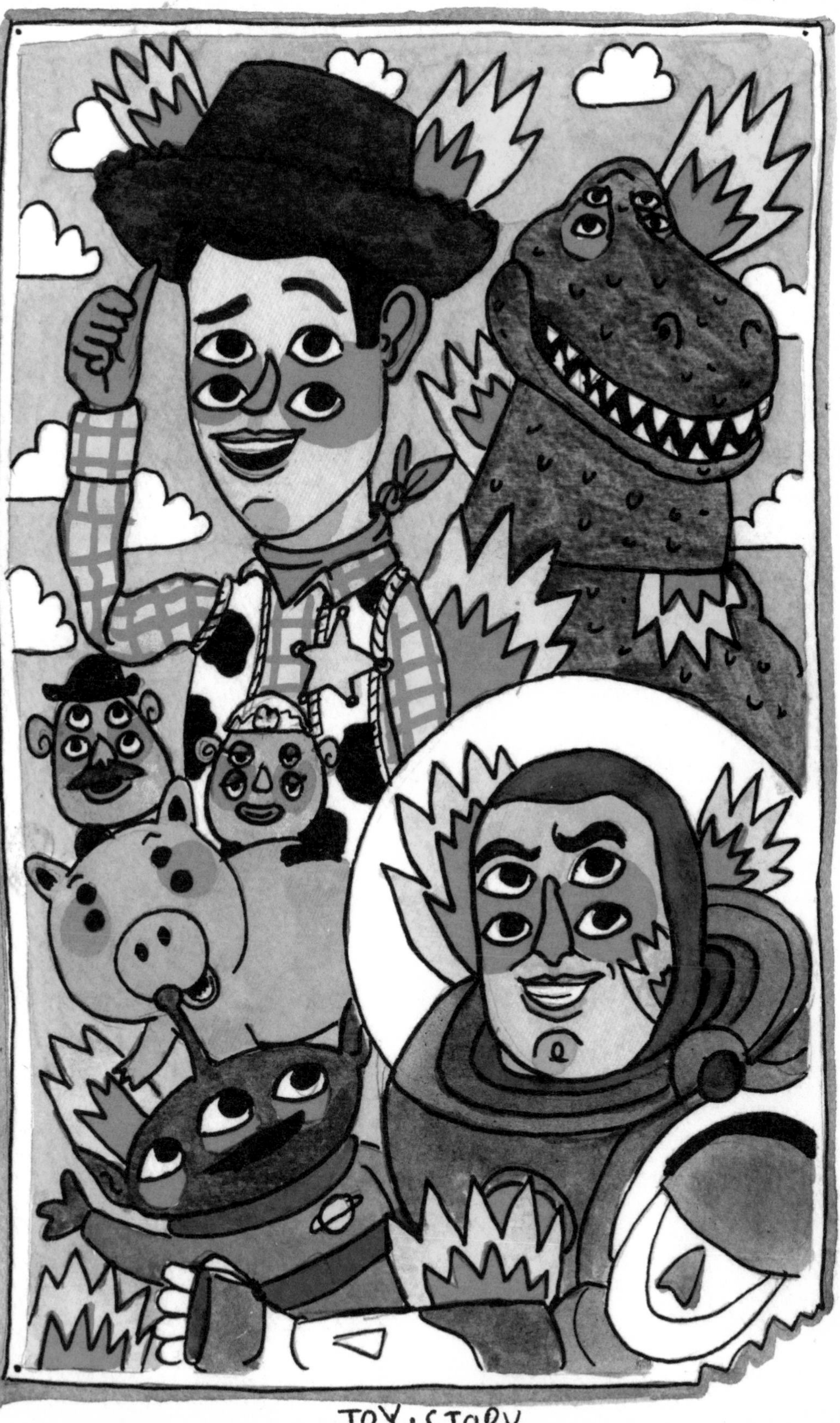

TOY · STORY

KIDS

(1995)

THERE COULD ~~NOT~~ BE NO BETTER MOVIE THAN
THIS TO COME OUT WHEN YOU ARE 13.
i WATCHED iT OVER AND OVER AGAIN, NOT KNOWING
WHAT TO MAKE OF iT BUT COMPLETELY BLOWN
AWAY BY THAT TEENAGE WORLD FULL OF SEX,
DRUGS AND FREE WiLL THAT i ~~DREAMED~~ DREAMED
OF. THERE WERE LOTS OF THINGS i RELATED TO.
AND WHEN YOU'RE SO YOUNG, AND THERE'S NO
SUCH THING AS THE INTERNET, iT WAS SORT OF
WEiRD TO FEEL A CONNECTION WITH A
MOViE ABOUT A BUNCH OF KiDS FROM SO FAR
AWAY. i'M GOiNG TO SAY HERE THAT i'VE NEVER
HAD ANY DOUBTS ABOUT THE iSSUE OF SAFE SEX, SO
iT WASN'T THAT PART OF THE MOViE THAT SHOOK
ME. i THINK iT WAS MORE THE OPPORTUNiTY TO
WATCH THE CULTURE i'D BEEN SO OBSESSED WiTH.
AND BY THAT AGE i WAS A SKATER, TOO, AND WORE
THE SAME CLOTHES AS THE KiDS iN "KiDS," AND
DiD MANY OTHER THINGS MY ~~XXXX~~ PARENTS
WOULDN'T HAVE APPROVED OF iF THEY'D FOUND
OUT (TOO LATE NOW, PARENTS! HA!). iT WAS LIKE
LOOKiNG iN A MiRROR. AND iN AN ERA WiTHOUT
iNTERNET, THAT WAS A REAL FEAT. WiTHOUT A
DOUBT, KiDS iS ONE OF THE MOViES THAT
SHAPED MY LiFE.   :ü:

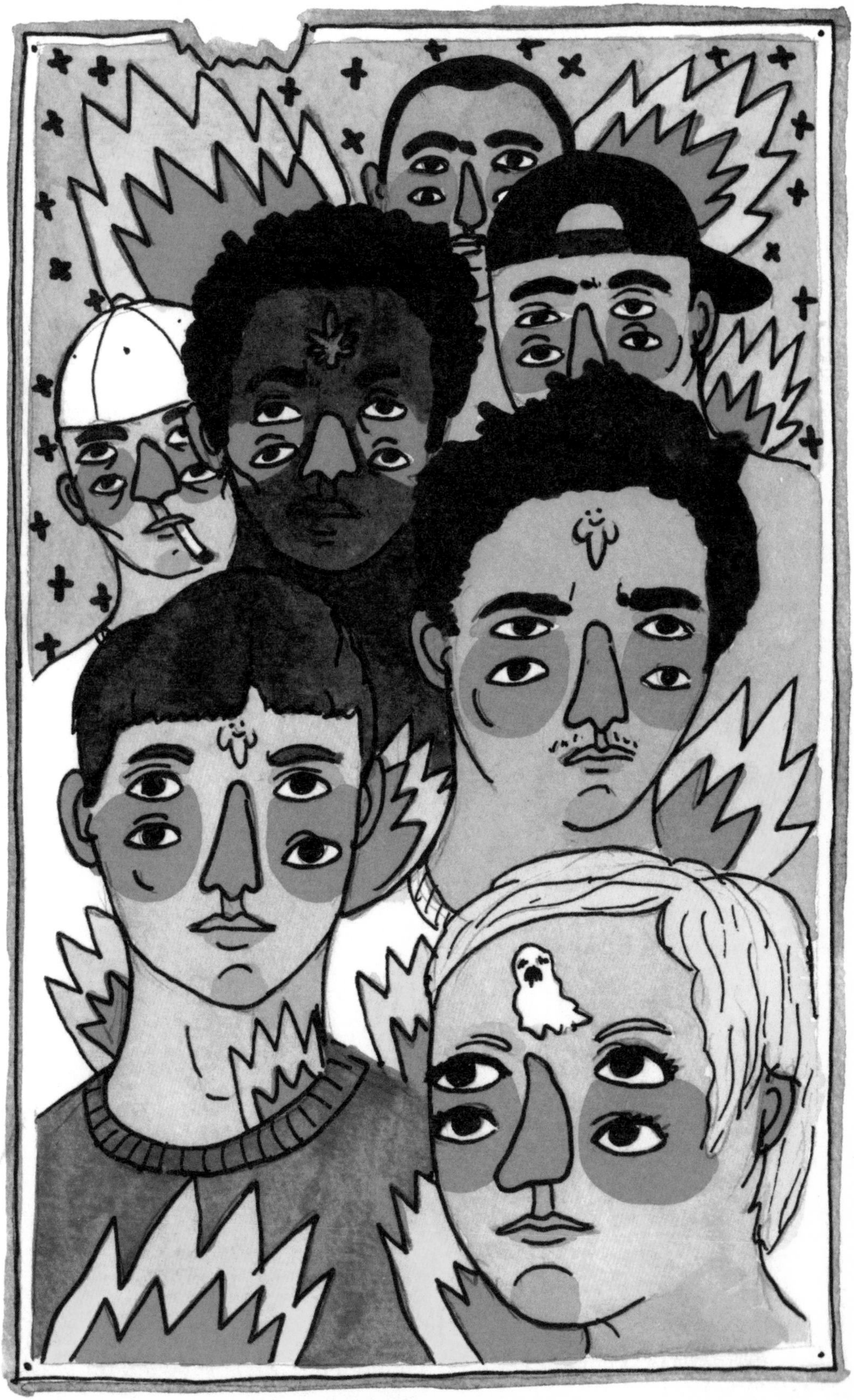

KIDS

CASINO

(1995)

BACK WITH MARTIN SCORSESE AND ANOTHER OF HIS TOUR DE FORCES. I'VE ALWAYS CONSIDERED CASINO TO BE AN EXTRA CHAPTER IN THE WORLD OF GOODFELLAS. IN FACT, ROBERT DE NIRO AND JOE PESCI PLAY THE LEADS AGAIN HERE. CASINO IS A PRIME EXAMPLE OF THE ITALIAN-AMERICAN MAFIA GENRE, ONLY NOW IT'S NOT WITHIN THE USUAL EAST COAST SETTING, BUT UNDER THE BRIGHT LIGHTS OF LAS VEGAS — A KIND OF THEME PARK FOR THOSE MODEL GANGSTERS. I GO CRAZY OVER THE OPENING OF THE MOVIE, WHERE IN THE FIRST 20 MINUTES THEY SHOW HOW THE WHOLE MAFIA BUSINESS IN VEGAS IS RUN. ROBERT DE NIRO HAS WORKED UMPTEEN TIMES WITH SCORSESE, AND IT SHOWS. IT'S AS IF HE WASN'T ACTING, LIKE HE REALLY WAS PART OF THE MAFIA. AND WHAT CAN I SAY ABOUT JOE PESCI? IN MY OPINION, IN BOTH GOODFELLAS AND CASINO HE'S EARNED HIMSELF THE TITLE OF ONE OF THE GREATEST MOVIE ACTORS OF ALL TIME. IT'S TRUE HE HASN'T APPEARED IN THAT MUCH, BUT WHEN HE DOES, IT'S LIKE A COMBINATION OF EARTHQUAKES, VOLCANOES TORNADOS AND ELECTRICAL STORMS. HE'S A GENIUS, LIKE DE NIRO, AND LIKE SCORSESE. JOE PESCI, I LOVE YOU.

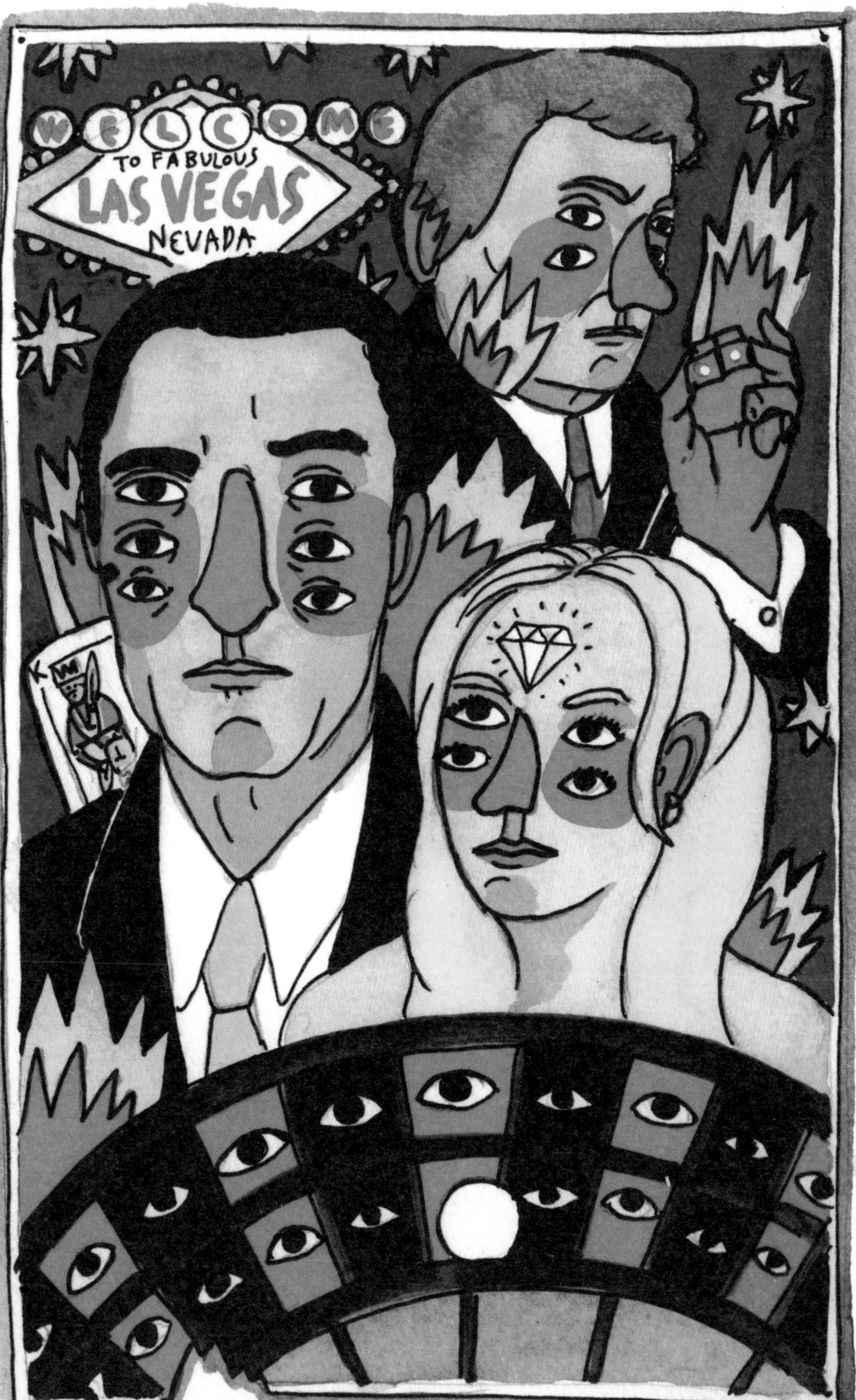
WELCOME
TO FABULOUS
LAS VEGAS
NEVADA

CASINO

se7en

(1995)

SEVEN IS A GREAT MOVIE. OR AT LEAST FOR MY INTERESTS IN 1995, IT WAS PERFECT. AND LIKE MANY OTHER MOVIES FROM MY TEENAGE YEARS, I STILL ENJOY IT TODAY. THE TYPE OF MURDERER PLAYED BY SPACEY HELPED PAVE THE WAY FOR A NEW KIND OF THRILLER — HE WAS A COMPLETE PSYCHOPATH, METHODICAL AND WITH DEPTH TO HIS CHARACTER. SO MUCH SO THAT YOU ALMOST WISH HE'D CARRY ON HORRIFYING US WITH HIS DESPICABLE DEEDS (WHICH IN HIS HEAD WERE SUFFUSED WITH HEAVENLY JUSTICE). NO SPOILERS, BUT I WILL SAY THAT ENDINGS DON'T REALLY GET MORE INTENSE THAN THIS ONE. MY HEART WAS IN MY MOUTH A COUPLE OF TIMES. CONFESSION... I KIND OF WISH THERE WERE 14 DEADLY SINS INSTEAD OF 7.

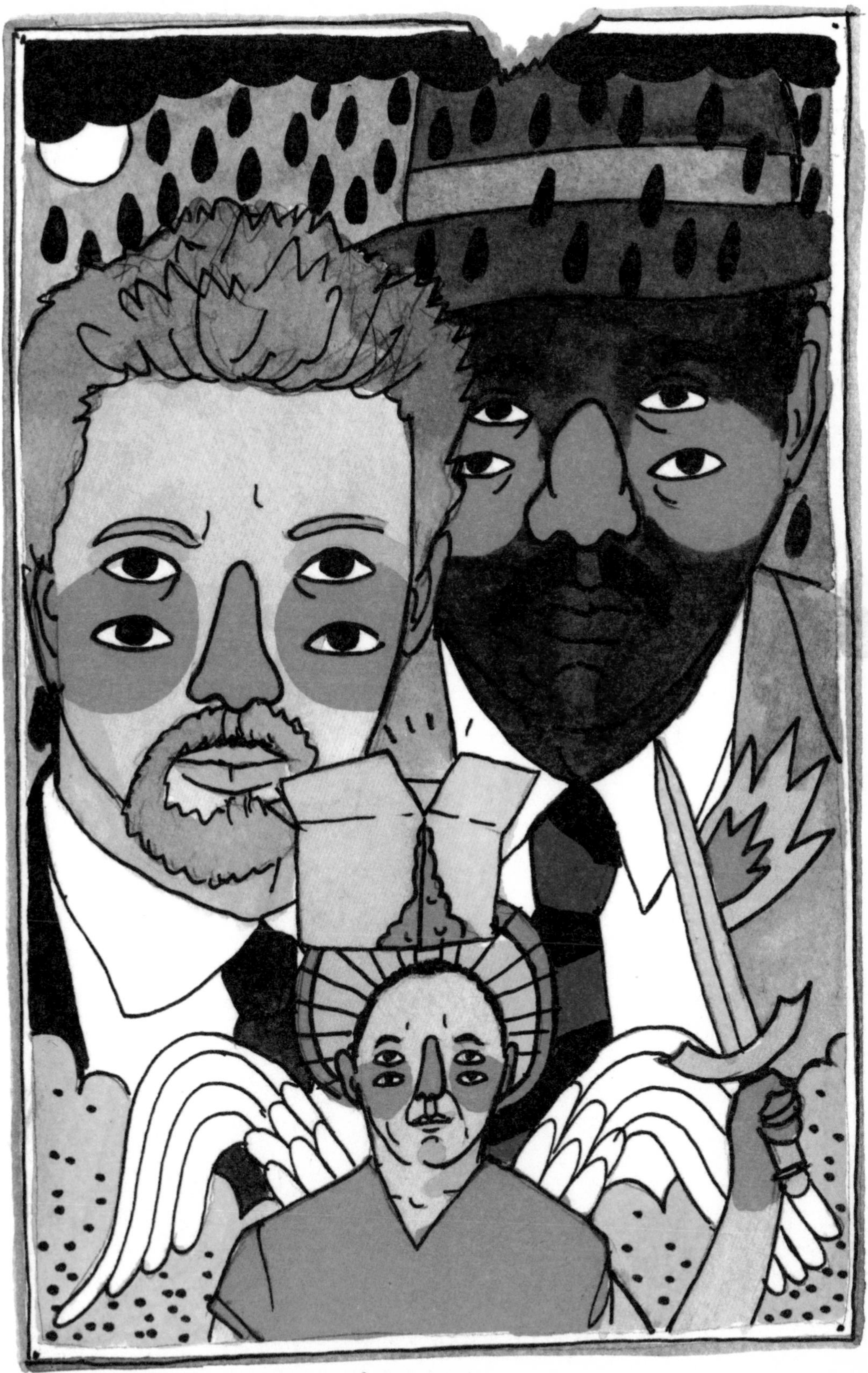

SEVEN

LA HAINE

(1995)

ANOTHER EXAMPLE OF THE WORLD i LIKE TO
DRAW IN MY WORK. ON A SMALL BUDGET, THIS
MOVIE FOLLOWS THE LiFE OF THREE YOUNG MEN
ALL CONDEMNED TO SURVIVE IN THE PARISIAN
SUBURBS BECAUSE OF THEIR ORIGINS (ONE IS JEWISH,
ONE ARAB AND ANOTHER BLACK). AND LiFE THERE
IS WORTH LESS THAN IN OTHER NEIGHBOURHOODS IN
THE FRENCH CAPITAL. 24 HOURS WITH THESE
CHARACTERS IS ALL THE DIRECTOR NEEDS TO
SHOW US HOW TOUGH IT IS FOR THE BOYS TO AVOID
GETTING ENSNARED IN THE SPIDERS' WEBS THAT LIE
ALL OVER PLACES LIKE THIS.
STYLISTICALLY, LA HAINE IS ALSO REALLY INTERESTING
– SHOT IN BLACK AND WHITE AND WITH OCCASIONAL
ECHOES OF PULP FICTION.
VINCENT CASSEL IS AMAZING. FEW WOULD
CHOOSE TO LIVE IN ONE OF THOSE NEIGHBOURHOODS,
BUT WE JUST CAN'T TAKE OUR EYES OFF WHAT GOES
ON THERE. IT'S LIKE WATCHING A METEORITE
APPROACHING EARTH BUT DOING NOTHING TO TRY
TO STOP IT. YOU JUST GAWP IN AWFUL WONDER
AT THE SCREEN.

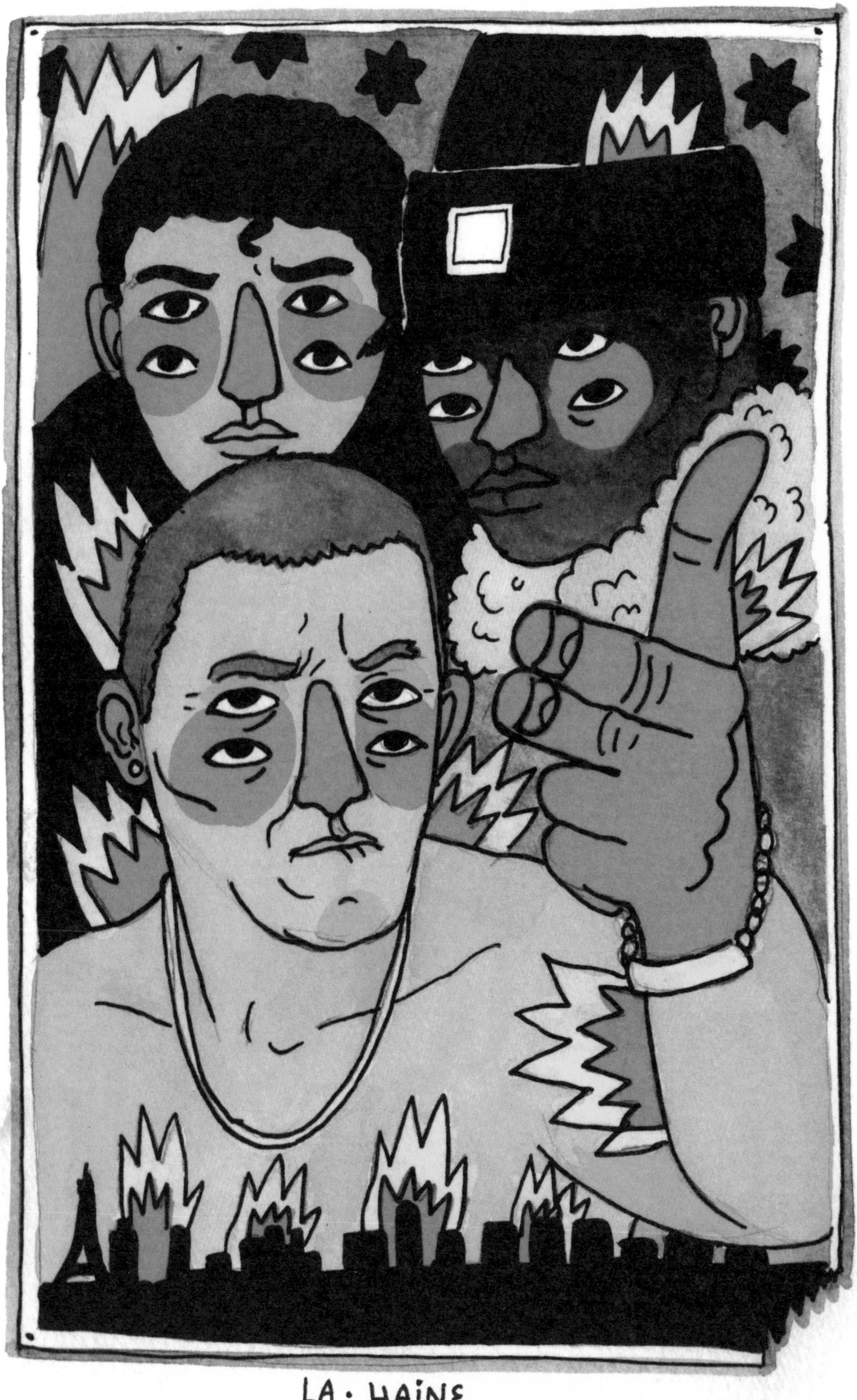

LA · HAINE

FARGO

(1996)

WHAT A FILM. THE COEN BROTHERS' SHOT IT WITH MINIMAL PLOT AND IN THE MIDDLE OF NOWHERE IN THE STATES. EVERY SINGLE DETAIL OF FARGO IS IMPECCABLE. THE CAST IS A MISHMASH OF UNREAL AND WHACKY ~~CHARACTERS~~ CHARACTERS ALONG WITH BELIEVABLE AND BLAND ONES. THE DIALOGUES ONLY SERVE TO REINFORCE THE COMPLEXITY AND INTERNAL UNIVERSE OF EACH CHARACTER. THE LOCATIONS AND LANDSCAPE SUIT THE MOVIE DOWN TO GROUND. THE MUSIC FLOWS PERFECTLY. AND THE SCRIPT IS COMPLETE, FLAWLESS, TIMELESS. I'M NOT SURE IF I'D LIVE IN FARGO, BUT I'D DEFINITELY PAY A VISIT@ EACH WINTER TO SEE WHAT'S COOKING ON ITS ICY STREETS.

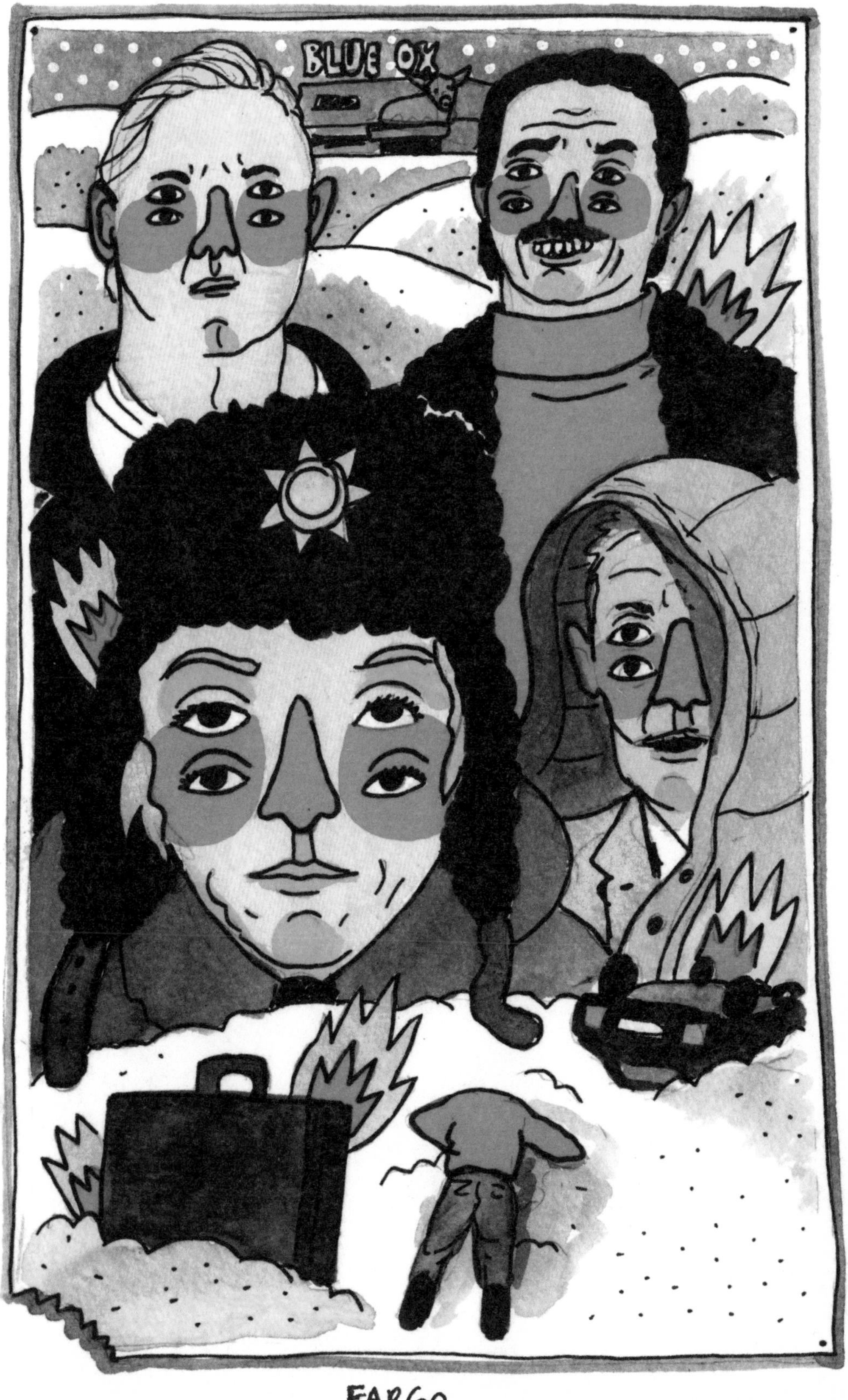
BLUE OX

FARGO

Trainspotting

(1996)

THIS IS ANOTHER MOVIE THAT LANDED IN MY
LIFE AT JUST THE RIGHT MOMENT. RENTON AND
HIS BAND HAD A BIG EFFECT ON 14-YEAR-OLD ME.
IT'S NOT LIKE I WANTED TO EMULATE THE KIND
OF LIFE THAT THE EDINBURGH GANG LIVED, BUT I
LOVED WATCHING IT ALL - THE HIGHS, THE LOWS,
THE EVEN LOWER LOWS... IF IT'S A PORTRAIT OF A
GENERATION, OF ONE ● CLOSE TO YOU, THEN IT'S
NATURAL THAT YOU WANT TO TRY TO UNDERSTAND
WHAT IT CAN ● TEACH YOU. ALL OF US WHO
WERE TEENAGERS IN THE MID-90S CARRY A
LITTLE ● BIT OF TRAINSPOTTING IN US, FOR BETTER
OR FOR WORSE. AND ● ON THE OTHER HAND,
TRAINSPOTTING MARKED THE START OF NEW
BRITISH CINEMA.
ONE DAY, I HOPE TO BE ABLE TO HAVE AS
AMAZING A TRIP AS RENTON, HIS HEAD DOWN
THE LOO, SWIMMING AROUND IN THE DARK WORLD
FULL OF "THOSE" SUPPOSITORIES.

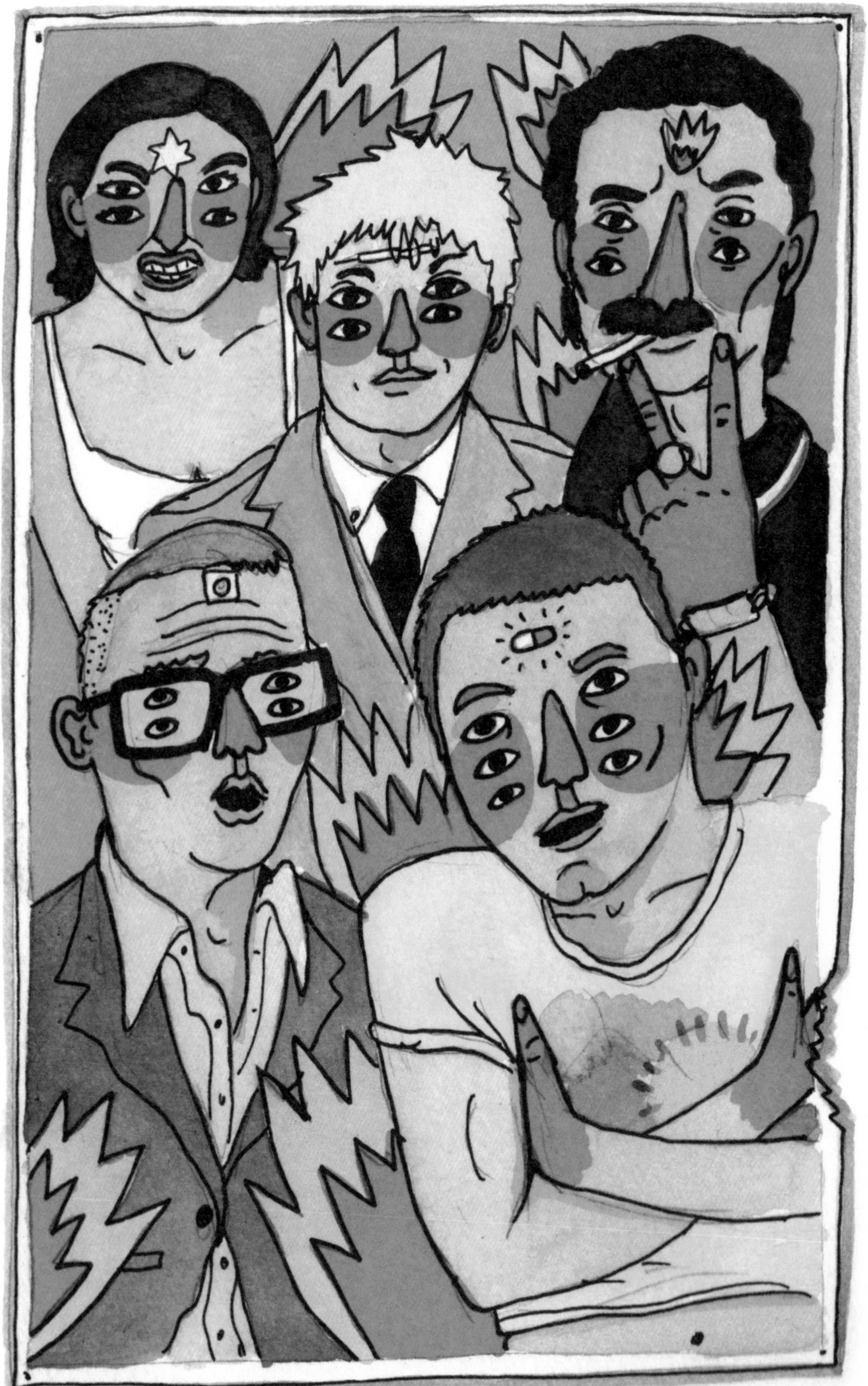

TRAINSPOTTING

LA·VITA·È·BELLA

(1997) (LIFE IS BEAUTIFUL)

WATCHING THIS MOVIE IS LIKE FINDING YOURSELF
~~STANDING~~ STANDING RIGHT UNDER A RAINBOW —
THE WORLD BECOMES MORE BEAUTIFUL. DIRECTOR
AND ACTOR ROBERTO BENIGNI REINCARNATES
THE ADORABLE AND HILARIOUS CHARLIE CHAPLIN
TO MAKE OUR HEARTS BURST. IF A FILM MOVES
ME, I'LL CRY. "LIFE IS BEAUTIFUL" MAKES ME
PUFFY FROM ALL THE CRYING. BENIGNI'S MOVIE
IS BEAUTIFUL, MOVING, SAD AND HAPPY ALL IN
ONE. THE CHARACTER HE PLAYS IS SO MAGICAL
I DON'T THINK HE'LL EVER NOT BE WITH ME.
I THINK IT'S THANKS TO THIS MOVIE THAT
I LEARNED HOW TO DEAL WITH CERTAIN
THINGS IN LIFE BETTER. IT'S A ~~HEART~~
HEART-WRENCHING STORY THAT I'LL NEVER
TIRE OF WATCHING. BENIGNI OFFERS MOVIEGOERS
A KIND OF KALEIDOSCOPE THROUGH WHICH TO
SEE THE OTHER SIDE OF THE COIN.
THANKS, ROBERTO, FOR MAKING ME A
BETTER PERSON.

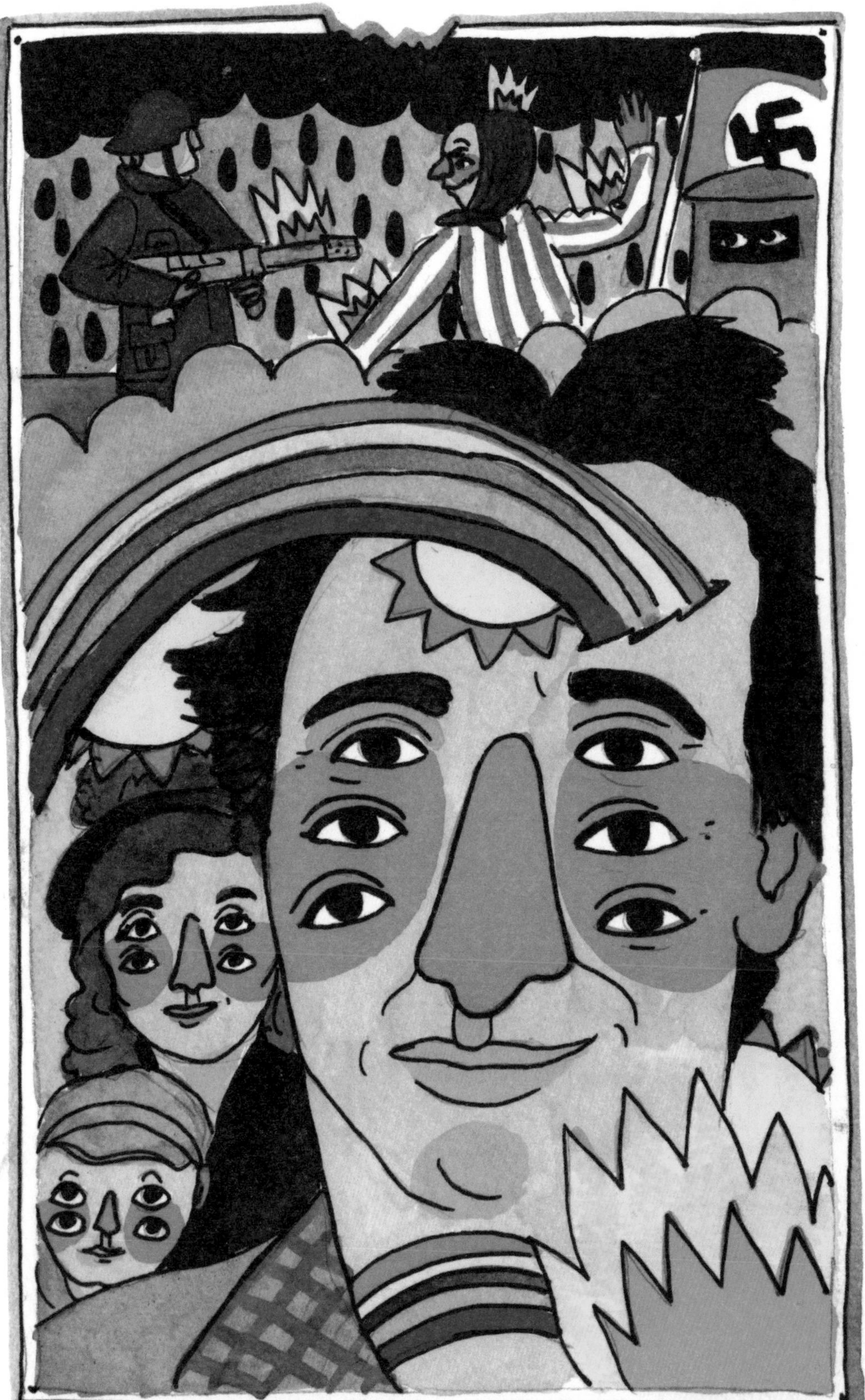

LA·VITA·É·BELLA

GUMMO

(1997)

HARMONY KORINE COULDN'T HAVE MADE A BETTER DEBUT. HE HAD ~~HIS~~ ALREADY SHOWN HIS CREDENTIALS WITH THE SCRIPT OF KIDS, BUT WITH GUMMO, HIS DARK, ~~HIS~~ UNUSUAL TASTES GO EVEN FURTHER. GUMMO IS ALMOST A DOCUMENTARY ABOUT THE AMERICAN HEARTLAND. IT'S A MERRY-GO-ROUND OF CHARACTERS, EACH ONE MORE OF AN OUTSIDER THAN THE NEXT, LIVING IN SOME TOWN IN THE MIDDLE OF NOWHERE IN OHIO. EACH CHARACTER REPRESENTS A DEMON OF SOCIETY. A DEMON WHO IS REALLY A VICTIM OF THE SYSTEM.

THE MOVIE IS LIKE A BAD DREAM THAT MAKES YOU FEEL QUEASY, BUT THAT YOU DON'T WANT TO WAKE UP FROM EITHER. KORINE MAKES US WANT TO COVER OUR EYES, BUT WE ALWAYS LEAVE A GAP TO PEEK THROUGH SO WE DON'T MISS A SECOND OF THE SPECTACLE. ALL OF THIS FORMS ONE OF THE CONCEPTUAL BASES OF MY OWN WORK, SO YOU'LL UNDERSTAND WHY KORINE'S MOVIE IS LIKE A HOLY BOOK FOR ME. I'VE ALWAYS THOUGHT THAT IF I EVER MADE A MOVIE, IT'D BE IN THE VEIN OF KORINE'S GUMMO.

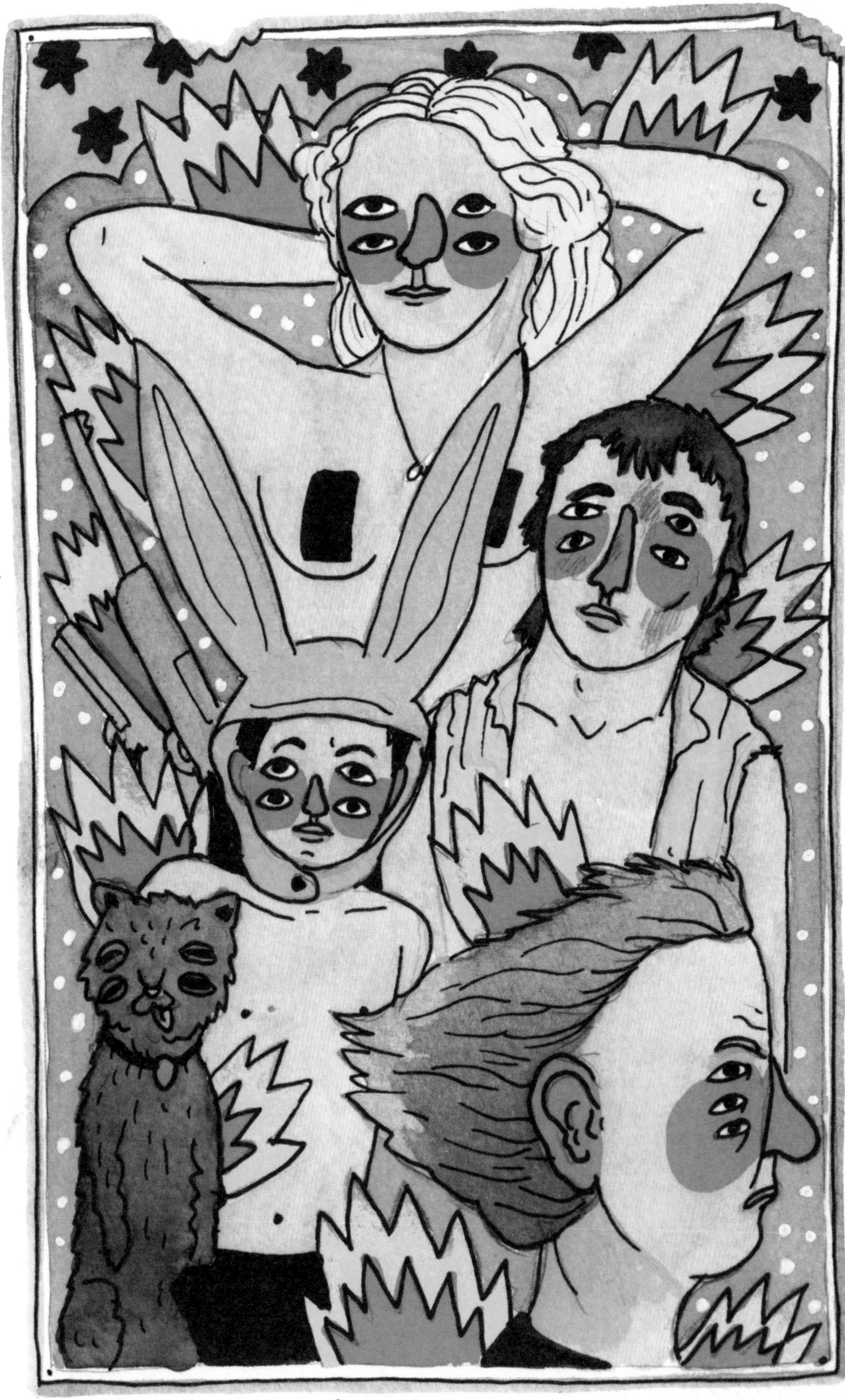

GUMMO

AMERICAN·HISTORY·X

(1998)

i REMEMBER MY FATHER AND i WERE ON
HOLIDAY IN THE NORTH OF SPAIN AND WE WENT
TO THE CINEMA TO WHILE AWAY THE EVENING.
WE LIKED THE POSTER SO WE JUST WENT IN,
NOT HAVING A CLUE WHAT THE MOVIE WAS ABOUT.
WHEN iT WAS OVER WE WALKED OUT AGAIN iN
SILENCE, AS iF WE HAD TO DIGEST WHAT WE'D
JUST SEEN.
THE STORY TOLD iN THIS MOVIE SEEMED ~~COMPLETE~~
~~COMPLETELY~~ COMPLETELY UNBELIEVABLE TO US.
BUT MORE ~~THE~~ UNBELIEVABLE STILL WAS
EDWARD NORTON. A NEW STAR HAD JUST BEEN
BORN iN OUR PANTHEON OF ACTORS.
~~THROUGH~~ iN THE FIRST PART OF AMERICAN
HISTORY X, NORTON HAS YOU GRIPPING YOUR SEAT
WITH FEAR. i WILL NEVER FORGET HIS FACE AS
THE POLICE CUFF HIM BY THE FRONT DOOR
TO HIS HOUSE. AND JUST AS INCREDIBLE iS THE
JOURNEY HE MAKES INSIDE THE PRISON, TO END
UP IN A PLACE NOT EVEN HE EXPECTED.

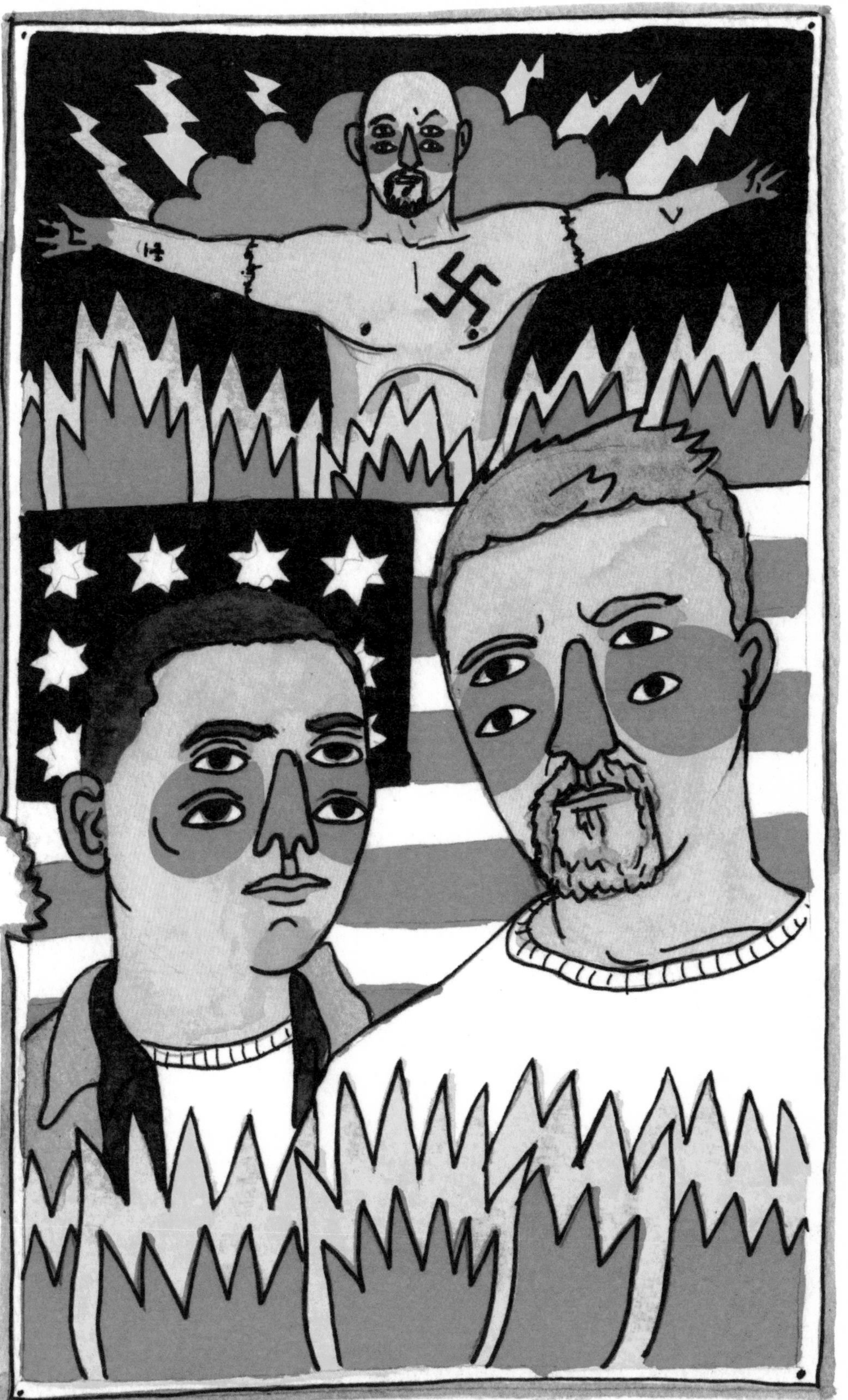

AMERICAN · HISTORY · X

BLACK CAT WHITE CAT

(1998)

NOW WE COME TO ANOTHER MOVIE THAT HAS
HAD A BIG INFLUENCE ON MY WORK.
EMIR KUSTURICA ONCE AGAIN BRILLIANTLY
DEPICTS ROMANI CULTURE. THE GOOD THING IS
THAT THIS TIME HE DOES SO FROM A MORE
PLAYFUL AND JOKEY STANCE. AND WE STILL HAVE
ALL THE MAGIC OF THE TRADITION AND THE
QUAGMIRE THAT IS THE REALITY FOR ROMANI
IN THE BALKANS. i REMEMBER THAT BACK
DURING MY TIME WITH ROMANI PEOPLE i
WAS ALWAYS LAUGHING, AND MY SHOES WERE
ALWAYS COVERED IN MUD. i'D HAPPILY SQUELCH
AROUND IN THE MUD EVERY DAY OF MY LIFE, AND
IF IT'S WITH A GENIUS LIKE KUSTURICA,
i WOULDN'T THINK TWICE ABOUT IT.
THIS MOVIE IS A VITAL LIFE LESSON, WHERE
YOU LAUGH, CRY, DANCE, WITNESS MISERY, GET
YOUR FEET MUCKY AND THEN LAUGH ALL
OVER AGAIN.

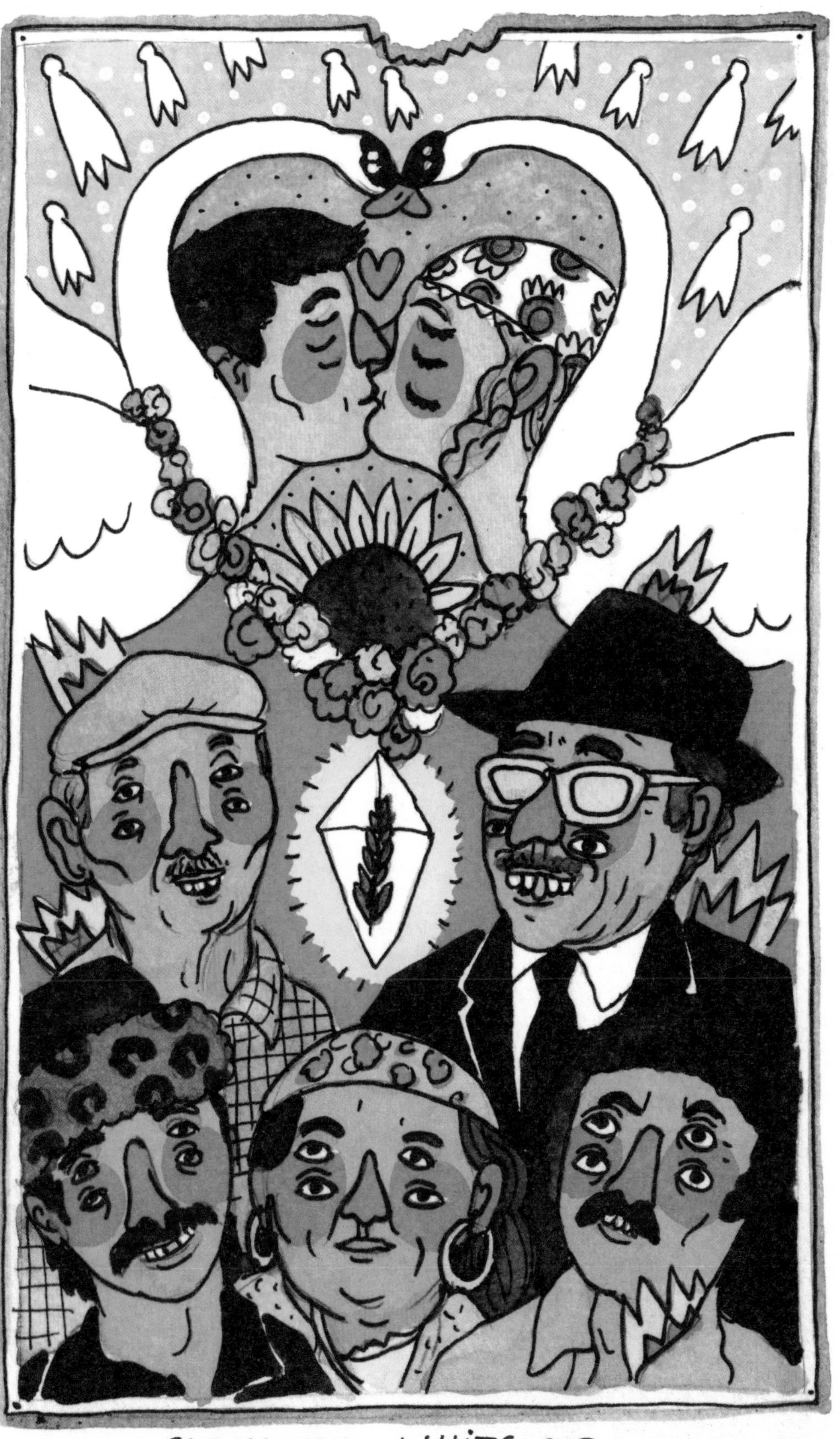

BLACK·CAT· WHITE·CAT

HAPPINESS

(1998)

i THINK THIS MOVIE FASCINATES ME SO MUCH BECAUSE, AMONG OTHER THINGS, iT DEPICTS SOCIETY'S "CORRECT" LiFESTYLE FALLING TO PiECES. A LiFE DEVOTED TO WORK OR CREATING A 2.4 FAMILY, WHERE THERE'S NO ROOM FOR SURPRISES OR iMPROViSATiON. iN HAPPINESS, WE SEE THAT NONE OF THAT iS REAL, THAT iT COLLAPSES AROUND THE CHARACTERS, AND THAT TERRIBLE DEMONS EMERGE. BUT HERE THE SET-UP iS ALMOST COMiCAL. THE CHARACTERS, WHEN THEY FiNALLY EXPLODE, ARE SO OVER THE TOP THAT THEY'RE FUNNY, EVEN THOUGH EVERYTHING AROUND THEM COULDN'T BE MORE BiTTER.

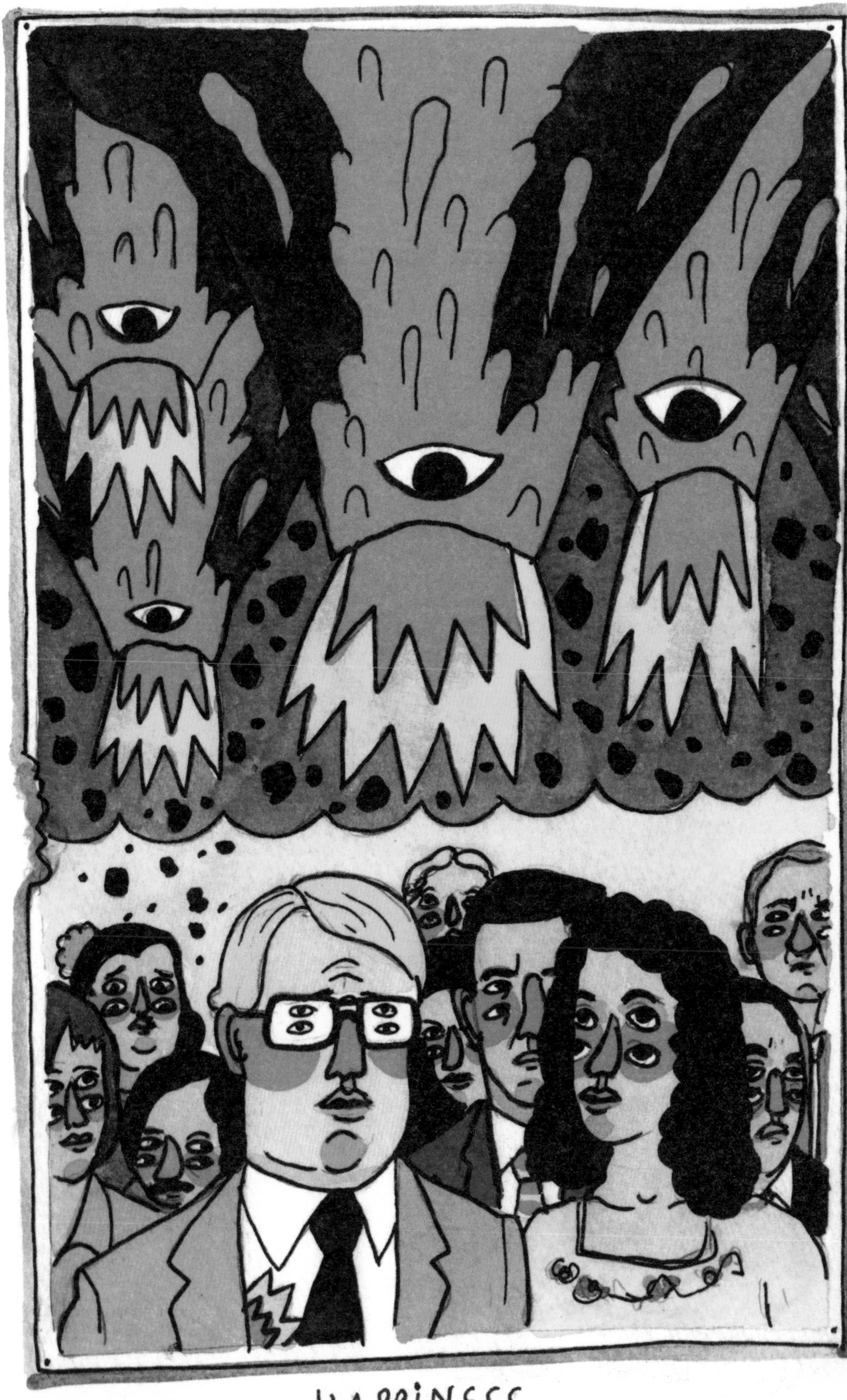

HAPPINESS

Buffalo '66

(1998)

IN BUFFALO'66, YOU GET A COMPLETELY DIFFERENT KIND OF LOVE STORY, DIRECTED BY AND STARRING THE MADMAN THAT IS VINCENT GALLO. THE PLOT ITSELF IS SLIGHT, WITH TWO INSIGNIFICANT CHARACTERS IN A COLD, NONDESCRIPT CITY, BUT GALLO CREATES AN ENTIRE COSMOS AROUND THEM.

YOU ALREADY KNOW THAT MY FIRST CINEMATOGRAPHIC LOVE WAS CHRISTINA RICCI, SO IT GOES WITHOUT SAYING ~~THE~~ THAT THE FACT THAT SHE IS ONE OF THE ~~MAIN~~ MAIN CHARACTERS MAKES THIS MOVIE EVEN MORE SPECIAL. VISUALLY SPEAKING, GALLO INCLUDES FRAMES THAT RIDICULE HIS CHARACTER EVEN MORE. HIS RED BOOTS, WHICH ~~THEY~~ DON'T GO WITH ANYTHING, STAND OUT AGAINST THE ICY, MUDDY GREYISH GROUND OF THAT BROKEN, USELESS CITY. AND RICCI APPEARS AS AN ANGEL RADIATING KINDNESS AND NAIVETY, WHICH ENDS UP RUBBING OFF ON MEAN OLD VINCENT GALLO. EVERY TWO OR THREE YEARS, I FEEL THE NEED TO RE-WATCH THIS MOVIE AND REMEMBER THE MAGIC THAT EXISTS IN THE MARGINAL STORIES THAT NOBODY ELSE WOULD NOTICE.

136

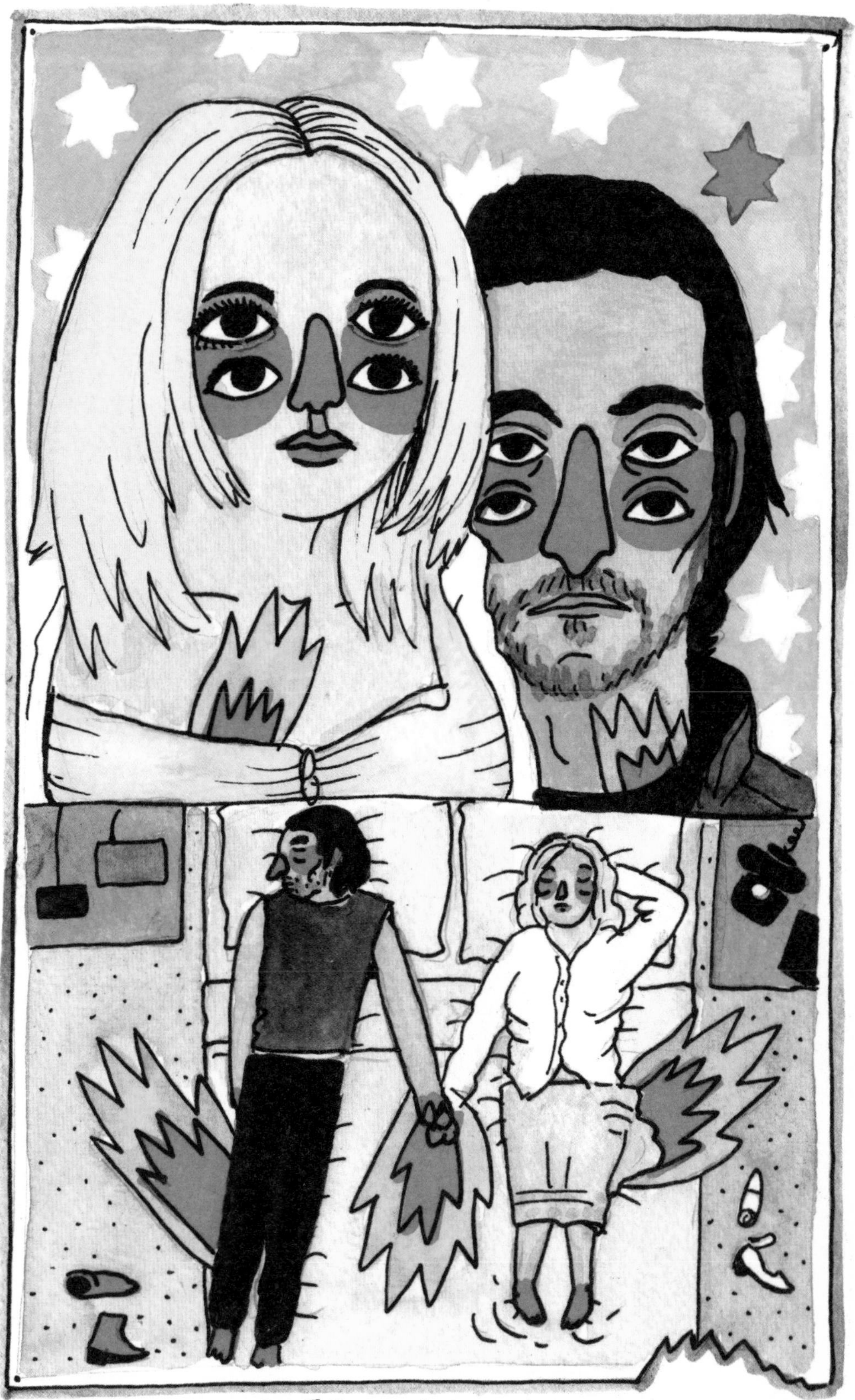

BUFFALO.'66

LA · VENDEDORA DE · R🌹SAS

(1998) (THE ROSE SELLER)

THIS ~~COLOMBIAN~~ COLOMBIAN MOVIE, LIKE MANY IN THIS DIARY, IS A STATEMENT OF PRINCIPLES WHICH I USE IN MY WORK AS AN ARTIST. LA VENDEDORA DE ROSAS NARRATES THE LIFE OF A GIRL LIVING IN TERRIBLE CONDITIONS IN SLUMS ON THE OUTSKIRTS OF MEDELLÍN, WHERE IT'S JUST AS DANGEROUS INSIDE THE HOUSE AS OUT ON THE STREETS. LIFE GETS HARDER STILL AND SHE ENDS UP SELLING ROSES ON THE ~~XXX~~ STREETS OF THAT BRUTAL AND HOSTILE CITY. THE MOVIE IS LIKE THE PITIABLE DANCE ROUTINE OF SOME WRETCHED KIDS ON THE STREET DANCING TO DEATH'S BEAT. IT'S NOT EASY VIEWING, BUT WE SHOULD WATCH THIS MOVIE TO GET A 🌹 BETTER ~~UNDERSTAND~~ UNDERSTANDING OF A REALITY THAT STILL EXISTS TODAY. WE'RE NOT GOING TO CHANGE ANYTHING BY WATCHING IT, BUT AT LEAST WE CAN BECOME AWARE OF WHAT GOES ON. THIS MOVIE MOVED ME SO MUCH THAT I ALWAYS KEEP IT IN MIND WHENEVER I CREATE CHARACTERS FOR MY ILLUSTRATIONS.

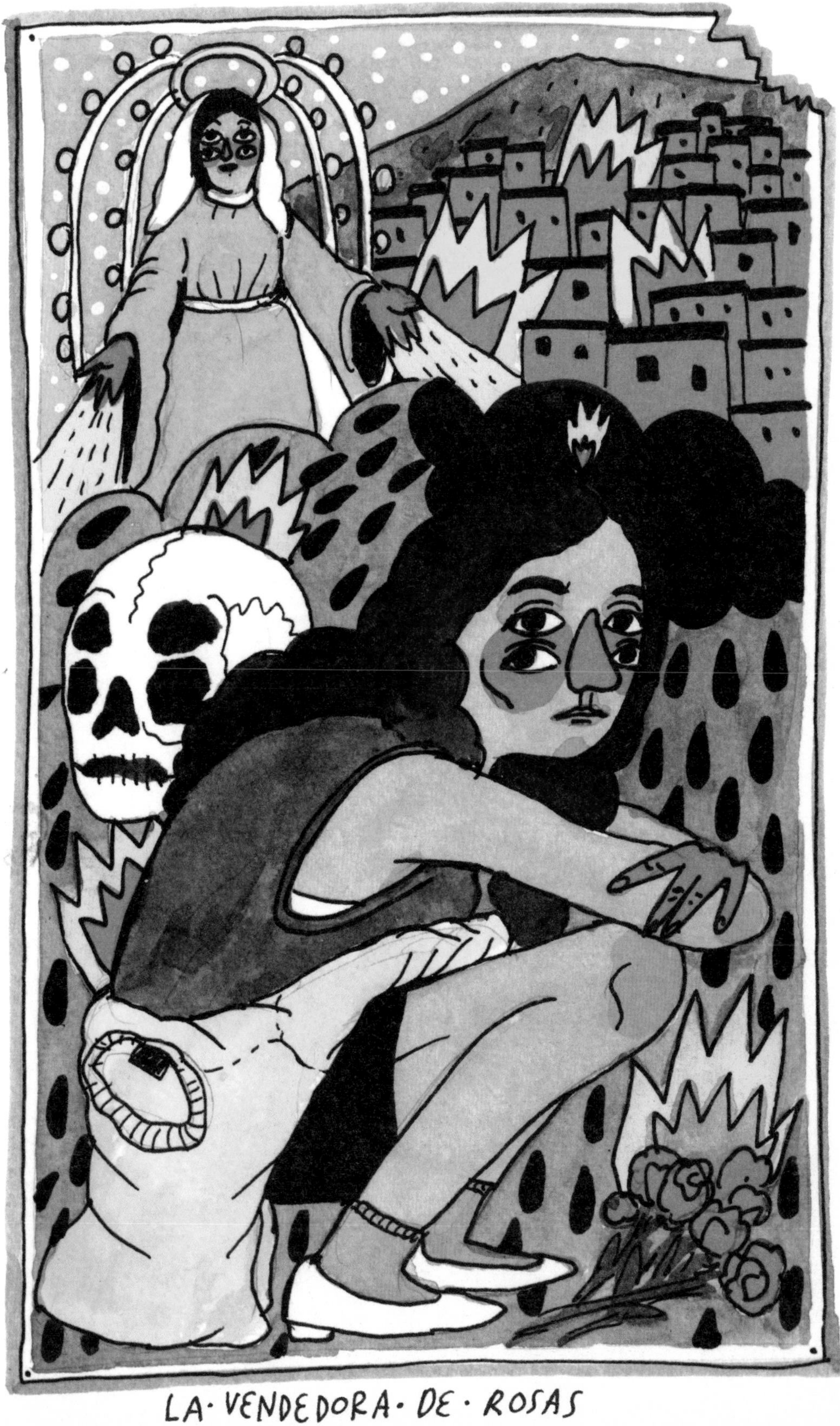

LA·VENDEDORA·DE·ROSAS

THE THIN · RED · LINE

(1998)

TERRENCE MALICK IS ONE OF CINEMA'S TRUE GENIUSES, WHICH IS PLAIN TO SEE IN THIS MOVIE. IN MY LIFE, WAR MOVIES HAVE OFFERED MANY HOURS OF ENTERTAINMENT. AND YET, AS WITH WESTERNS, THE ROLES AND STRUCTURES TEND TO REMAIN UNCHANGED FOR DECADES. MALICK OPTS FOR AN IMPRESSIVE ENSEMBLE CAST AND LETS THEM LOOSE IN THE PACIFIC DURING THE SECOND ~~WAR~~ WORLD WAR. EACH OF HIS CHARACTERS REINFORCES AN IDEA, A PHOBIA, A GRIEVANCE OR A SMALL JOY DIFFERENT FROM THE NEXT ONE. IT'S LIKE HE'S CONDENSED THE HUMAN SPECIES INTO A SMALL GROUP OF SOLDIERS, THEN STRETCHED IT TO THE LIMIT. A WONDERFUL STRATEGY BY MALICK, AS EVER, TO ADDRESS SOMETHING MUCH BIGGER THAN THE ACTUAL STORY TOLD IN THE MOVIE.

140

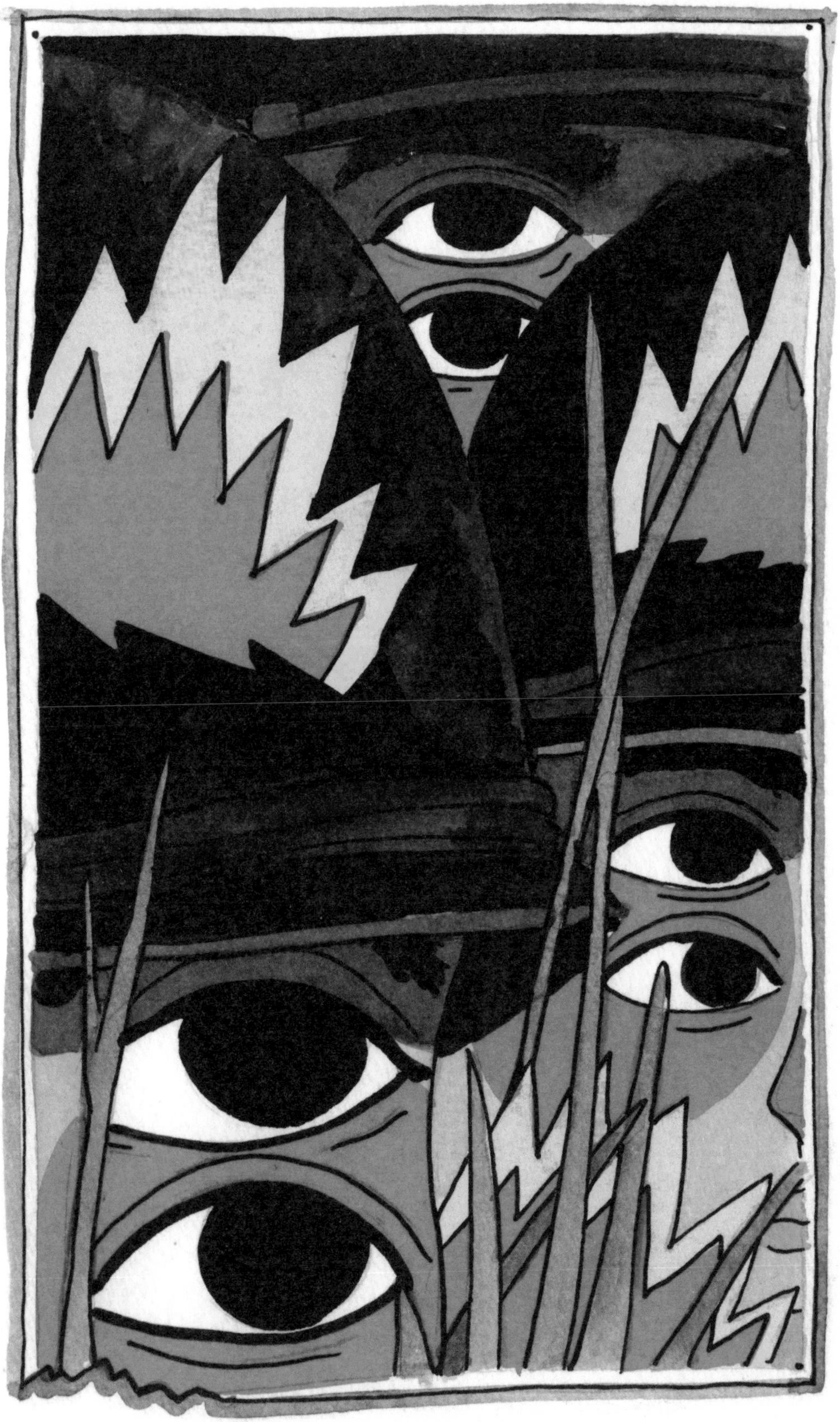

THE·THIN·RED·LINE

AMERICAN PIE

(1999)

I ALSO JUST LOVE HAVING A GOOD OLD GIGGLE, YOU KNOW? I LOVE PUERILE HUMOUR: POO, BUTTS, BOOBIES AND WILLIES, AND WITH AMERICAN PIE THAT KIND OF SILLY FUN IS A GIVEN. IVE ~~ALWAYS~~ ALWAYS ENJOYED AMERICAN MOVIES ABOUT KIDS IN COLLEGE PLAYING AT BEING GROWN-UPS AND OBSESSED WITH SEX, POPULARITY OR BEING DIFFERENT FROM EVERYONE ELSE.

THIS MOVIE MAKES FUN OF ALL OF THAT, WHILE PLAYING AT THE SAME GAME. THE U.S. MOVIE INDUSTRY HAS MANAGED TO MAKE IT SO THAT ITS TEENAGE STANDARDS ARE KNOWN AND REVERED ALL OVER THE WORLD. THAT'S WHY IT FEELS SO FAMILIAR, AND WE TAKE PLEASURE (OR AT LEAST I DO) IN WATCHING THESE HORMONE-CHARGED CHARACTERS. AMERICAN PIE DOESN'T STRAY ONE ~~MILLIMETRE~~ MILLIMETRE OUTSIDE OF THIS MODEL, AND THAT MAKES IT EVEN MORE ENJOYABLE AND HILARIOUS.

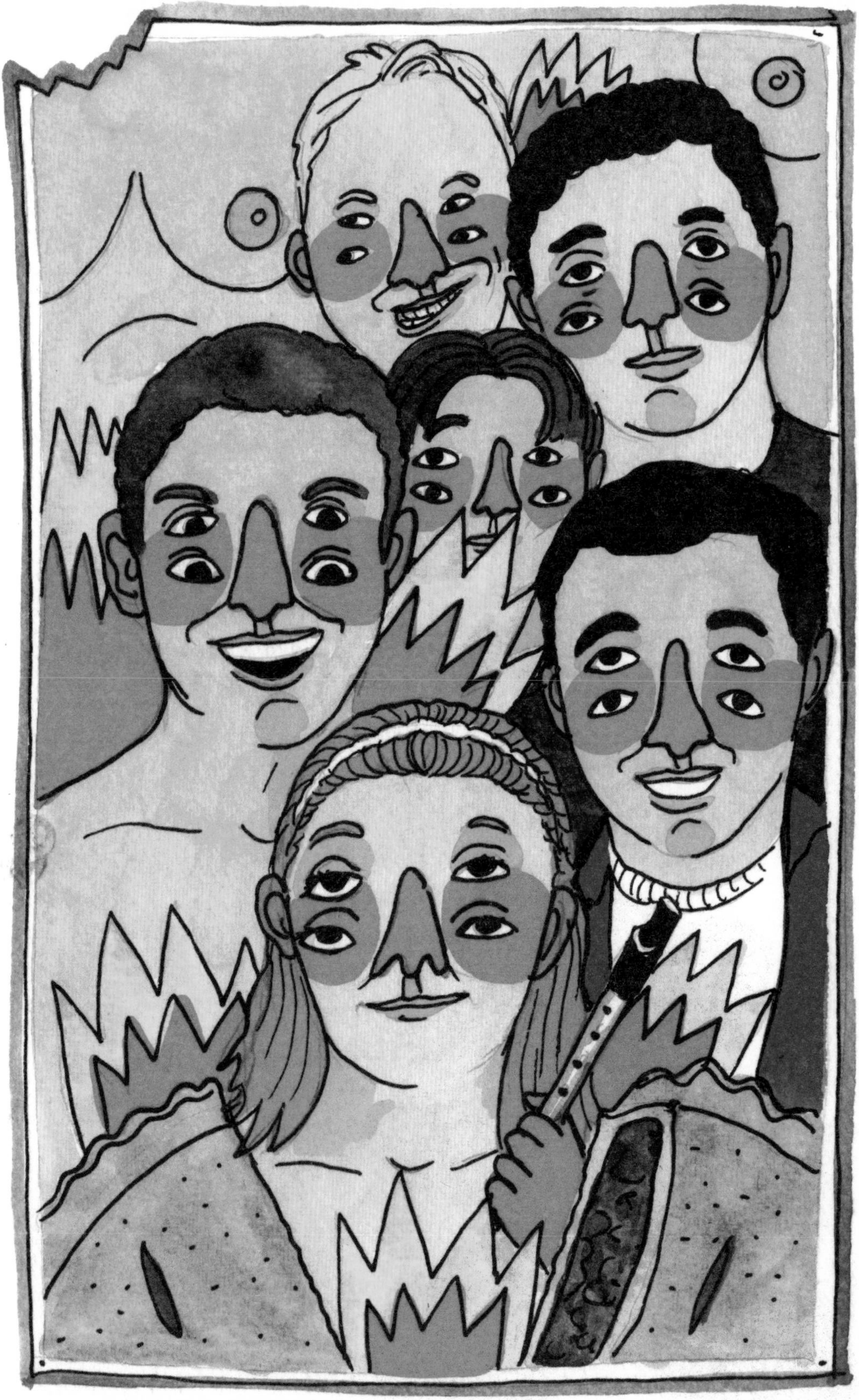

AMERICAN·PIE

(1999)

THIS MOVIE STAYED ETCHED ON MY RETINAS AND BRAIN FOR A LONG TIME AND MADE ME AN EVER BIGGER FAN OF DAVID FINCHER. i ALREADY LOVED EDWARD NORTON, BUT WITH THE RELEASE OF THIS MOVIE i BECAME A NORTON FAN FOR LIFE. AND BRAD PITT ~~WAS~~ WAS NOW THE COOLEST ACTOR IN MY CINEMA UNIVERSE. EVERYTHING, ABSOLUTELY EVERYTHING, IN THIS MOVIE WAS RIGHT UP MY STREET. IT LANDED LIKE A RIVAL'S RIGHT HOOK, SMACK BANG AGAINST MY JAW AND KNOCKED ME FOR SIX, AS IF i HAD COME OUT OF ONE OF THOSE UNDERGROUND FIGHTS MYSELF. i LOVED THAT WHOLE BACKDROP OF A SECRET ORDER THAT ALTERS REALITY ON ~~DIFFE~~ DIFFERENT LEVELS. AND i WANTED TO BE THERE. i EVEN LOOKED ONLINE FOR FIGHT CLUBS IN SPAIN. i WON'T EVEN GO INTO WHAT i FOUND — THAT'D BE A WHOLE OTHER BOOK. WHAT? YOU WANNA FIGHT?

144

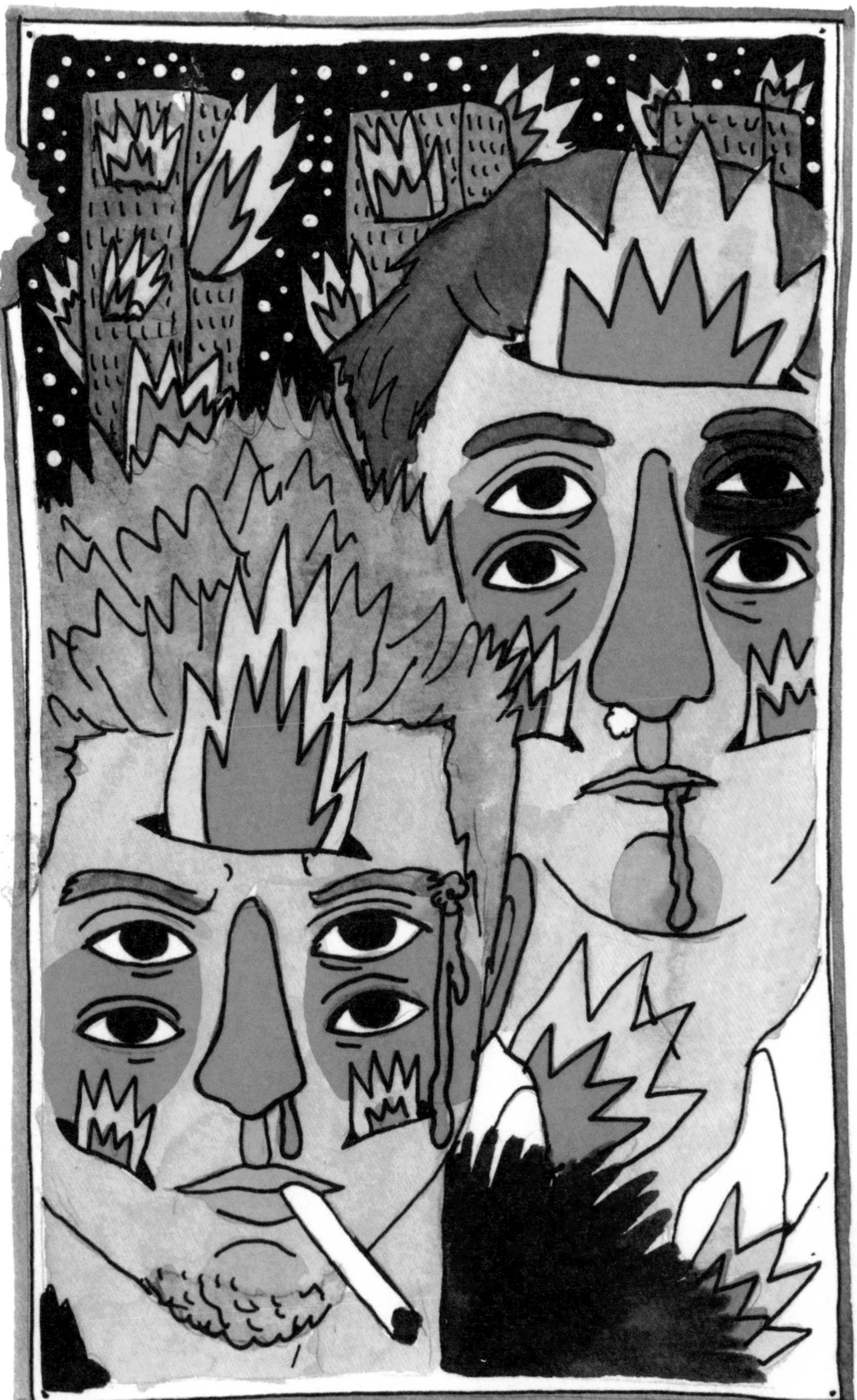

FiGHT· CLUB

AMERICAN BEAUTY

(1999)

THE TRUTH IS THAT WHEN I SAW THIS MOVIE IT REALLY CAPTIVATED ME, BUT I WASN'T EXACTLY SURE WHY. THERE WAS SOMETHING ABOUT THAT ATMOSPHERE OF ROTTEN PERFECTION THAT I FOUND REALLY POWERFUL. I THINK YOU UNDERSTAND THE MOVIE BETTER ONCE YOU'RE A BIT OLDER. SAM MENDES CAPTURED AN ABYSS IN THE MIDDLE OF A PICTURE-PERFECT AMERICAN SUBURB. AND I THINK THAT ABYSS IS A LITTLE HARDER TO UNDERSTAND WHEN YOU'RE THE AGE I WAS WHEN I SAW AMERICAN BEAUTY AT THE CINEMA.

I ALSO REMEMBER THAT THORA BIRCH WENT DOWN WELL WITH THAT 17-YEAR-OLD BOY. I WAS PRETTY PLEASED THAT INSTEAD OF BEING INTO THE OFFICIALLY HOT BLONDE, IT WAS "THE OTHER ONE" WHO I FOUND REALLY ATTRACTIVE — THE DIFERENT ONE, THE BRUNETTE WITH A WHOLE SECRET WORLD GOING ON INSIDE HER HEAD. JUST AS IN THE MOVIE HAPPINESS, MENDES LAYS BARE SOCIETY'S IMAGE OF THE IDEAL LIFE, REVEALING JUST HOW FAKE AND FRAGILE IT IS.

146

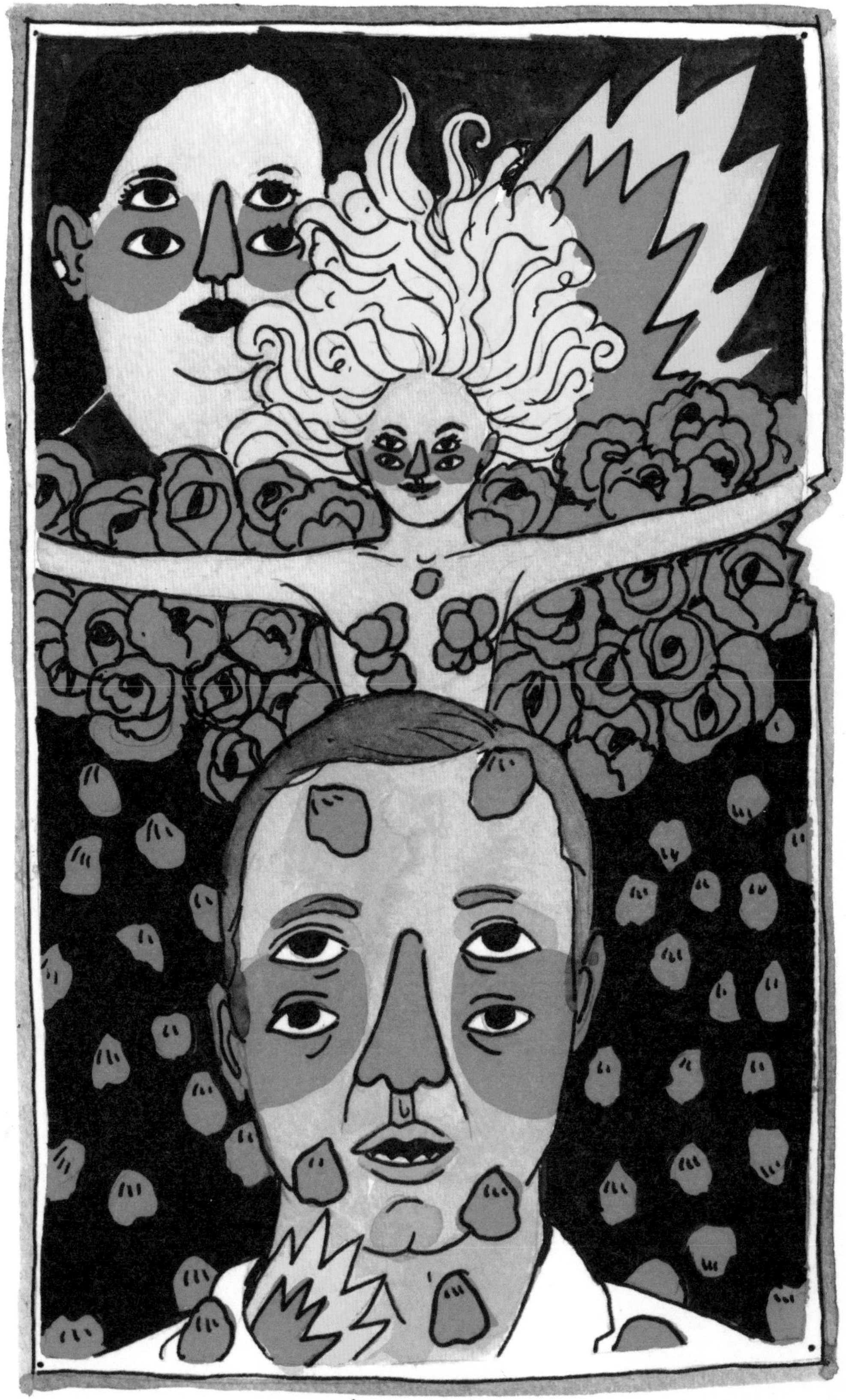

AMERICAN · BEAUTY

The Virgin Suicides

(1999)

SOFIA COPPOLA IS DEFINITELY ONE OF MY FAVOURITE DIRECTORS. EVERY MOVIE SHE'S MADE HAS TOUCHED SOME DEEP PART OF ME. IT'S AS IF SHE KNOWS HOW TO READ AND UNRAVEL A CERTAIN WAY OF BEING, LIVING, THINKING, AND CREATES A MAP OUT OF THAT WITH EVERY MOVIE. THE VIRGIN SUICIDES LEFT ME IN A KIND OF GENTLE SHOCK. I THINK IT'S QUITE A FEAT THAT COPPOLA IS ABLE TO DEPICT HOW PEOPLE FROM YOUNGER GENERATIONS BEHAVE. IT'S NOT EASY. AND IN THIS MOVIE SHE DOES IT SO PERFECTLY, SWITCHING BETWEEN THE NAIVETY OF A LITTLE GIRL TO THE BURNING DESIRES OF A TEENAGE WOMAN. FROM A SKELETON PLOT, AND ALMOST WITHOUT LEAVING THE HOUSE, SHE CREATES AN ENTIRE GALAXY AROUND THOSE FIVE SUNS THAT ARE THE LISBON SISTERS. A COSMOS FULL OF THE VITAL STAGES OF GIRLHOOD, FROM PYJAMAS AND BLONDE LOCKS, TO PHOTO CUT-OUTS AND NAIL POLISH. A COSMOS HIDING FIVE BLACK HOLES.

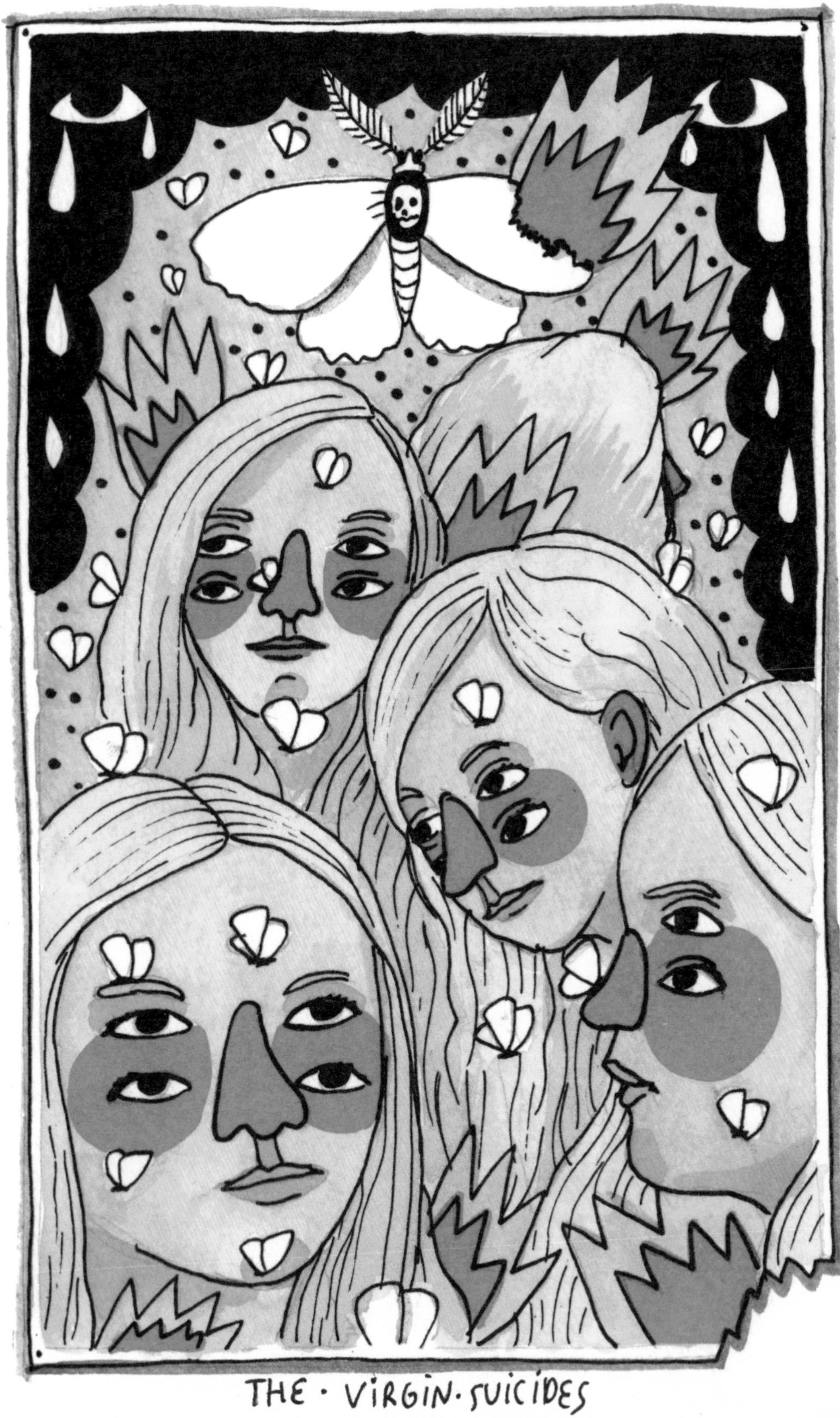
THE · VIRGIN · SUICIDES

THE MATRIX

(1999)

ADMIT IT, WE ALL WENT CRAZY OVER THE MATRIX. THERE WERE TWO MAIN ELEMENTS THAT MADE THIS MOVIE SO INCREDIBLE (ALTHOUGH WE DON'T TALK ABOUT IT NOW). THE FIRST IS THE PLOT - THE FACT THAT EVERYTHING IN FRONT OF US IS A PRODUCT OF SOFTWARE ENGINEERING. EVERYTHING IS JUST ONES AND ZEROS WHILE OUR BODY RESTS ALIVE IN A COFFIN. AND THEN THE AESTHETIC AND THE SPECIAL EFFECTS MEANT THAT THE MATRIX REALLY WAS LANDMARK CINEMA - THERE WAS A BEFORE AND AN AFTER. WHO HASN'T THROWN THEMSELVES BACKWARDS, IMITATING NEO DODGING BULLETS? AND THAT HIGH KICK FROM TRINITY IN 360°? EVEN TODAY, WHEN I'M WALKING ALONG THE STREET, I TRY TO LOOK FOR SOME KIND OF BUG IN THE MATRIX.

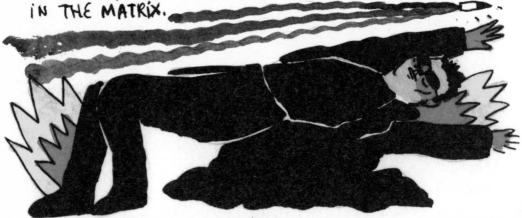

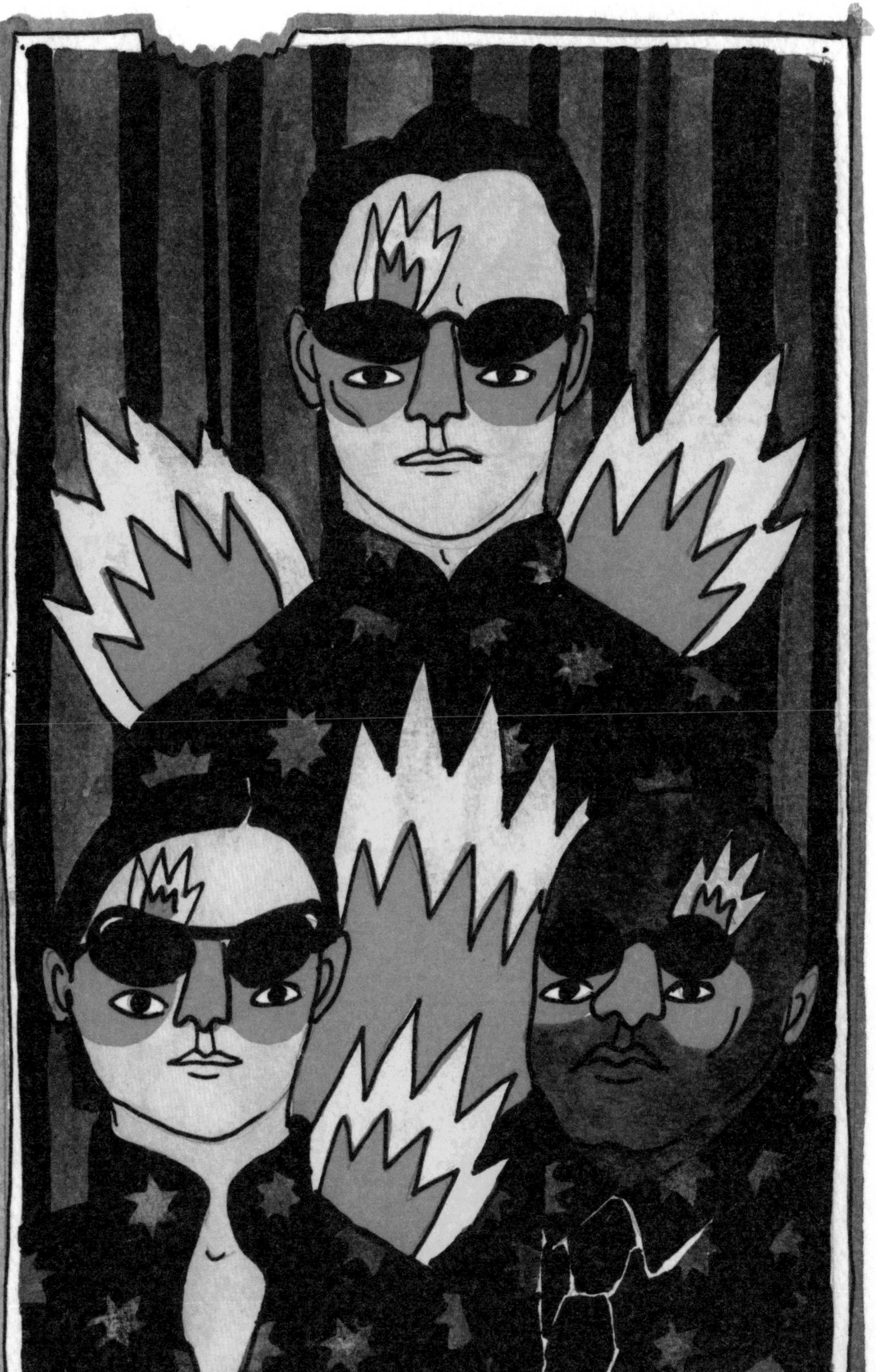

THE MATRIX

snatch

(2000)

MAN, I LOVE WATCHING THIS MOVIE. IT'S THANKS TO GUY RITCHIE THAT WE'RE ABLE TO ENTER SOME OF THE DARKEST STREETS AND SUBURBS OF ENGLAND, SWARMING WITH THUGS, GAMBLERS, FIGHTS AND PINTS UPON PINTS OF BEER. I LOVE THAT DIRTY, BADLY BEHAVED SIDE OF ENGLAND WITH ITS STAINED CARPETS THAT IS SO AT ODDS WITH THE VICTORIAN HOUSES AND THOSE PERFECT MANNERS. I LOVE RITCHIE'S BRAND OF PUNK HOOLIGANISM WHICH, WHEN MIXED WITH HIS HOMAGE TO PULP FICTION, CREATES A STORY WORTH REVISITING OVER AND OVER AGAIN. AND A SHOUT-OUT TO BRAD PITT'S IRISH TRAVELLER. ONE OF MY FAVOURITE CHARACTERS IN CINEMA HISTORY. I'VE ALWAYS THOUGHT YOU COULD DO A GREAT SPIN-OFF OF MICKEY, KING OF GLOVELESS BOXING, CONSTANTLY SURROUNDED BY A DOZEN COUSINS AND LIVING OUTSIDE IT ALL.

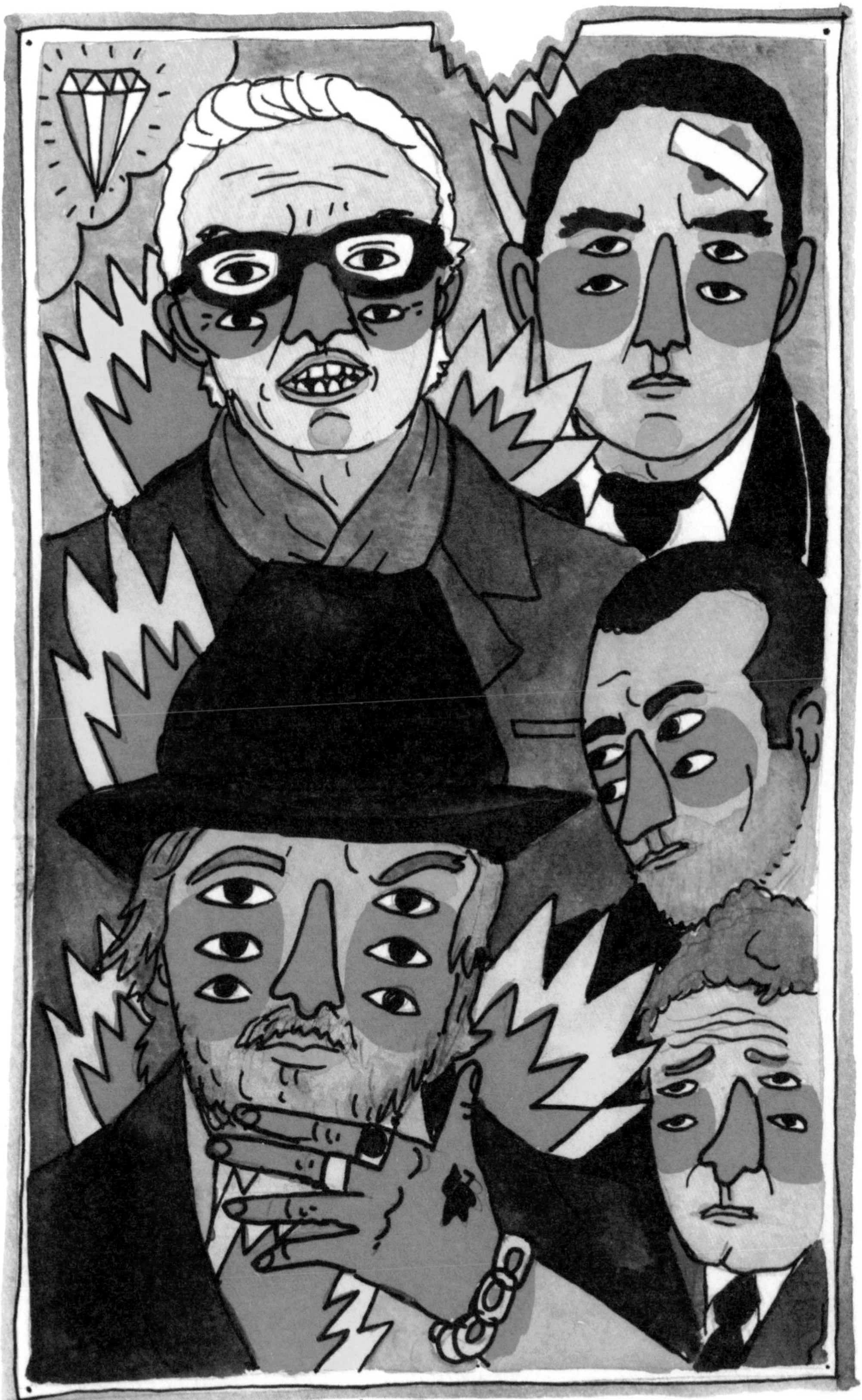

SNATCH

amoresperros

(2000) (LOVE'S A BITCH)

I LOVE MEXICO, NATURALLY. I LOVE ITS TRADITIONS, BUT EVEN MORE THAN THAT I LOVE THE BUBBLING VOLCANO THAT IT IS TODAY. AND AMORES PERROS IS ONE OF THOSE TRAILS OF SMOKE SIGNALLING AN ACTIVE VOLCANO. WHEN I FIRST SAW IT I COULDN'T HELP BUT SEE ITS SIMILARITIES TO PULP FICTION. THOSE THREE STORIES THAT INTERLINK BECAUSE OF A CAR CRASH ARE THE PERFECT WAY TO UNDERSTAND MODERN-DAY MEXICO, FAR REMOVED FROM ITS ANCIENT TRADITIONS. MODERN MEXICO IS JUST LIKE THIS MOVIE —VORACIOUS, WILD, BEAUTIFUL, AND ~~🖤~~ INTENSE. SINCE HIS VERY FIRST MOVIES, IÑÁRRITU HAS BEEN ONE OF MY FAVOURITE DIRECTORS. WHEN I WENT TO WATCH HIS DEBUT AT THE CINEMA, I THINK IT WAS THE FIRST ~~AC̶T̶IO̶N̶~~

MEXICAN MOVIE I'D ~~of~~ EVER SEEN ON THE BIG SCREEN AND IT WAS A HISTORICAL MOMENT IN MY PERSONAL CINEMA HISTORY.

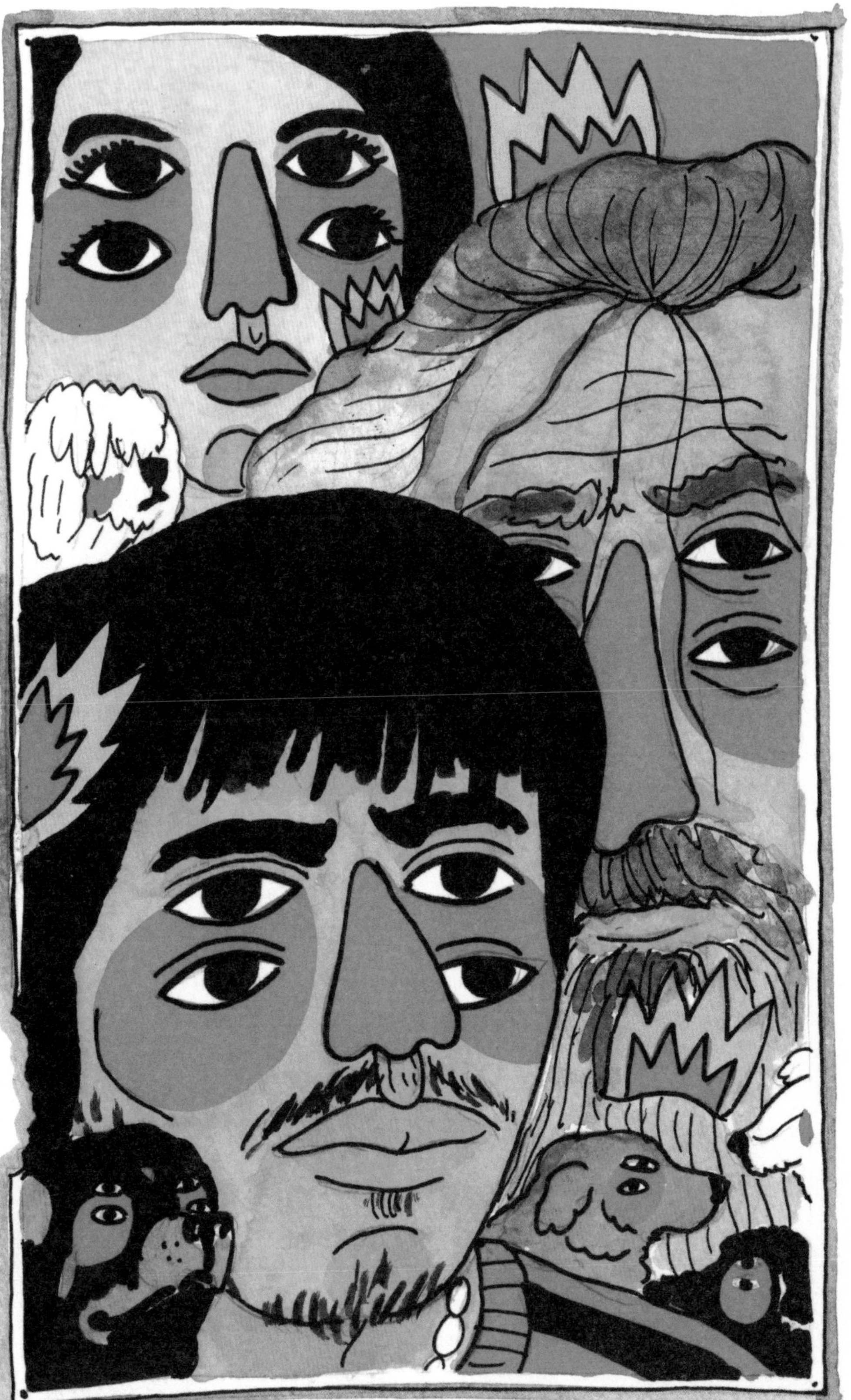

AMORES · PERROS

Harry Potter

(I, II, III, IV, V, VI, VII, VIII / 2001-2011)

i FIRST CAME INTO CONTACT WITH HARRY POTTER
ON THE PAGE. AND WE ALL KNOW THE OLD SAYING
THAT THE BOOK IS BETTER THAN THE MOVIE
(i BELIEVE THAT TOO, AT LEAST IN MOST CASES). BUT
WITH THE HARRY POTTER MOVIES, THEY CONJURED
UP ANOTHER DIMENSION THAT WAS SEPARATE FROM THE
BOOKS. I'M LUCKY IN THAT EVEN THOUGH i WAS QUITE
A BIT OLDER THAN HARRY WHEN i READ THE FIRST
NOVEL, i GREW UP ALONGSIDE HIM AS THE REST OF
THE SERIES CAME OUT. AND THAT'S WHY EVERY NEW
INSTALMENT OF HIS MAGICAL ADVENTURE BECAME
DARKER AND MORE DANGEROUS. THESE EIGHT MOVIES
HAVE BECOME A MARVELLOUS WORLD i CAN DISAPPEAR
INTO FOR A WHOLE WEEK. i'M SUCH A FAN THAT
~~FEELS~~ i CAN WATCH ALL EIGHT MOVIES IN ONE GO
AND STILL WANT MORE MAGIC. MY HARRY POTTER SESSIONS
HAVE BECOME SUCH A GREAT MOMENT IN MY LIFE
THAT i LIKE TO DO ONE EVERY NOW AND THEN.
IT'S BECOME A KIND OF TRADITION. HARRY POTTER IS PART
OF ME.

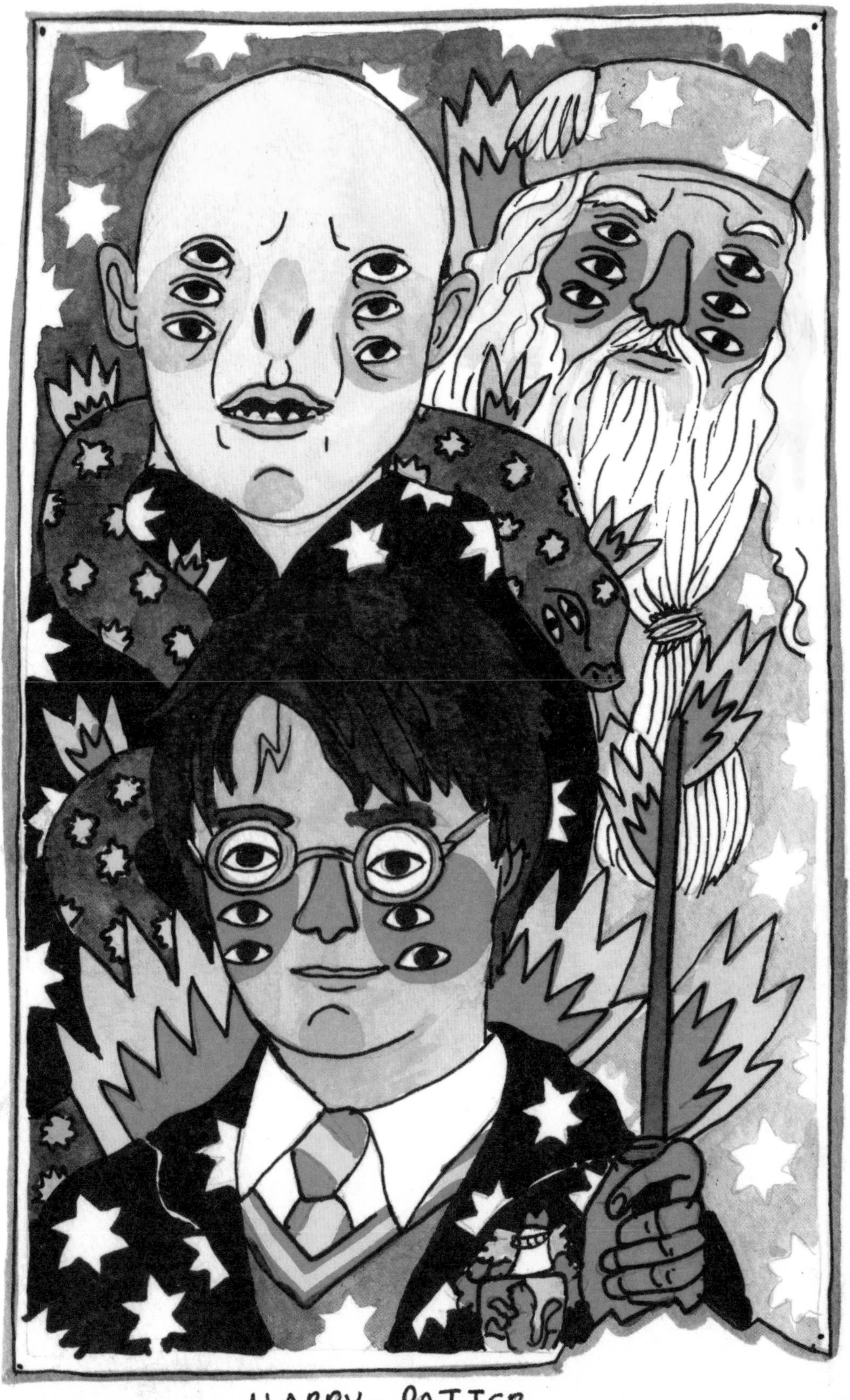

HARRY · POTTER

MONSTERS, INC.

(2001)

i HAVE TO SAY i COULD WATCH PRETTY MUCH
ANYTHING iN THE ANiMATED MOViE GENRE.
BUT MONSTERS, iNC. iSN'T JUST ANY ANiMATED MOViE.
EACH AND EVERY MONSTER iS AN UNDENiABLE
DELiGHT, EVEN THOSE WHO JUST POP UP iN THE
BACKGROUND. SULLEY iS BRiLLiANT, BUT WAZOWSKi
iS MY BUDDY. i REALLY LOVE HiM. AND BOO'S PLACE
iN THE ANNALS OF CiNEMA iS ALREADY RESERVED.
ON TOP OF THE EXCELLENT ViSUALS AND CHARACTERS,
i THiNK THE PLOT iS PERFECTiON, ONE OF THE
GREATEST OF iTS KiND.

i'M TELLiNG YOU, EVERY NOW AND
THEN, i FLiNG OPEN THE DOOR TO MY
WARDROBE AT NiGHT, HOPiNG TO
FiND WAZOWSKi THERE WAiTiNG
TO COME iNTO MY ROOM.
(WiTH BOO BY HiS SiDE,
HOLDiNG HiS HAND,
iF POSSiBLE.)

158

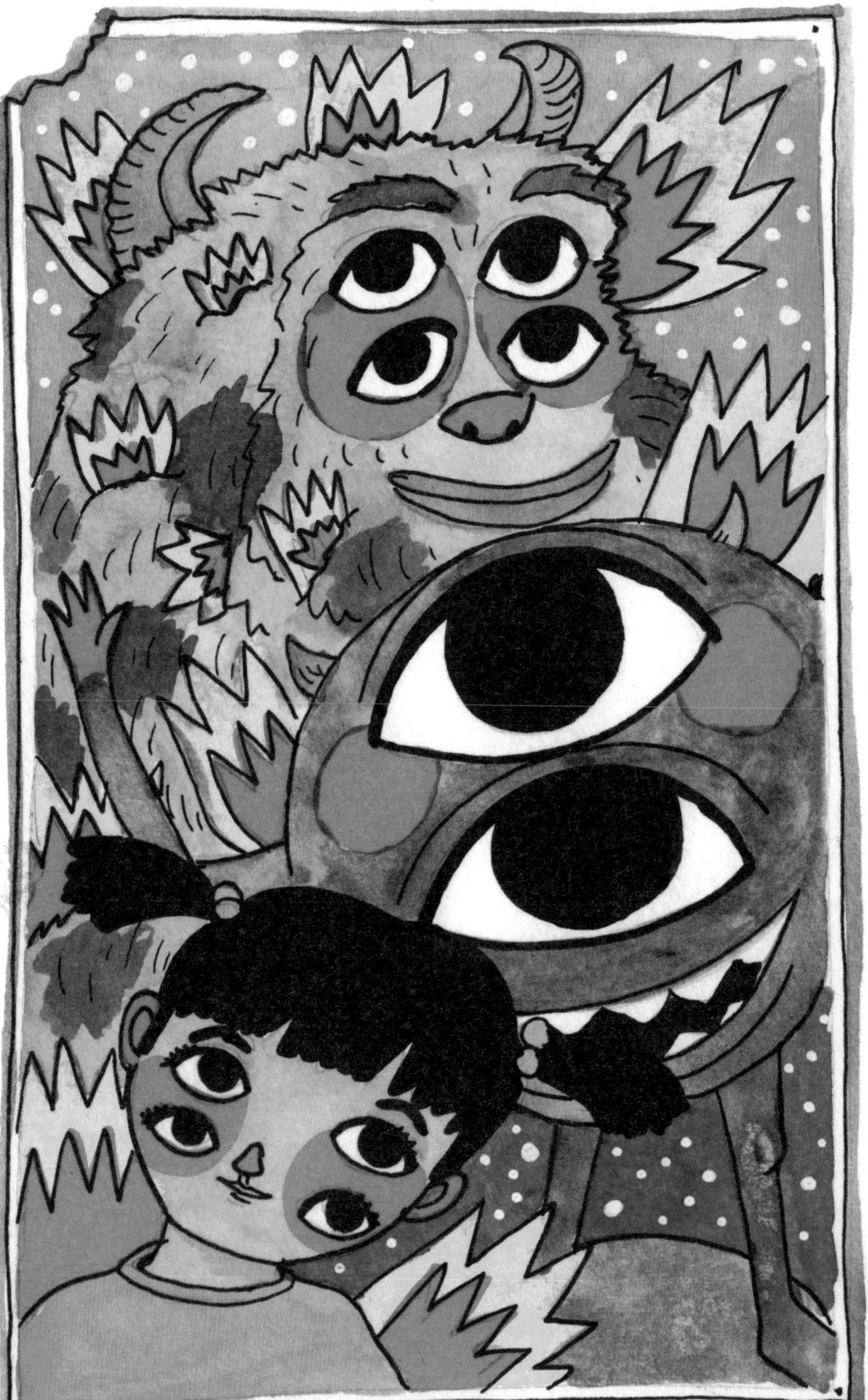

MONSTERS, INC.

THE·ROYAL·TENENBAUMS

(2001)

WES ANDERSON IS A GENIUS. IF I WORKED IN THE MOVIE-MAKING BUSINESS, I'D TRY TO ACHIEVE WHAT WES ANDERSON DOES. I'M FASCINATED BY HIS OBSESSION FOR SCENOGRAPHY, AND THAT SUBLIME, EXQUISITE AND UNIQUE ART DIRECTION. HE ALMOST MAKES THE PLOT SURPLUS TO REQUIREMENT, BECAUSE THERE'S SO MUCH VISUAL INFORMATION TO ENJOY. THIS IS WHAT MAKES YOU WANT TO WATCH AND RE-WATCH HIS MOVIES. IT'S LIKE GOING UP TO A DOLL'S HOUSE AND FINDING THAT IT HAS COME TO LIFE —IN EVERY ROOM, SOMETHING SO REMARKABLE IS GOING ON THAT YOU JUST CAN'T MISS IT.

EVEN THOUGH ANDERSON HAD ALREADY MADE AWESOME MOVIES LIKE RUSHMORE BY THEN, IN THE ROYAL TENENBAUMS HIS COMPANY OF CHARACTERS ARE EACH SO INTERESTING AND COMPLEX THEY COULD BE LEADING ROLES IN THEIR OWN MOVIES.

THE SUICIDE SCENE WITH RICHIE AND "NEEDLE IN THE HAY" BY ELLIOTT SMITH PLAYING IN THE BACKGROUND STILL MAKES MY HAIR STAND ON END.

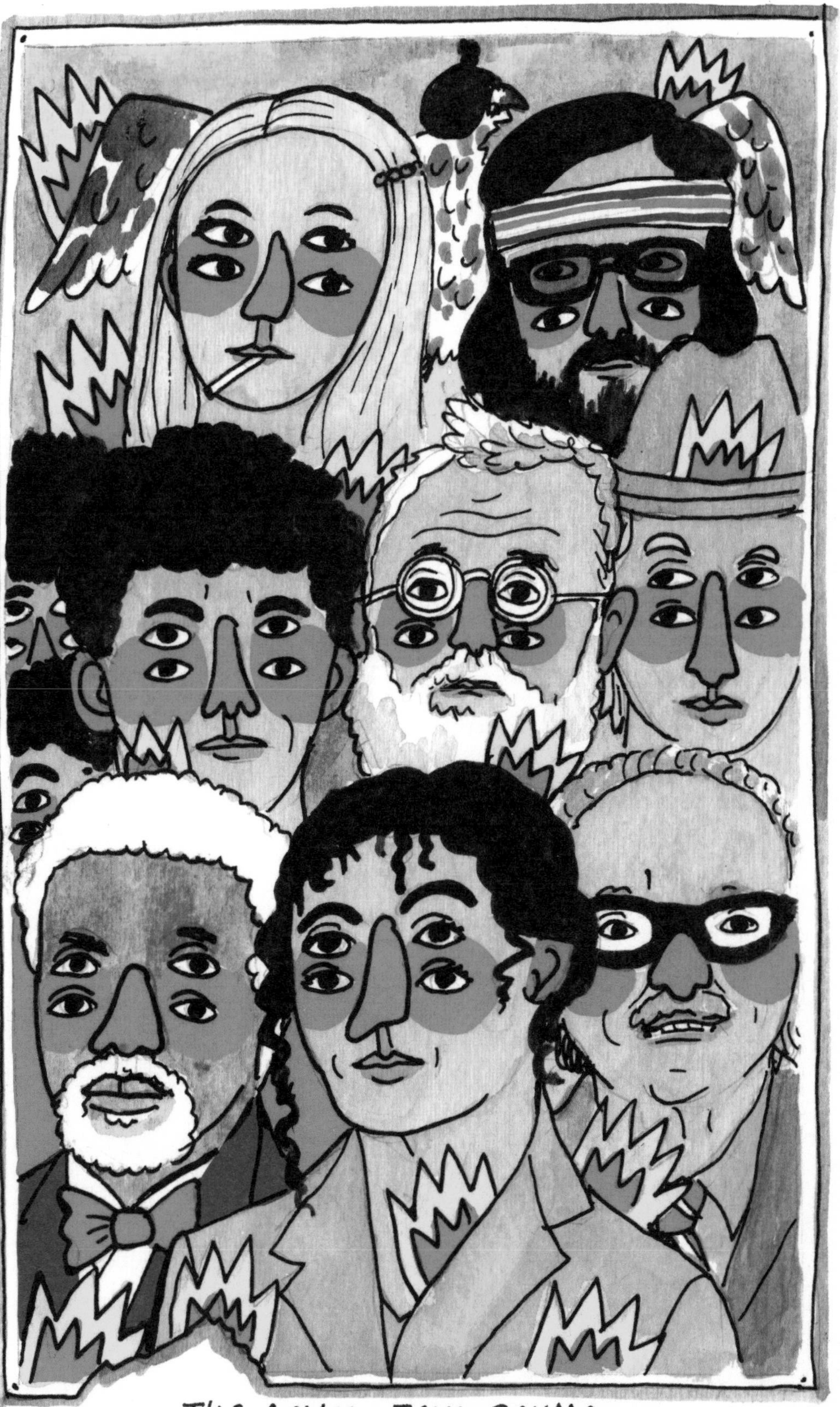

THE · ROYAL · TENENBAUMS

GHOST WORLD

(2001)

I'M NOT GOING TO LIE - I READ THE COMIC AFTER WATCHING THE MOVIE. BACK IN ~~THE ONLY~~ THOSE DAYS I WAS LIVING IN THE MIDDLE OF NOWHERE, AND I DON'T THINK I ~~██~~ WOULD HAVE HAD ACCESS TO DANIEL CLOWES'S ORIGINAL COMIC. I DID KNOW, THOUGH, THAT THE MOVIE WAS BASED ON IT. I IMAGINE THERE ARE A LOT OF HATERS WHO SAY THE MOVIE ISN'T AS GOOD AS THE COMIC, BUT I LIKED THE MOVIE - A LOT. THEN I READ THE COMIC, AND I LIKED IT - A LOT. I IDENTIFIED WITH ENID (THORA BIRCH), AND NOT JUST BECAUSE SHE WAS MY MOVIE CRUSH (AND HAD BEEN

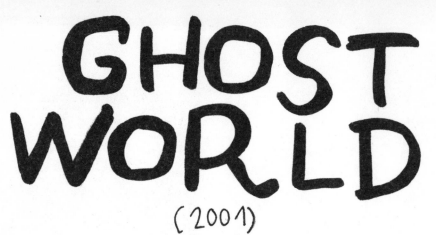

SINCE AMERICAN BEAUTY). IT'S AS IF WEDNESDAY FROM THE ADDAMS FAMILY HAD GROWN UP AND NOW LIVED IN TYPICAL U.S. SUBURBIA. AND THE PART PLAYED BY STEVE BUSCEMI IS TOO GOOD FOR WORDS - NOT EVEN SEYMOUR FROM THE COMIC BEATS BUSCEMI'S SEYMOUR FROM THE MOVIE.
I WOULD HAVE BEEN IN ENID AND REBECCA'S MINI GANG, AND I WOULD HAVE LOVED TO GO AND CHAT WITH SEYMOUR EVERY AFTERNOON.

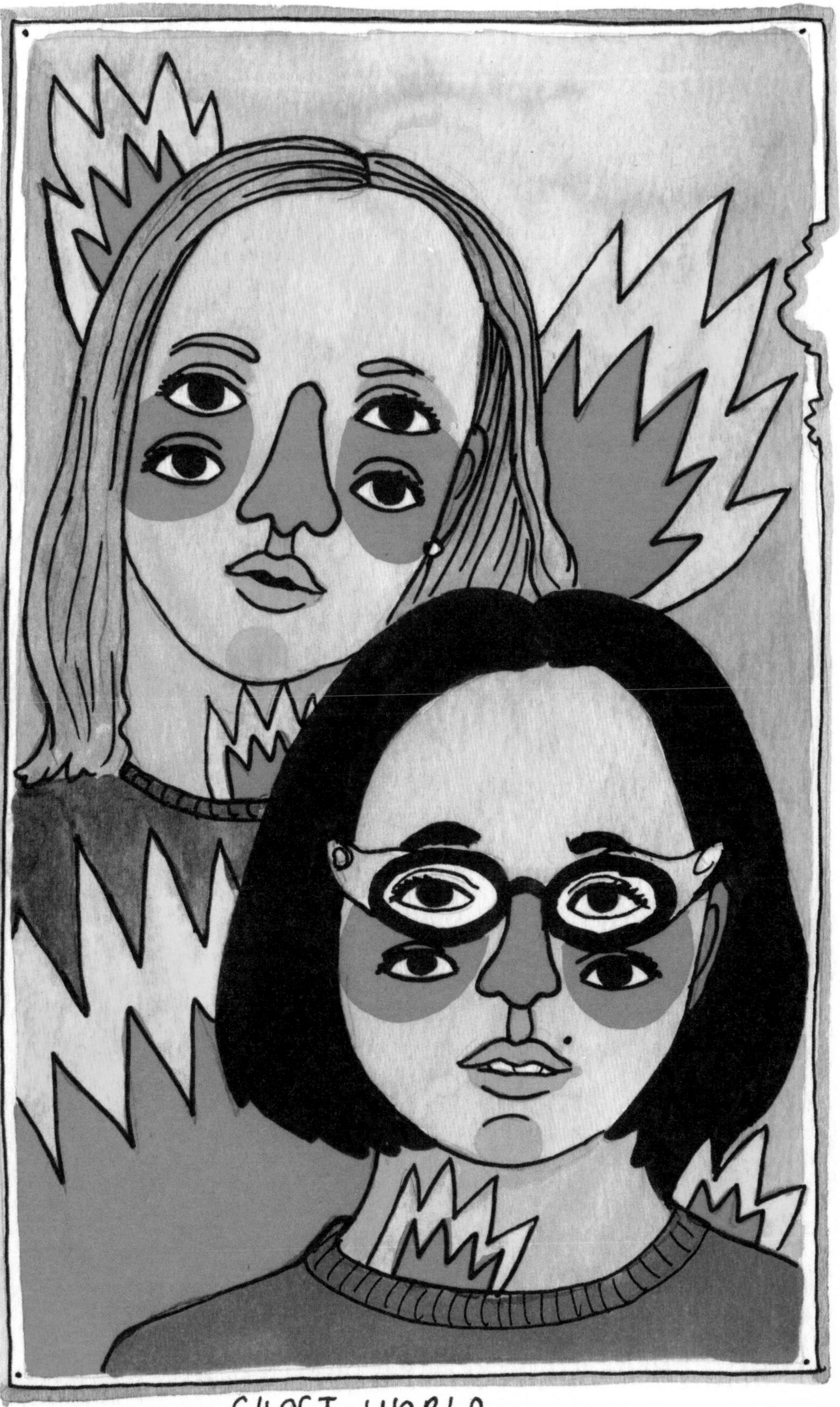

GHOST · WORLD

SPIRITED·AWAY

(2001)

I'M NOT A HUGE FOLLOWER OF JAPANESE ANIMATION, BUT I REALLY THINK THIS MOVIE IS A MASTERPIECE. THIS JAPANESE-STYLE ALICE IN WONDERLAND IS A SUPERB EXAMPLE OF THE COMPLEX WORLD OF JAPANESE SPIRITS, MONSTERS AND DEMONS. EVERY TIME I WATCH SPIRITED AWAY, I HAVE A PAPER AND PEN WITH ME AND MAKE NOTES OF EACH DEVILISHLY MAD AND PERFECT BEING, ALL CREATED IN THE YŌKAI TRADITION. ON TOP OF THAT, ALL THESE CREATURES ARE BROUGHT TO LIFE BY THE MAGICIAN THAT IS DIRECTOR HAYAO MIYAZAKI, RESULTING IN AN ENCHANTING, BEAUTIFUL MOVIE, BRIMMING WITH MAGIC.

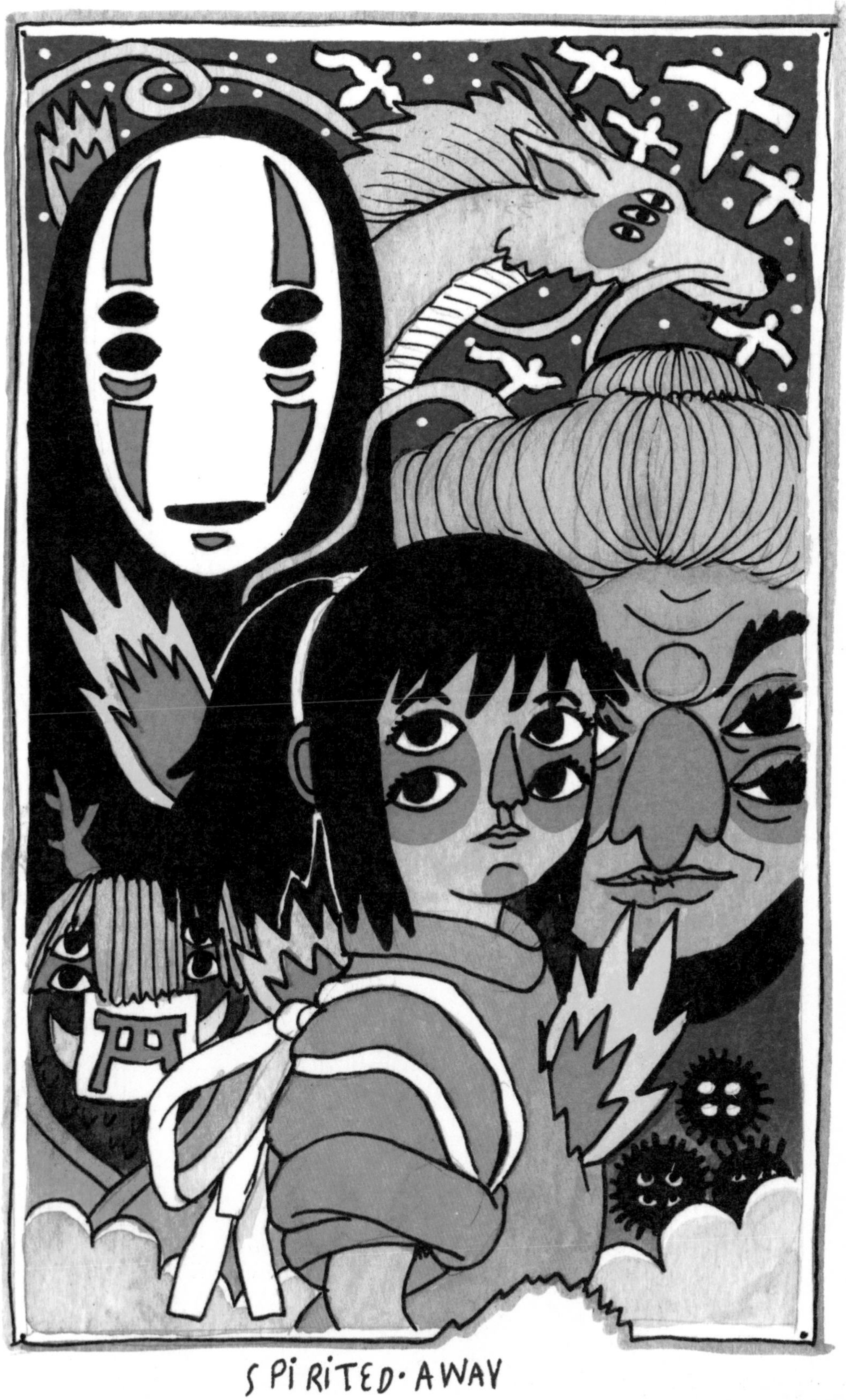

SPIRITED·AWAY

THE LORD OF THE RINGS

(I, II, III, 2001-2003)

I PLAYED DUNGEONS AND DRAGONS, MAGIC: THE
GATHERING, AND ALL THE ROLE-PLAYING GAMES
I COULD AS A BOY. BY THE TIME I WAS TEN I'D
ALREADY READ JRR TOLKIEN'S LORD OF THE RINGS
TRILOGY THREE TIMES. I WAS OBSESSED WITH
THE SWORD FIGHTS, THE ORCS, THE DWARVES AND THE
ELVES. MIDDLE EARTH WAS MY STOMPING GROUND, AND I
WAS A RANGER OF THE NORTH. PETER JACKSON'S TRILOGY
IS NOT THE SAME AS THE BOOKS, GRANTED, BUT THE MOVIES
ARE A WHOLE OTHER BALL GAME. AND I GET BUTTERFLIES
IN MY TUMMY EVERY TIME ONE OF MY MARATHONS BEGINS.
THE LORD OF THE RINGS MAKES ME INTENSELY HAPPY.
ENOUGH SAID. THAT'S WHAT CINEMA IS FOR. THESE MOVIES
TAKE ME BACK TO MY CHILDHOOD. THE RUSSIAN POET RILKE
SAID IT FIRST: SOMETHING ABOUT YOUR CHILDHOOD BEING YOUR
TRUE MOTHERLAND. AND PETER JACKSON LETS ME GO BACK
TO MY CHILDHOOD WHENEVER I FEEL LIKE IT. THANK YOU.

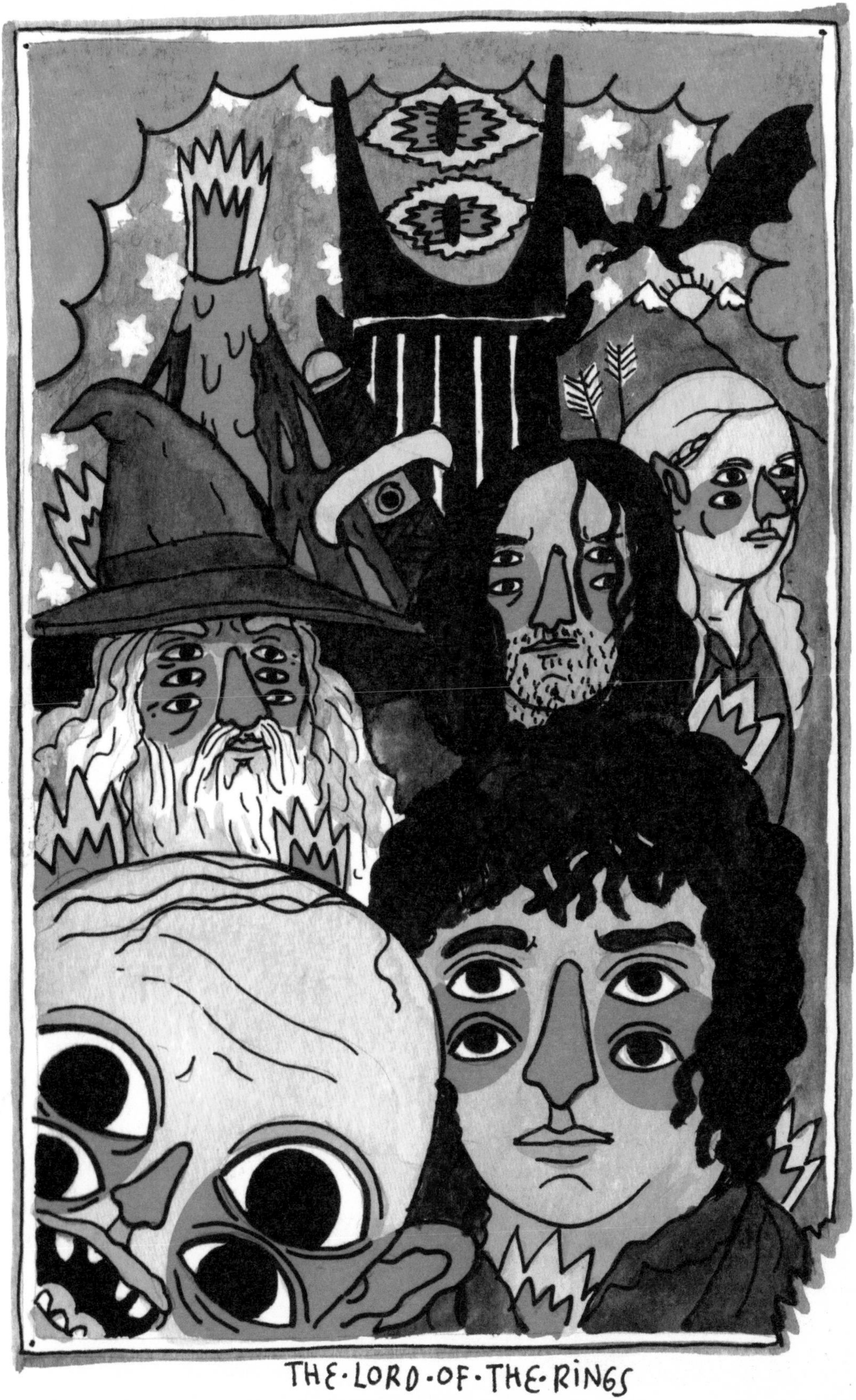

THE·LORD·OF·THE·RINGS

CIDADE DE DEUS

(2002) (CITY·OF·GOD)

I REMEMBER LEAVING THE CINEMA AFTER WATCHING THIS, COMPLETELY STUNNED. I ALREADY KNEW ABOUT THE REALITY OF BRAZIL'S FAVELAS, BUT THIS MOVIE SHONE A LIGHT ON THEM IN A NEW WAY —IT HAD A SPECIFIC STORY AND AN EXTRA SOMETHING TO ADD. IT HAD THAT TOUCH OF PULP FICTION ~~THAT~~ THAT A LOT OF MOVIES USED ~~~~~~ (QUITE RIGHTLY) IN THE YEARS FOLLOWING THE RELEASE OF TARANTINO'S HIT. I'VE ALWAYS BEEN INTO STORIES SET IN THE OUTSKIRTS (PROBABLY BECAUSE TO SOME EXTENT I LIVED THERE MYSELF). TO ME THEY FEEL LIKE HOME-GROWN STORIES; MINE. THE FACT THAT THEY TELL ME SOMETHING ABOUT WHERE I COME FROM, BUT HAPPEN IN ANOTHER CONTINENT, KEEPS ME GLUED TO THE SCREEN. AND IF THE MOVIE HAS DIRECTOR FERNANDO MEIRELLES'S CRAZY, FURIOUS RHYTHM, I'M AN EASY TARGET.

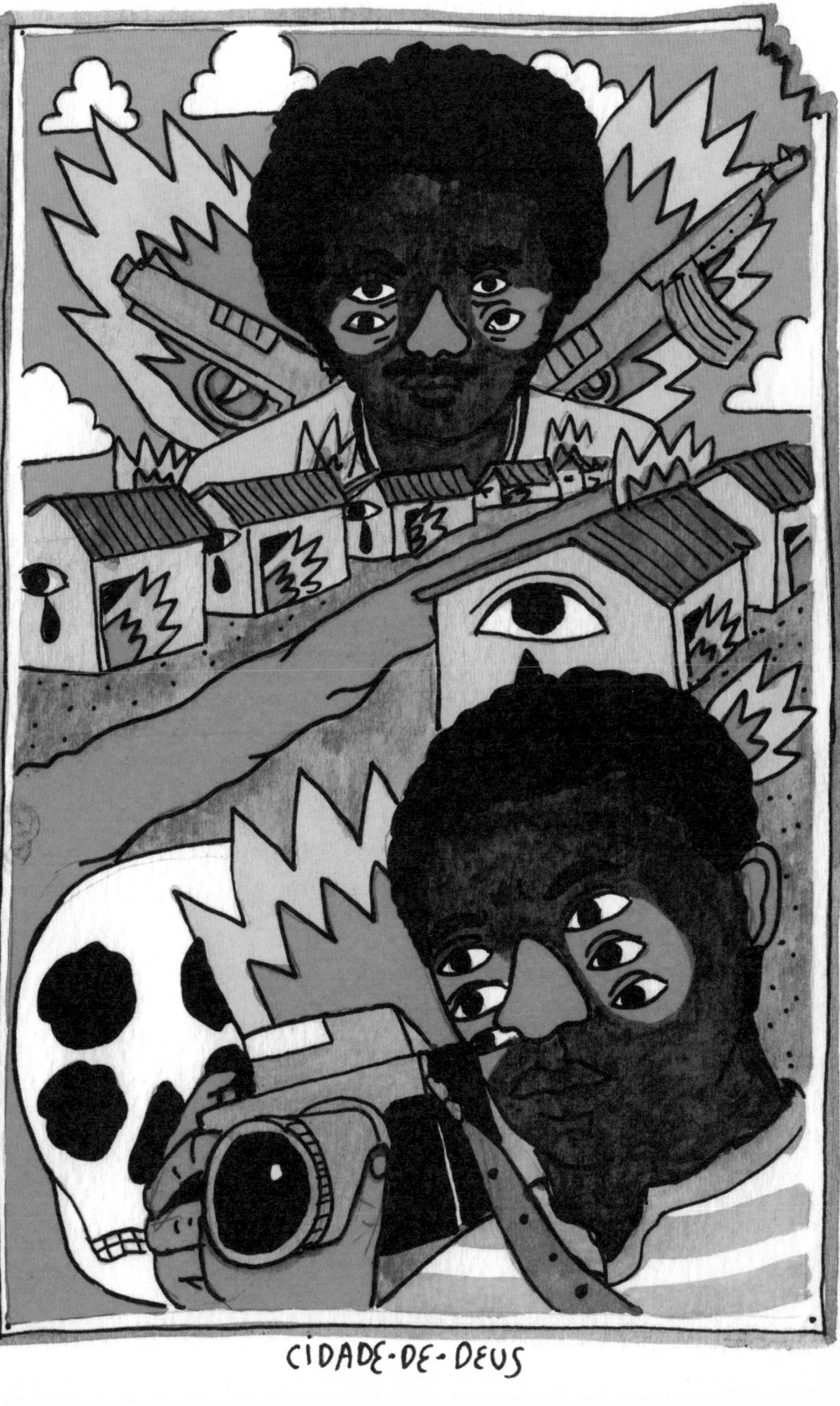

CIDADE-DE-DEUS

Lost In Translation

(2003)

ANOTHER MARVEL FROM SOFIA COPPOLA.

i HAVE TO TRAVEL A LOT FOR WORK, AND THERE ARE A LOT OF THINGS ABOUT THIS MOVIE THAT i RELATE TO AT A BASIC LEVEL. SOMETIMES i LIKE TO BE BILL MURRAY, LOOKING AT EVERYTHING IN THAT SPECIAL WAY OF HIS — WITH RESPECT BUT ALSO WITH HUMOUR.

THE STORY SHOWS TWO PEOPLE WHOSE PERSONAL LIVES AREN'T AS BRILLIANT AS THEY WANT THEM TO BE AND WHO FIND THEMSELVES IN THE OCCASIONALLY INHOSPITABLE CITY OF TOKYO. LOST EMOTIONALLY, AND LOST IN A CITY OF SEVERAL MILLIONS OF INHABITANTS. THEY BOND LIKE TWO MOTHS FLUTTERING TO THE ONLY LAMP LIGHTING UP THE NIGHT. SOFIA COPPOLA KNOWS EXACTLY HOW TO DEPICT THE HUMAN CHARACTERISTICS OF TODAY — PEOPLE WHO ARE SOMETIMES EMPTY, SOMETIMES BORED AND SOMETIMES LETTING THEMSELVES GO.

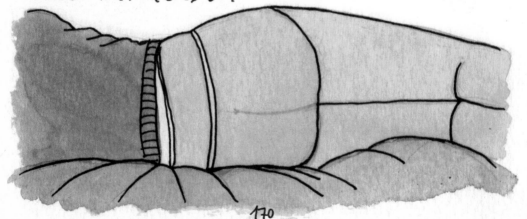

170

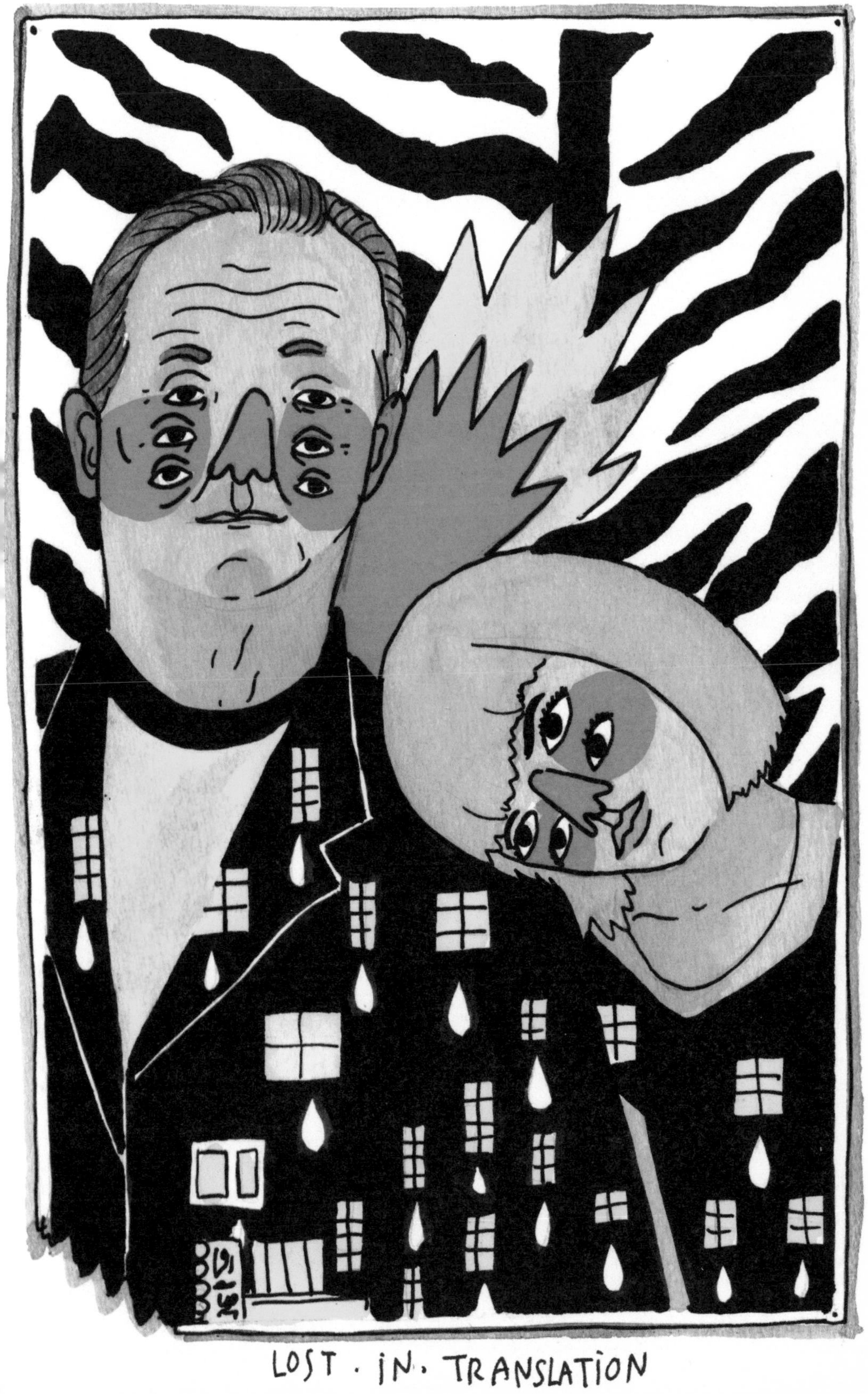

LOST . IN . TRANSLATION

KILL BILL

(2003)

AND SO WE FIND OURSELVES BACK WITH THE GREAT QUENTIN TARANTINO AND A REAL PEACH IN TWO INSTALMENTS, RELEASED A YEAR APART. AFTER HIS TRIUMPH WITH PULP FICTION, IT'S LIKE HE DIDN'T HAVE ANYTHING TO PROVE SO HE MADE THE MOVIE HE WANTED TO MAKE. HE IMITATES LOTS OF GENRES LIKE HONG KONG MARTIAL ARTS MOVIES AND SPAGHETTI WESTERNS, TOGETHER WITH A BIG OLD LOAD OF ~~####~~ SEXUAL FETISHES AND A HODGEPODGE OF CHARACTERS THAT LEFT ME ASTOUNDED.

THE PLOT ITSELF IS SIMPLE, LIKE THE B-MOVIES TARANTINO SO ENJOYS. HE WANTED TO CREATE A HIGH-OCTANE VISUAL FEAST. AFTER ~~####~~ THE ENDLESS (AND PERFECT) DIALOGUES IN PULP FICTION, THE DIRECTOR OPTS FOR THE OPPOSITE IN KILL BILL: LESS TALKING, MORE KILLING, WITH PERFECTLY CHOREOGRAPHED SCENES.

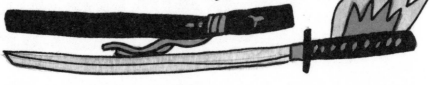

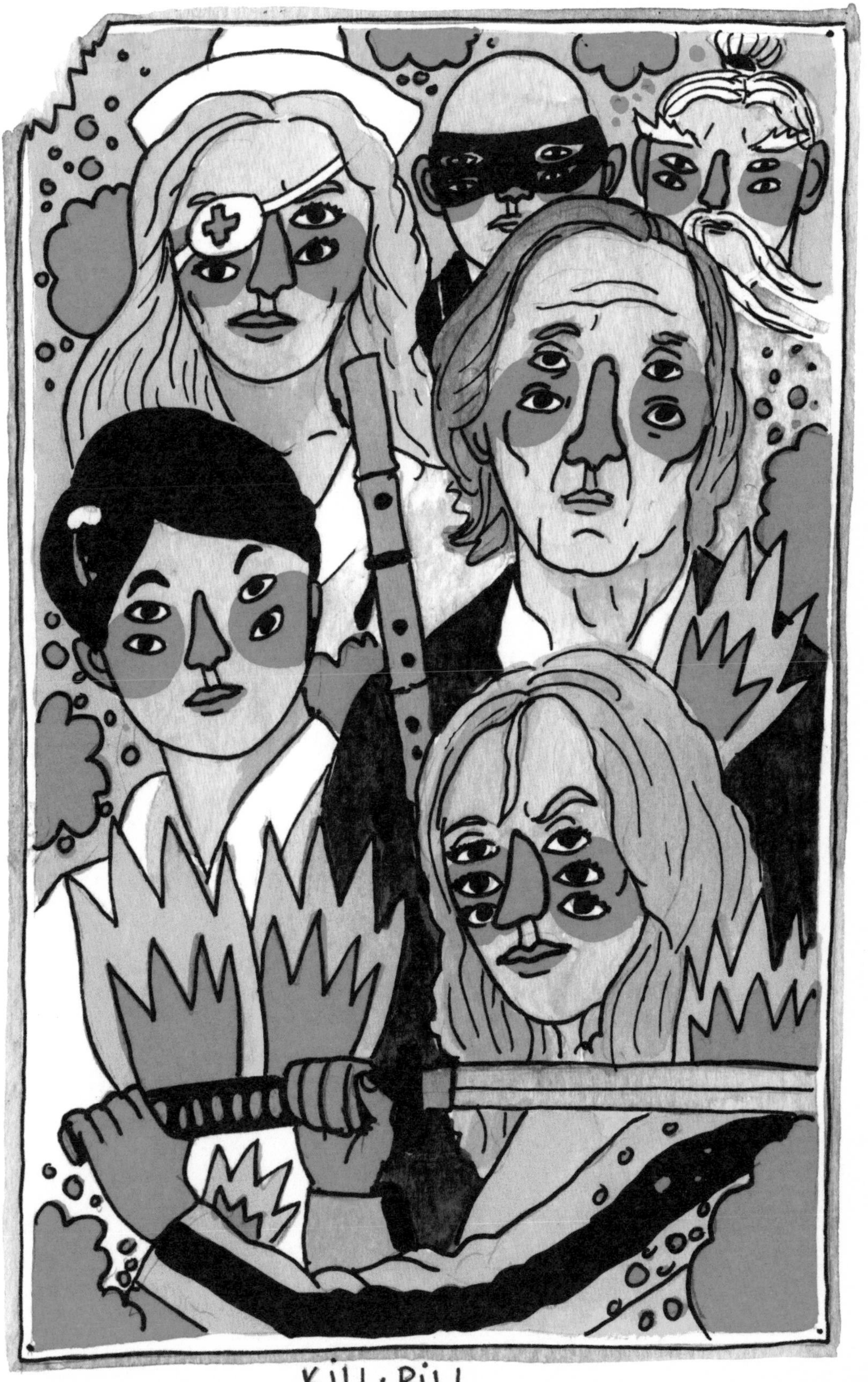

KILL · BILL

BIG FISH

(2003)

I KNOW IT'S A BIT ODD FOR THIS MOVIE TO
BE IN HERE — IT'S GOOD, BUT PERHAPS NOT
QUITE UP THERE WITH MOVIES LIKE CASABLANCA OR
THE GODFATHER. BUT WHAT I HAVE WITH THIS MOVIE IS
A RELATIONSHIP SO INTIMATE IT'S ALMOST ~~SOME~~
EMBARRASSING. AS WELL AS TIM BURTON'S TYPICAL
SURREAL~~ISM~~ FLAIR, THERE'S A TALE HERE I FEEL
VERY CONNECTED WITH, AND I'M DAMN PROUD OF IT.
IT TELLS THE STORY OF EDWARD BLOOM, OR RATHER
IT TELLS THE STORY OF HOW HE TELLS HIS OWN
STORY. FROM WHAT HE EXPLAINS TO US, HE'S
LIVED A LIFE FULL OF ENCOUNTERS WITH ESSENTIALLY
MAGICAL BEINGS, AND HAS BEEN PART OF THINGS WORTHY
OF SOME KIND OF OTHERWORLDLY MYTHOLOGY. NOBODY
BELIEVES HIM, BUT HE REALLY HAS BEEN THROUGH IT ALL.
PERHAPS HE JUST SEES THINGS DIFFERENTLY TO OTHER
PEOPLE, AND NOTICES THINGS THAT OTHERS DON'T. LIFE
SEEMS A LOT MORE BEAUTIFUL AND INTERESTING WHEN STORIES
HAVE A ~~DASH~~ DASH OF MAGIC AND EMBELLISMENT.
YES TO MAGIC, NO TO DULLNESS.

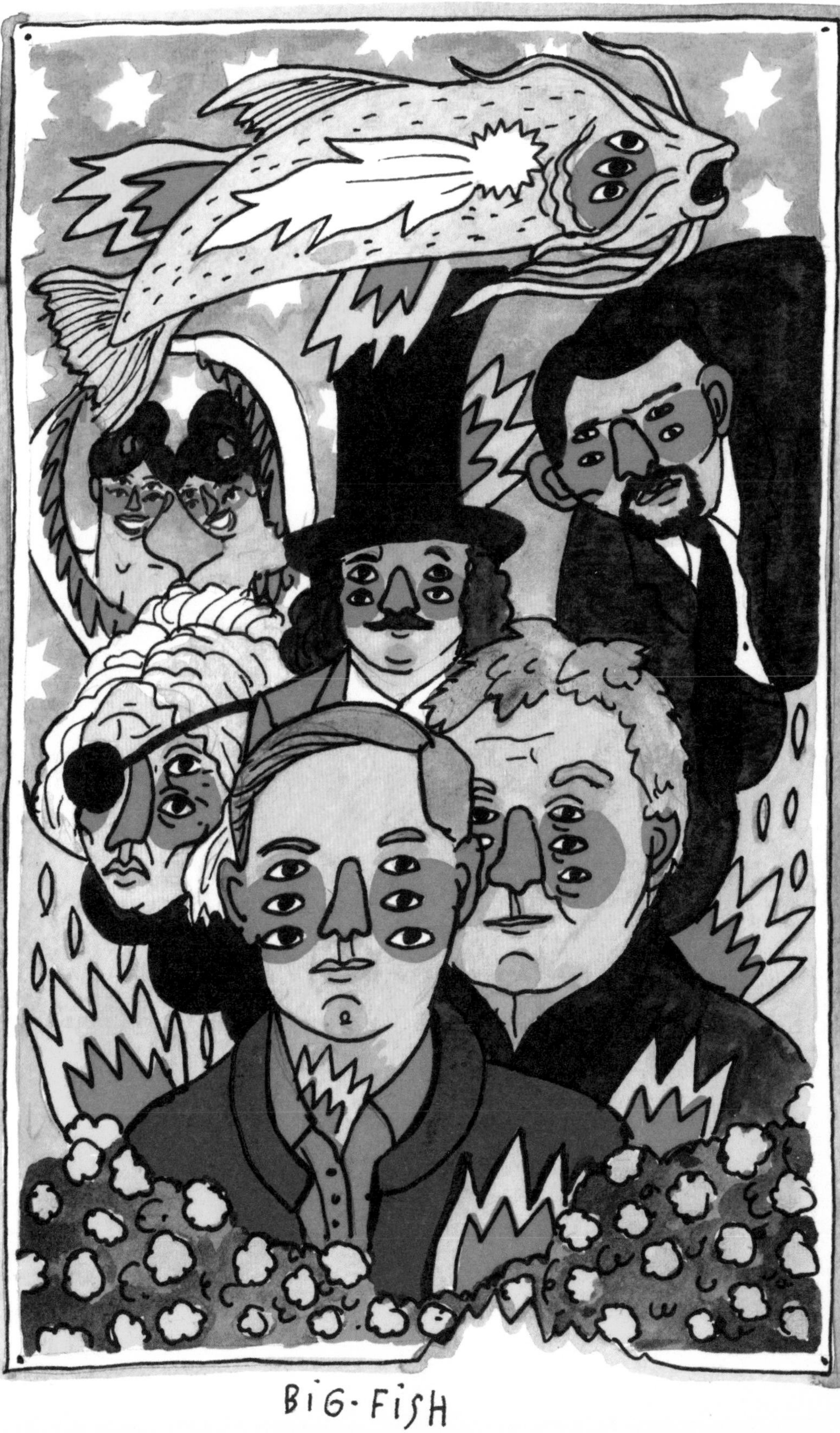

BIG·FISH

Elephant

(2003)

A MASTERFUL MOVIE DIRECTED BY GUS VAN SANT,
PORTRAYING THE MASSACRES THAT HAVE BOOMED
IN RECENT YEARS IN COLLEGES IN THE UNITED
STATES. MORE SPECIFICALLY, IT FOCUSES ON THE
NOTORIOUS SHOOTING AT COLUMBINE. IT FOLLOWS
SEVERAL TEENAGERS FROM THE COLLEGE ON ONE
DAY OF THEIR LIVES -IN FACT, ON "THE DAY" THAT
TWO FELLOW STUDENTS DECIDED TO ARM THEMSELVES
WITH ALL THE GUNS THEY COULD AND KILL AS
MANY PEOPLE AS THEY COULD. I'M INTERESTED
IN THIS MOVIE BECAUSE IT SEEMS TO ME THAT
KIDS DON'T TEND TO BE UNDERSTOOD AS BEING
WORTHY SUBJECTS IN MOVIES UNLESS THEY'RE ON
SOME KIND OF ADVENTURE. AND IN ELEPHANT,
GUS VAN SANT PORTRAYS AN AVERAGE TEENAGER
LIVING IN AN AVERAGE TOWN GOING THROUGH
SOMETHING AS CATASTROPHIC AS A SHOOTING
WHEN ALL THEY SHOULD REALLY BE GOING
THROUGH IS TEDIOUS, ROUTINE LIFE. THERE IS
SOMETHING HE DOES A LOT IN THE MOVIE, AND
THAT IS DRAWING OUT EVERY SHOT AS IF HE WERE
GIVING YOU TIME TO THINK AND REFLECT ON ~~WHAT~~
WHAT'S HAPPENING.

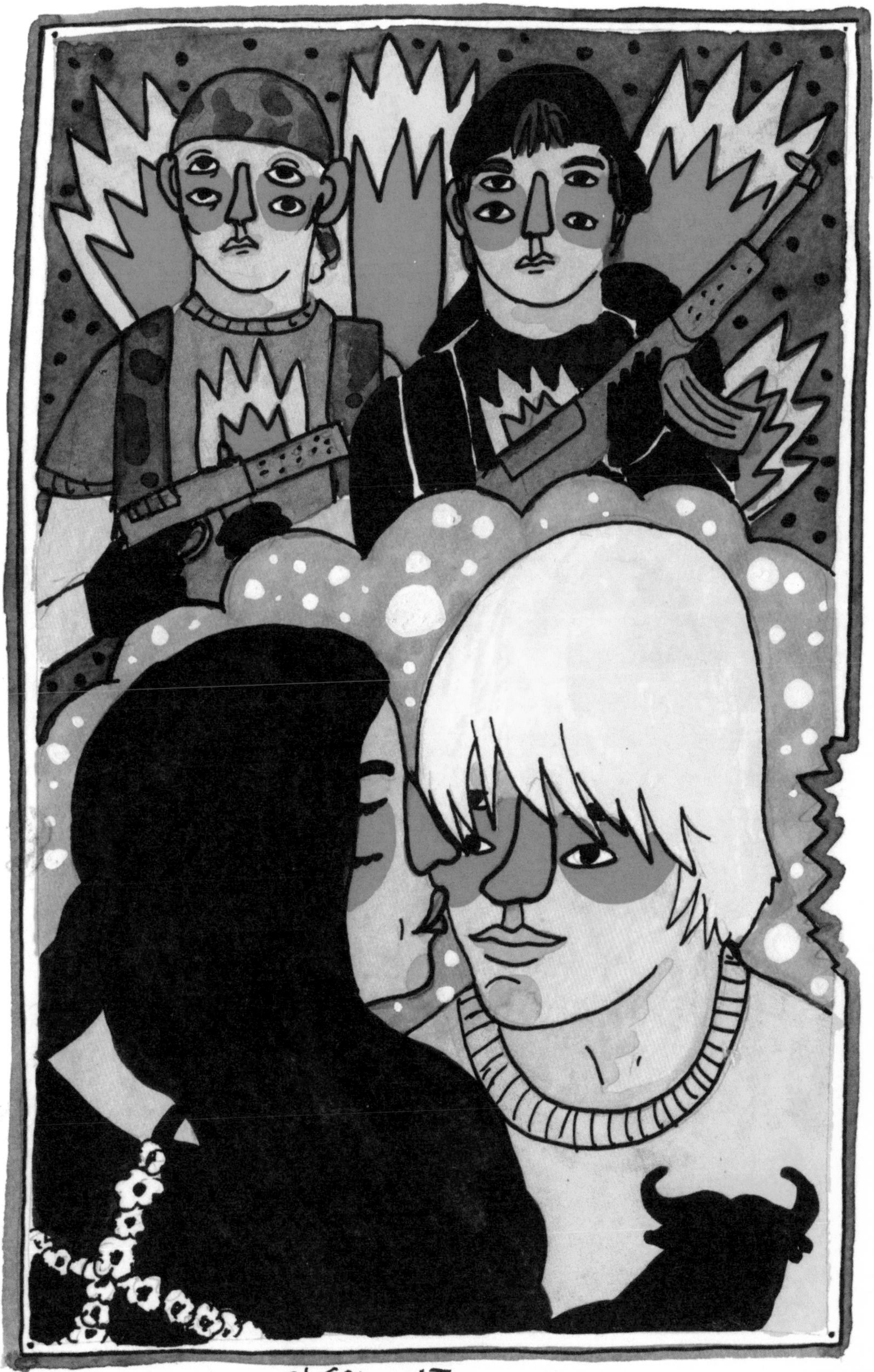

ELEPHANT

BATMAN

(THE · DARK · KNIGHT · TRILOGY/2005-2012)

I'VE ALREADY SAID THAT I'M A HUGE BATMAN FAN. AND TO TELL THE TRUTH, I NEVER THOUGHT I'D SEE ANYTHING BETTER THAN BURTON'S TWO MOVIES BASED ON THE DARK KNIGHT. THE FOLLOWING ONES WERE TERRIBLE. BUT WHO BETTER THAN CHRISTOPHER NOLAN TO ~~AD~~ AT LAST CREATE A DARK TRILOGY TRULY DESERVING OF MY NOCTURNAL HERO? I GIVE HIM MY FULL BLESSING, AND IN FACT I FIND MYSELF HAVING TO ~~REW~~ RE-WATCH THE TRILOGY EVERY NOW AND THEN TO FEED MY THIRST FOR BATS. FOR ME, CHRISTIAN BALE PLAYED THE BEST BATMAN IN CINEMA HISTORY. THE PURISTS AMONG YOU MIGHT TELL ME THAT NOTHING TOPS JACK NICHOLSON'S JOKER. WHILE IT MAY BE TRUE THAT WITHOUT NICHOLSON BEFORE HIM, HEATH LEDGER WOULDN'T HAVE PERFORMED THE JOKER IN THE SAME WAY, NEVERTHELESS HERE THE JOKER IS ACTUALLY SCARY-HE TERRIFIES YOU, BUT YOU CAN'T LOOK AWAY. A PERFECT TRILOGY IN EVERY RESPECT. AND I DON'T WANT TO LEAVE OUT THE BRILLIANT MICHAEL CAINE AS ALFRED OR GARY OLDMAN AS SERGEANT GORDON. SERIOUSLY, BRAVO!!!

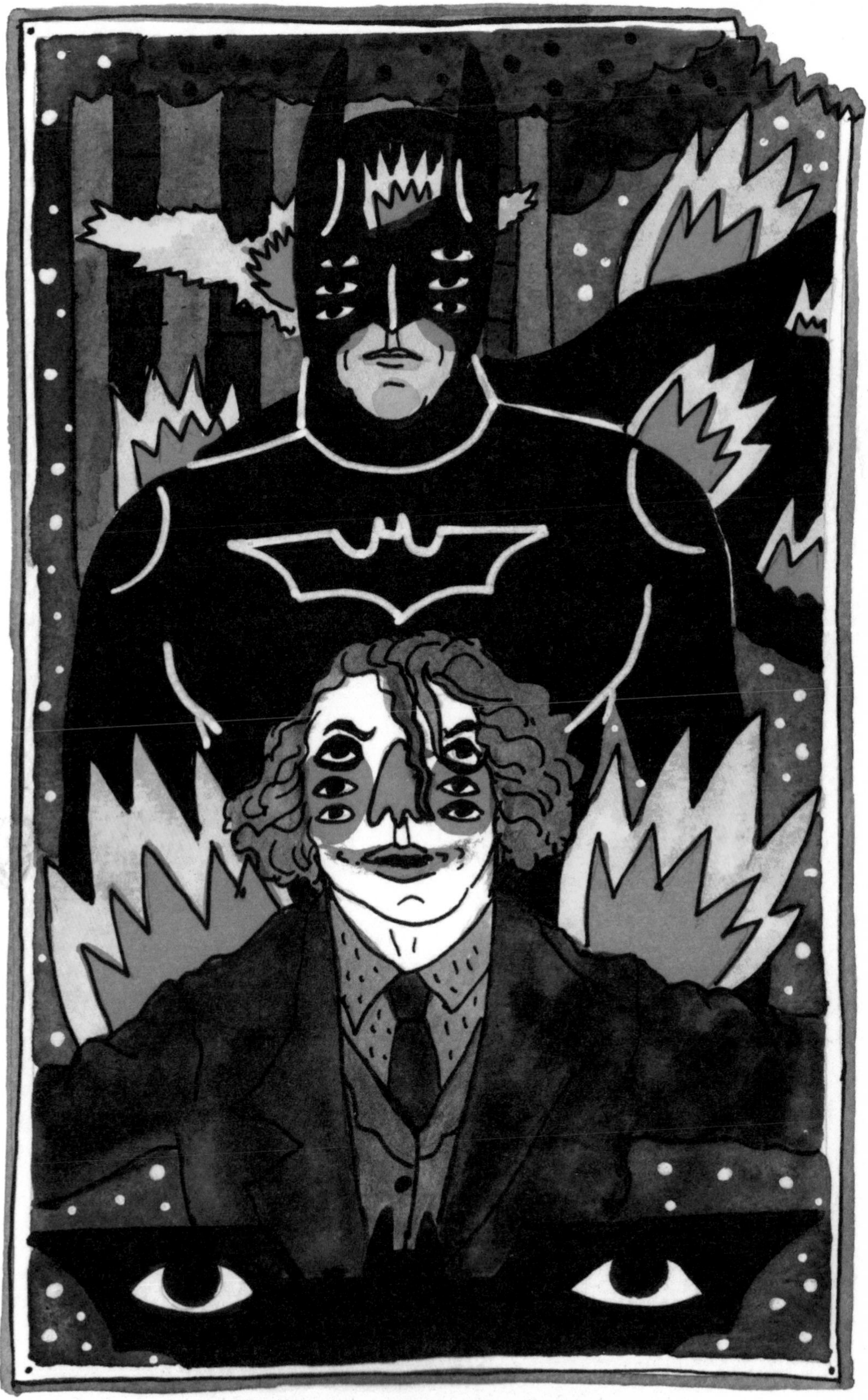

NOLAN'S. BATMAN

WALK THE LINE

(2005)

JOHNNY CASH MIGHT JUST BE MY FAVOURITE SINGER AND MUSICIAN OF ALL TIME. WHICH MEANS THAT A BIOPIC ABOUT HIM WAS ALWAYS GOING TO BE RISKY FOR ME. i WAS CONVINCED i'D BE DISAPPOINTED. BUT NO. LUCKILY, i HAD A HAPPY SURPRISE IN STORE. THEY CHOSE THE BEST POSSIBLE ~~XXXX~~ ACTOR - JOAQUIN PHOENIX. HE'S FLAWLESS IN THIS. i RECOGNIZE CASH'S GESTURES AND EXPRESSIONS - PHOENIX REPLICATES THEM TO A T. iT'S AS IF THE SPIRIT OF JOHNNY WERE INSIDE HIM AND HE ONLY HAD TO LET iT FLOW OUT. REESE WITHERSPOON IS GREAT AS JUNE CARTER, TOO.

i WAS REALLY CHUFFED ALL ●ROUND, BECAUSE i THINK IF JOHNNY CASH HIMSELF HAD SEEN THE MOVIE, HE'D BE HAPPY WITH IT.

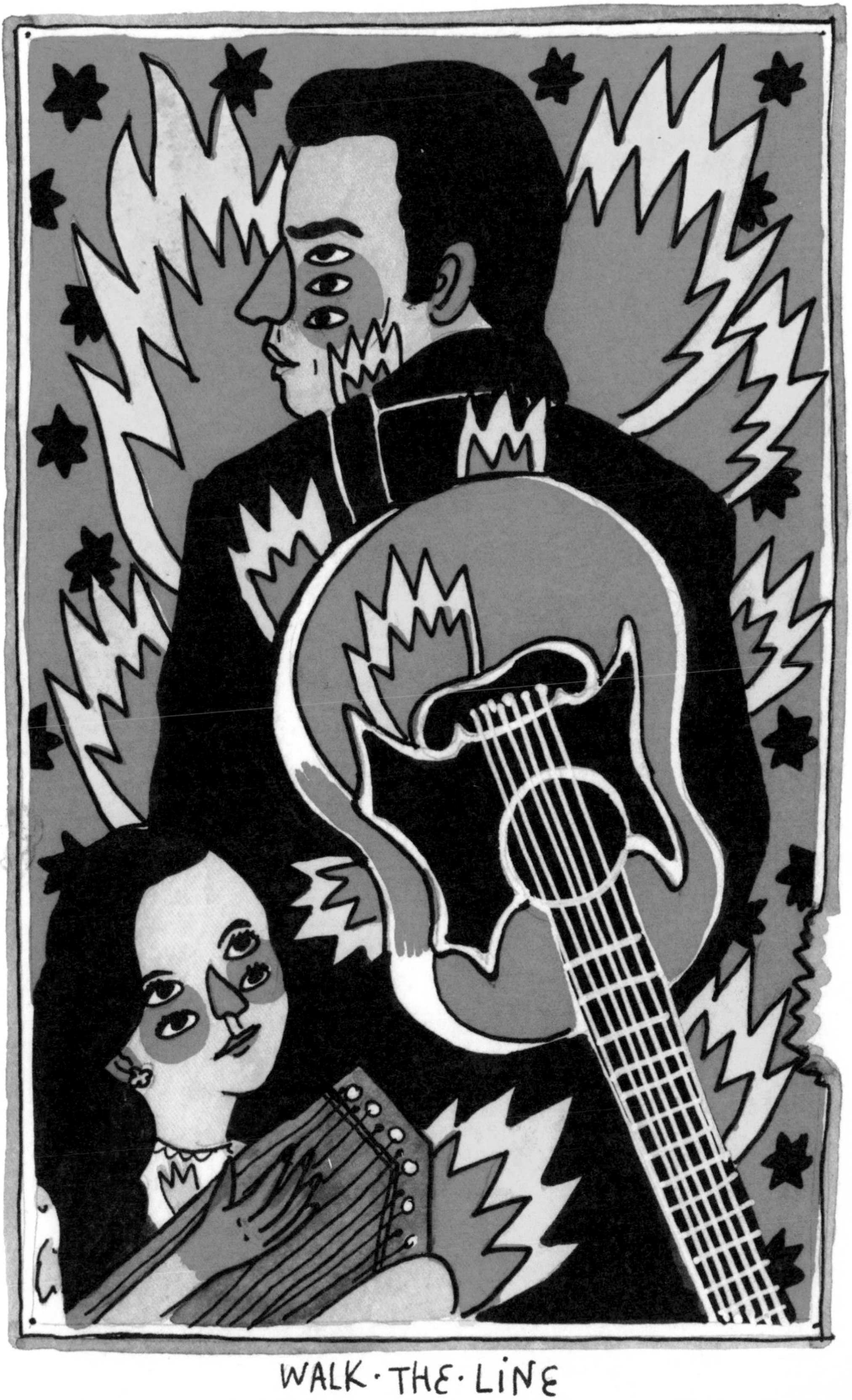

WALK · THE · LINE

MARIE ANTOINETTE

(2006)

SOFIA COPPOLA DID IT AGAIN. THROUGH THE REAL STORY OF MARIE ANTOINETTE, SHE NARRATES THE LIFE OF A GIRL WHO GOES THROUGH SOMETHING AKIN TO WHAT HAPPENS TO THE BLONDE SISTERS IN THE VIRGIN SUICIDES. SOMEONE LIVING AS A PRISONER IN THEIR OWN HOME, EVEN IF THIS TIME THAT HOME HAPPENS TO BE THE ENTIRE PALACE OF VERSAILLES AND THE GIRL IN QUESTION IS THE QUEEN OF FRANCE. COPPOLA HAS A SPECIAL SKILL FOR SEEING THE HIDDEN DETAILS OF A PERSON'S INNER LONELINESS AND ISOLATION, AND THE WAY THEY CAN TRY TO BURST FREE. AND FOR THAT I LOVE THIS MOVIE, AS WELL AS THE MOVIE'S AESTHETIC... THE COMPOSITION, COLOURS, LIGHT. EVERY SINGLE SCENE IS AN ODE TO THE LUXURIOUS AND IDEAL VERSAILLES BEAUTY, BUT AT THE SAME TIME WITH DASHES OF BONHOMIE AND LAUGHTER. THE MOVIE WAS CRITICIZED BECAUSE IN ONE SCENE YOU CAN SEE A PAIR OF HIGH TOP CONVERSE SEEMINGLY BELONGING TO MARIE ANTOINETTE. I PERSONALLY LOVE THIS DETAIL, WHICH CREATES A BRIDGE FOR THE VIEWERS BETWEEN THOSE "OLDEN TIMES" AND OUR OWN. MARIE WAS JUST LIKE ANY OTHER YOUNG GIRL WHO WANTED TO LET HER HAIR DOWN AND HAVE FUN.

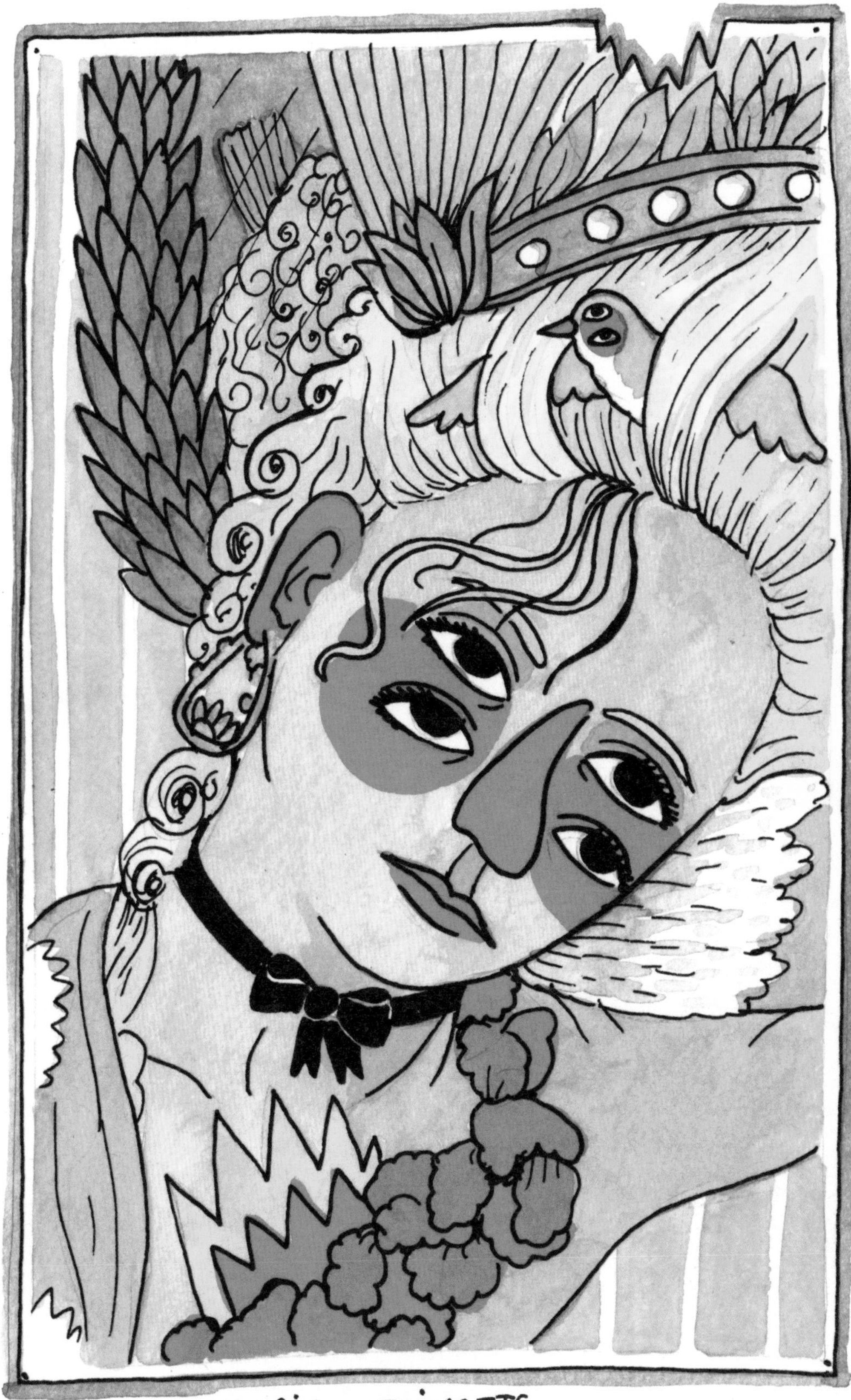

MARIE-ANTOINETTE

LITTLE·MISS·SUNSHINE

(2006)

I'VE GOT A REAL SOFT SPOT FOR THIS MOVIE. AND EVEN MORE SO THAN FOR THE STORY ITSELF, THAT SOFT SPOT IS FOR OLIVE, THE LITTLE GIRL WHO PLAYS THE MAIN PART. I ABSOLUTELY ADORE HER CHARACTER. HER INNOCENCE, HER ZANINESS, HER HOPES, HER FEARS, HER COURAGE. SHE OVERRULES ALL OF SOCIETY'S PREDETERMINED RULES TO SING THE SEXY SONG SHE'S PRACTICED WITH HER ~~GRUMPY OLD GIT~~ GRANDFATHER IN A RIDICULOUS CHILD BEAUTY CONTEST. I'D LOVE TO HAVE OLIVE FOR A DAUGHTER. YOU CAN LEARN SO MUCH FROM SOMEONE LIKE HER: SO FREE-SPIRITED, SO HAPPY, SO BRIMMING WITH ENTHUSIASM, AND THAT SMILE... I'M GOING TO MAKE A CONFESSION — THERE'S A SCENE WHEN OLIVE LISTENS TO A VOICE MESSAGE TELLING HER THAT SHE'S BEEN ACCEPTED TO TAKE PART IN THE LITTLE MISS SUNSHINE BEAUTY CONTEST. HER FACE LIGHTS UP AND BUILDS INTO A SHRIEK OF SHEER JOY. WELL, I FILMED THAT SCENE ON MY PHONE TO BE ABLE TO WATCH THE JOY OVER AND OVER.

I DON'T WANT TO BE A LOSER.

ANOTHER SPECIAL MENTION FOR PAUL DANO, WHO PLAYS OLIVE'S OLDER BROTHER, AND BEAUTIFULLY SO.

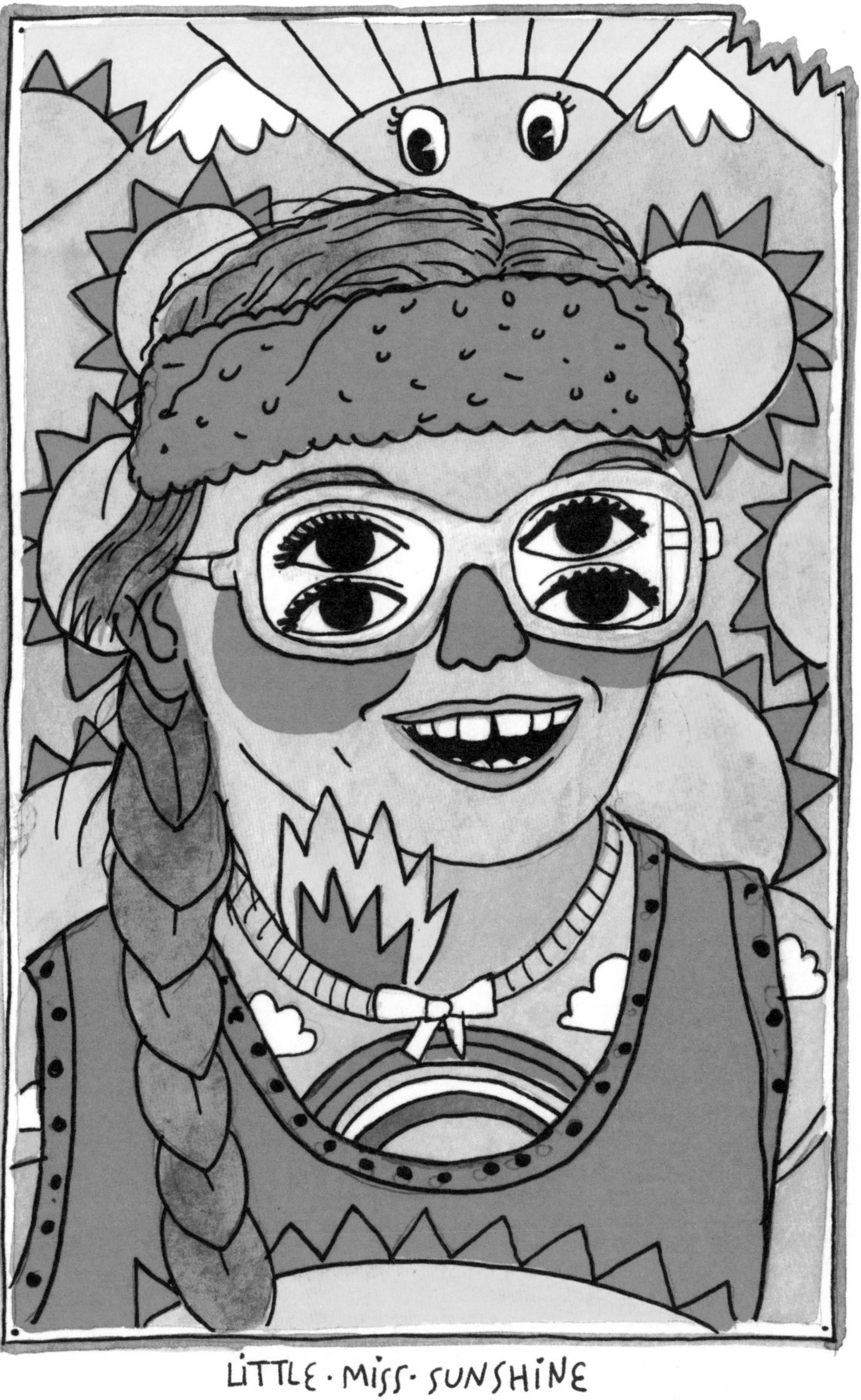

LITTLE · MISS · SUNSHINE

THE DEPARTED

(2006)

MY BELOVED MARTIN SCORSESE AGAIN. HE NEVER FAILS. AGREED, THIS ISN'T TECHNICALLY HIS MOVIE AS IT'S A REMAKE. THE ORIGINAL IS FROM HONG KONG (INFERNAL AFFAIRS), BUT HE ~~KNEW~~ KNEW HOW TO ADAPT IT TO MOBSTER FRANK COSTELLO'S BOSTON SETTING LIKE THE WIZARD HE IS. A MOVIE WITH VARIOUS LEVELS OF ESPIONAGE AND COUNTERESPIONAGE, RATS, MOLES, COMINGS AND GOINGS. I LOVE THIS GENRE, AND IF THE CAST IS AS BADASS AS THIS ONE, IT IS PERFECTION IN THRILLER FORM. I'LL ADD THAT I ALSO HAVE A SOFT ● SPOT FOR DICAPRIO AND MATT DAMON. WATCHING THIS MOVIE IS ONE OF THE BEST POSSIBLE WAYS TO SPEND A COUPLE OF HOURS. IT GIVES ME A BURNING DESIRE TO GET CAUGHT UP IN SOME KIND OF MAFIA PLOT AND START CHASING PEOPLE IN SOME DINGY NEIGHBOURHOOD ON THE EAST COAST.

~~IT'S~~ IT'S GOT ALL THE ELEMENTS TO MAKE SOMETHING AS SIMPLE AND TOUGH AS "A GOOD MOVIE". EVERY TIME, SCORSESE. EVERY TIME.

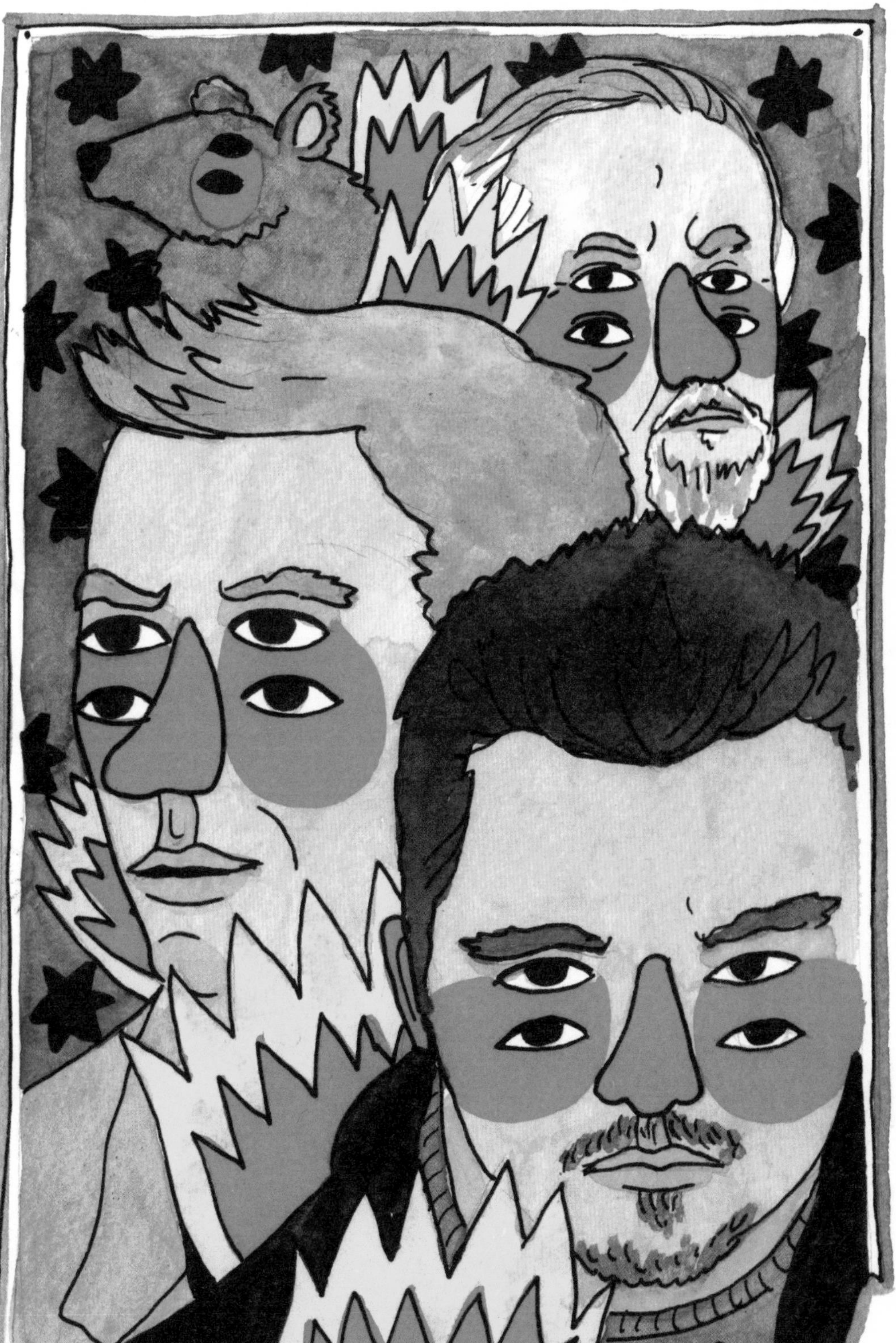

THE · DEPARTED

INTO·THE·WILD

(2007)

i PUT THIS MOVIE ON EVERY NOW AND
THEN AS IF IT WERE MEDICINE - A PRESCRIPTION
TO HELP ME PUT EVERYTHING AROUND ME INTO
PERSPECTIVE. IT'S LIKE A MEDITATION EXERCISE
WHERE i TURN INTO A BOY WHO HAS ~~FROM A~~
FORSAKEN HIS LIFE TO GO AND DISAPPEAR IN
THE MIDDLE OF ALASKA. IT'S A JOURNEY
TOWARDS FREEDOM, TO A STRIPPED DOWN
INNER SELF. WHEN YOU MAKE THIS JOURNEY,
IN THE OPPOSITE DIRECTION TO CIVILIZATION,
IT'S ABOVE ALL A MENTAL JOURNEY, ON WHICH
YOU'RE ALONE WITH YOURSELF AND NOBODY
ELSE. THE BEST WAY TO GET TO KNOW YOURSELF.
SEAN PENN CREATED A WONDERFUL, MULTI-
LAYERED VOYAGE. iT FEELS REALLY GOOD
TO ESCAPE FROM TIME TO TIME AND
LEAVE iT ALL BEHIND, AT LEAST TO GET
SOME PERSPECTIVE ON THE WORLD AROUND US.

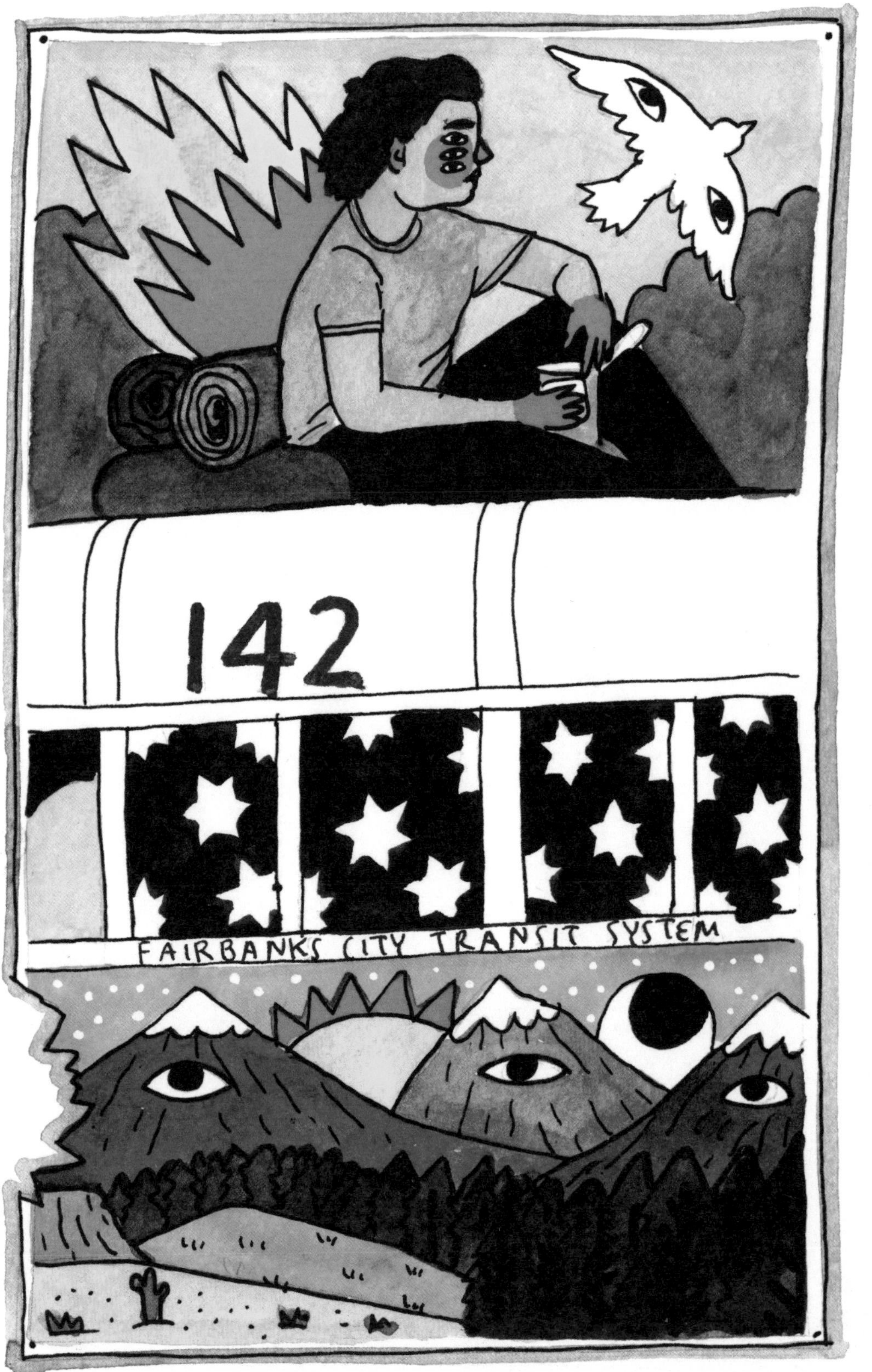
142
FAIRBANKS CITY TRANSIT SYSTEM
INTO· THE· WILD

There Will Be Blood

(2007)

MY GOD, WHAT A MOVIE. EPIC. ONCE AGAIN, A
FEATURE FILM FOLLOWING ONE PERSON'S LIFE
STORY. IN THIS CASE IT'S A POOR, DESTITUTE
MINER AT THE START OF THE 20TH CENTURY
~~WHO~~ WHO ENDS UP BEING ONE OF THE BIGGEST
OIL MAGNATES IN THE UNITED STATES. DANIEL DAY-
LEWIS EMBODIES HIM TO PERFECTION. HE'S SIMPLY
BREATHTAKING. YOU HATE HIM, YOU LOVE HIM, YOU
FEEL SORRY FOR HIM... ALL FOR ONE PERSON.
I ALSO LOVE THIS MOVIE BECAUSE THANKS TO IT,
I LEARNT A WHOLE NEW AREA OF THE COUNTRY'S
HISTORY. A SOMEWHAT DARK PIECE OF THE PUZZLE,
AND CAKED IN DESERT DUST. I CAN'T FORGET
ABOUT PAUL ~~████~~ DANO AND THE PENTECOSTAL
PREACHER HE PLAYS. I'D GO AS FAR AS TO SAY
THAT THIS YOUNG ACTOR IS AT THE SAME HEIGHT
AS DAY-LEWIS IN THIS STORY. IT'S A JOURNEY OF
EGOTISTICAL OUTBURSTS AND POWER STRUGGLES IN
THE MIDDLE OF NOWHERE IN THE STATES, WITH A
LEVEL OF POVERTY AND ARCHAISM WORTHY OF
A BIBLICAL STORY.

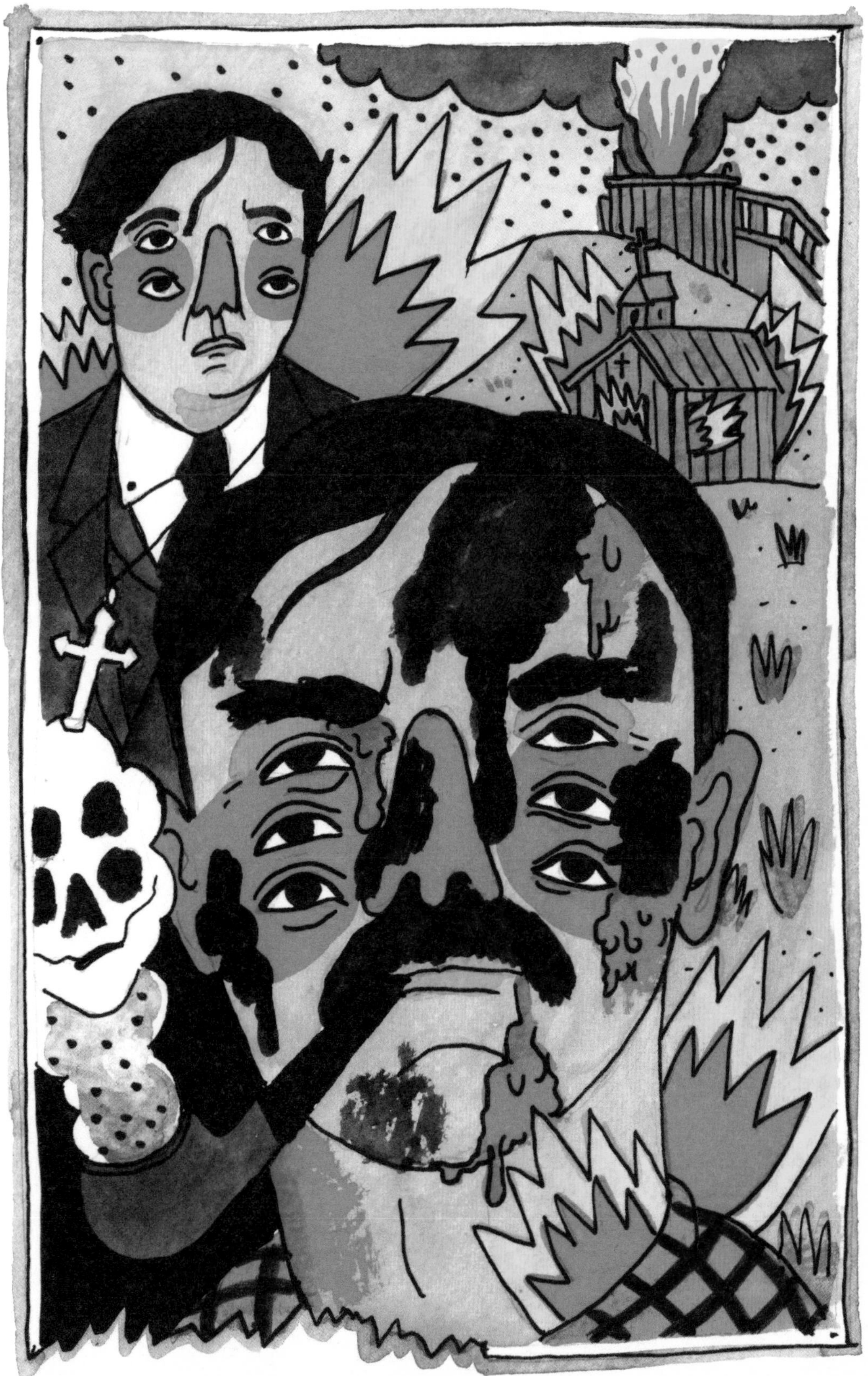

THERE· WILL· BE · BLOOD

THE WRESTLER

(2008)

i admit i have a penchant for stories about people with sordid, wasted lives, people who have settled – and not without frustration – for a life of frozen food in a trailer park. ~~and this movie~~

~~and this movie~~ and this movie is a perfect example of all that. Aronofsky does this better than anyone. He presents us with the life of this wasted wrestler... a one-time hero some thirty years ago and now working unloading boxes, he sleeps in a trailer or in his camper and the only chink of light in his dreary life is a third-rate fight in a fifth-rate city.

i love that they revived Mickey Rourke in this movie. it's ~~like~~ like he doesn't act – like he plays himself in a spiral of desolation and memories. i'm always moved by the duct tape he wears like improvised patches all over his bomber jacket. Randy "the ram" forever in my heart.

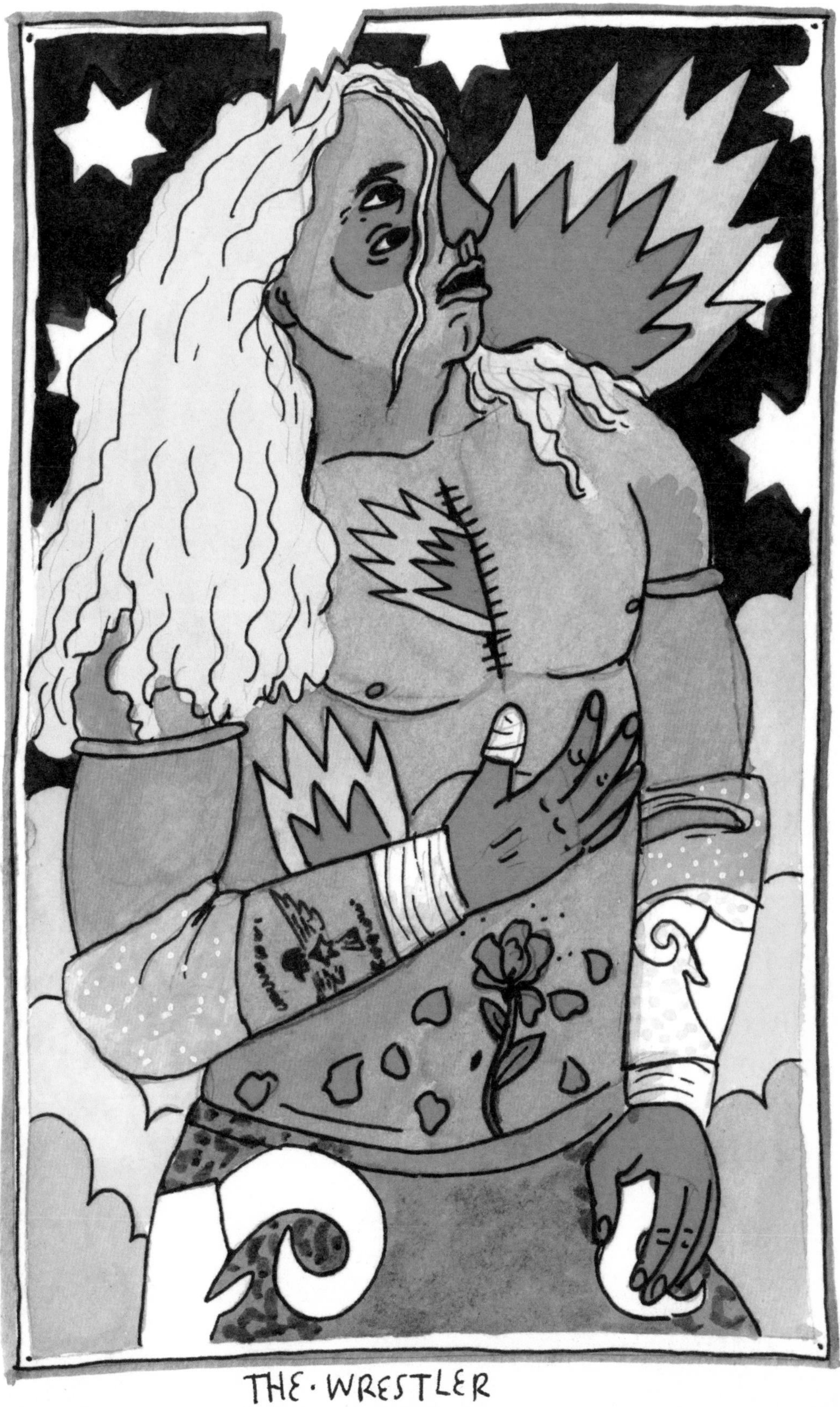

THE · WRESTLER

FANTASTIC MR. FOX

(2009)

WES ANDERSON AGAIN. WES FOREVER. EVEN
WHEN IT COMES TO ANIMATED MOVIES. ROALD
DAHL'S BOOK WAS ALREADY A JOY, BUT WES
ANDERSON MANAGED TO DRESS IT UP EVEN
MORE DELIGHTFULLY. THERE ARE MOMENTS WHEN
IT FEELS LIKE A WOODY ALLEN MOVIE. OTHER
MOMENTS HAVE SHADES OF TIM BURTON. BUT YOU
CAN REALLY SPOT ANDERSON'S DELICATE AND
DETAIL-CRAZY TOUCH. PLUS IT'S VERY LAUDABLE
THAT THE ANIMATION IS STOP MOTION —NO
COMPUTERS, JUST MILLIONS OF PHOTOGRAPHS
OF EVERY SINGLE MOVEMENT AND NUANCE.
MR. FOX IS SUPERB. CHARMING, A SMART
ALECK, CLASSY, BRAVE. EVERY TIME I SEE
THIS MOVIE IT MAKES ME WONDER WHAT
SMALL WOODLAND CREATURE I'D ~~BE~~
~~BE~~ BE IN A PARADISE LIKE THAT. i THINK
I'D LIKE TO BE THE WOLF THAT APPEARS NEAR
THE END, BUT MAYBE IT'S TOO MUCH
RESPONSIBILITY.

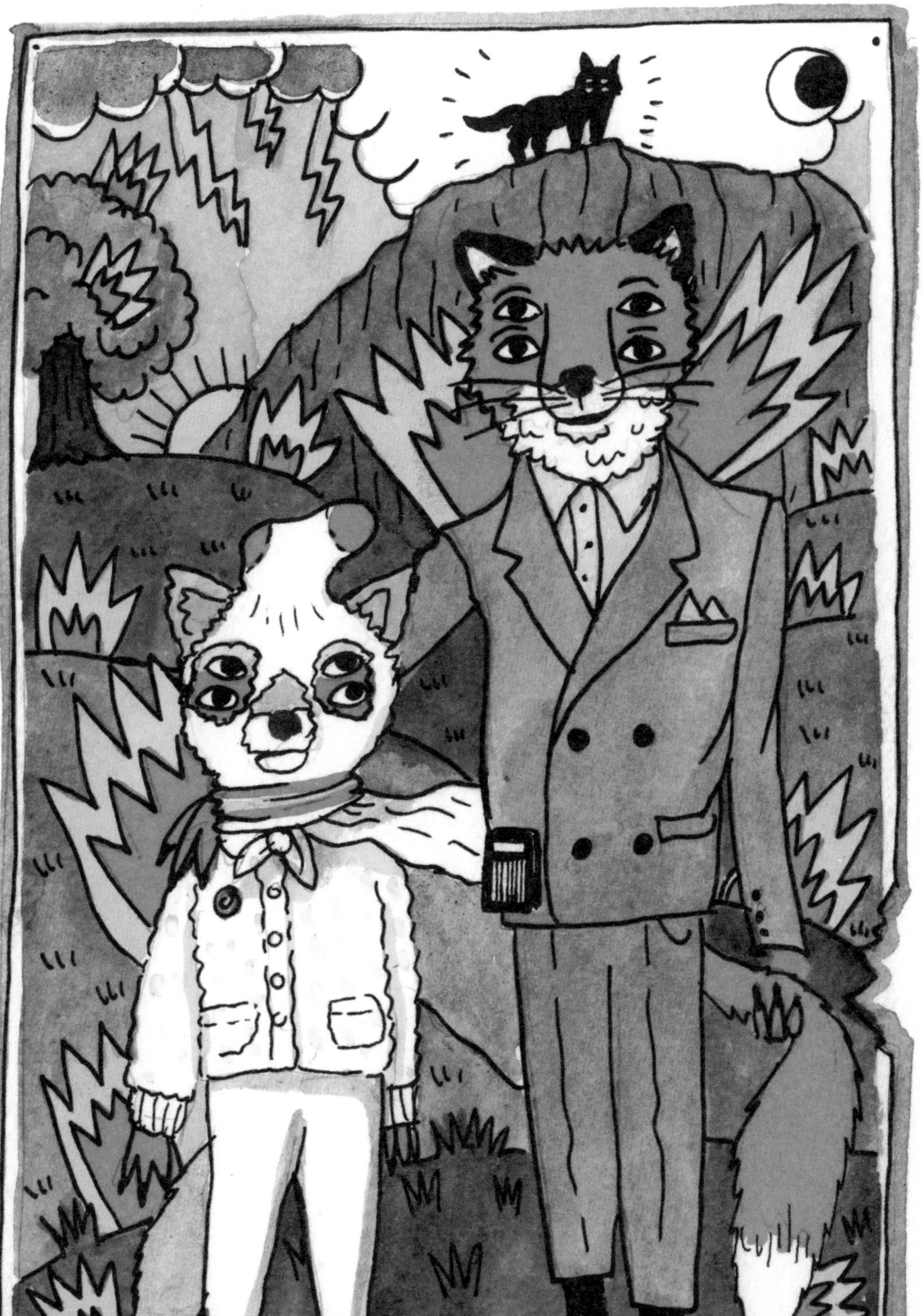

FANTASTIC · MR. · FOX

precious

(2009)

ANOTHER STORY OF SOMEONE LIVING IN A DISMAL, MISERABLE, PAINFUL ENVIRONMENT. PRECIOUS HAS SO MANY BULLET WOUNDS YOU CAN'T BELIEVE SHE'S STILL WALKING. WE ALMOST FEEL ASHAMED TO WATCH ██ SUCH ABUSE. THROUGH HER, THE DIRECTOR LEE DANIELS PRESENTS US WITH A SERIES OF THEMES THAT COME TOGETHER TO MAKE PRECIOUS' LIFE HELL: RACISM, FRUSTRATION, SOCIAL REJECTION FOR BEING OVERWEIGHT, SEXUAL ABUSE, ████ IMMIGRATION, SEXUALLY TRANSMITTED DISEASE, RELIGION, EDUCATION. AND SEEMINGLY, PRECIOUS SHOULDERS IT ALL. DESPITE THE HARDSHIP, THE FEELING THAT STICKS WITH ME AT THE END IS SOMETHING POWERFUL — A FEELING OF HOPE. AND EVEN THOUGH THAT SHINING LIGHT IS FACED WITH AN OVERWHELMING AMOUNT OF SHIT, THAT FEELING OF HOPE IS ALWAYS MUCH MORE POWERFUL.

196

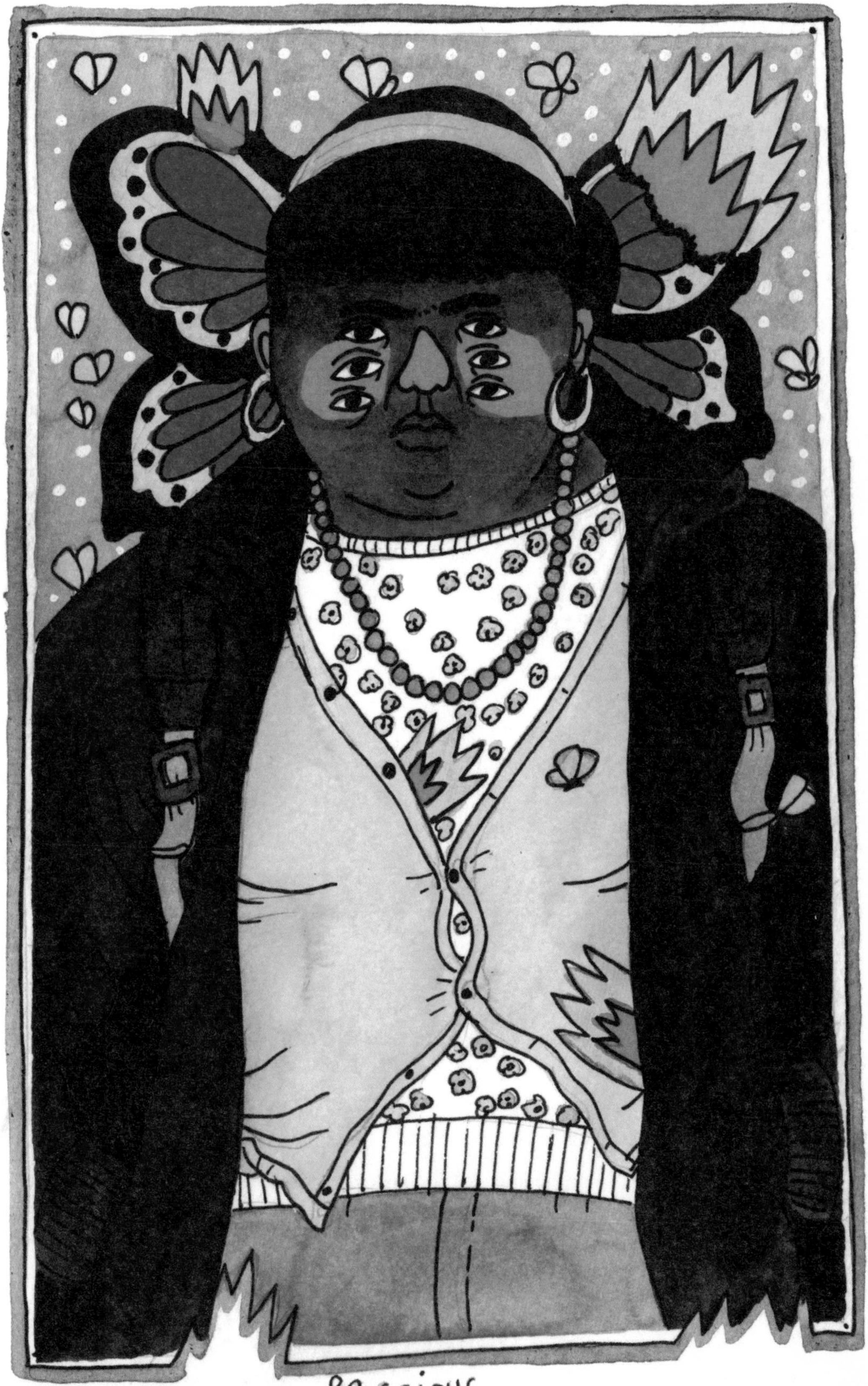

PRECIOUS

WHERE·THE·WILD·THINGS·ARE

(2009)

WILD. REALLY WILD. AND CRAZY. WHEN i SAW THiS
MOViE FOR THE FIRST TIME i HAD HiGH HOPES
BECAUSE i'M A FAN OF SPiKE JONZE, AND THE
BOOK iT'S BASED ON iS A CLASSIC. BUT i DON'T
THINK i TOTALLY CONNECTED WITH iT. AND NOW
i KNOW WHY. BACK THEN, BECAUSE OF THINGS
THAT WERE GOING ON iN MY LiFE, i HAD
REALLY BLOCKED OUT MY EMOTIONS. AND THiS MOVIE
iS JUST THAT—A CONSTANT EMOTIONAL WORKOUT,
AN EMOTION BINGE WITH THE CORRESPONDING
HANGOVER.
ONLY NOW THAT i'VE SORTED OUT THAT BLOCK AND
iVE LET PART OF ME BE, DO i FULLY RELATE TO
JONZE'S MOVIE. AND HE DOES ALL THiS BY MEANS
OF A BOY AND SOME MONSTERS. BUT THEN, i
SUPPOSE WE'RE ALL STILL THE LiTTLE BOY OR
GiRL WE WERE, AND WE ALL HAVE OUR OWN
MONSTERS, BOTH GOOD AND BAD.
AND i CAN'T WRAP THiS UP WITHOUT MENTIONING
THE ART. THE iMAGES ARE SUBLiME, THE
MONSTERS iNCREDIBLE, AND THE BOY EXACTLY AS
HE SHOULD BE. ~~~~ i THINK JONZE HAS
TAKEN THE ORiGiNAL BOOK FROM THE 60s
AND RAISED iT TO A WHOLE NEW LEVEL. WHERE
THE WiLD THINGS ARE iS A LiFE MANUAL. 🖐❤⚡

198

WHERE·THE·WILD·THINGS·ARE

THE FIGHTER

(2010)

ALMOST BEFORE STARTING THIS BOOK, THIS MOVIE WAS UP THERE IN MY TOP 101. BUT, FOR HONESTY'S ~~SAKE~~ SAKE, I'LL SAY THAT I'M NOT SURE WHAT'S SO ~~EXCEPTIONAL~~ EXCEPTIONAL ABOUT THIS MOVIE. IT JUST IS. AND IF I WROTE THIS BOOK ALL OVER AGAIN IT'D STILL BE HERE. IT'S THE STORY OF TWO BROTHERS WHO ARE BOXERS, BUT THE MOVIE ISN'T ~~ALL~~ ABOUT BOXING, NOR IS IT AN EPIC ABOUT OVERCOMING YOUR DESTINY. IT'S A MINOR, FAMILY DRAMA. IT'S ONE OF THOSE STORIES THAT COULD ~~BE~~ BELONG TO PRETTY MUCH ANY NAMELESS COLD GREY CITY ON THE NORTH EAST COAST OF AMERICA. I REALLY ENJOY THESE MOVIES THAT AREN'T GOING TO CHANGE THE WORLD ONE IOTA, BUT BOMBARD ME WITH REALITY, THE REALITY I LOVE SO MUCH — THAT GREY REALITY, WHERE IT'S SO WONDERFUL TO FIND A SPOT OF MAGIC, BECAUSE IT SHINES OUT AS THE LOVELIEST MAGIC IN THE WORLD.
ALL THE ACTORS HERE PLAY THEIR ROLES TO ~~PERFECTION~~ PERFECTION. REAL LIFE —REALITY— COULDN'T BE MORE INTERESTING.

200

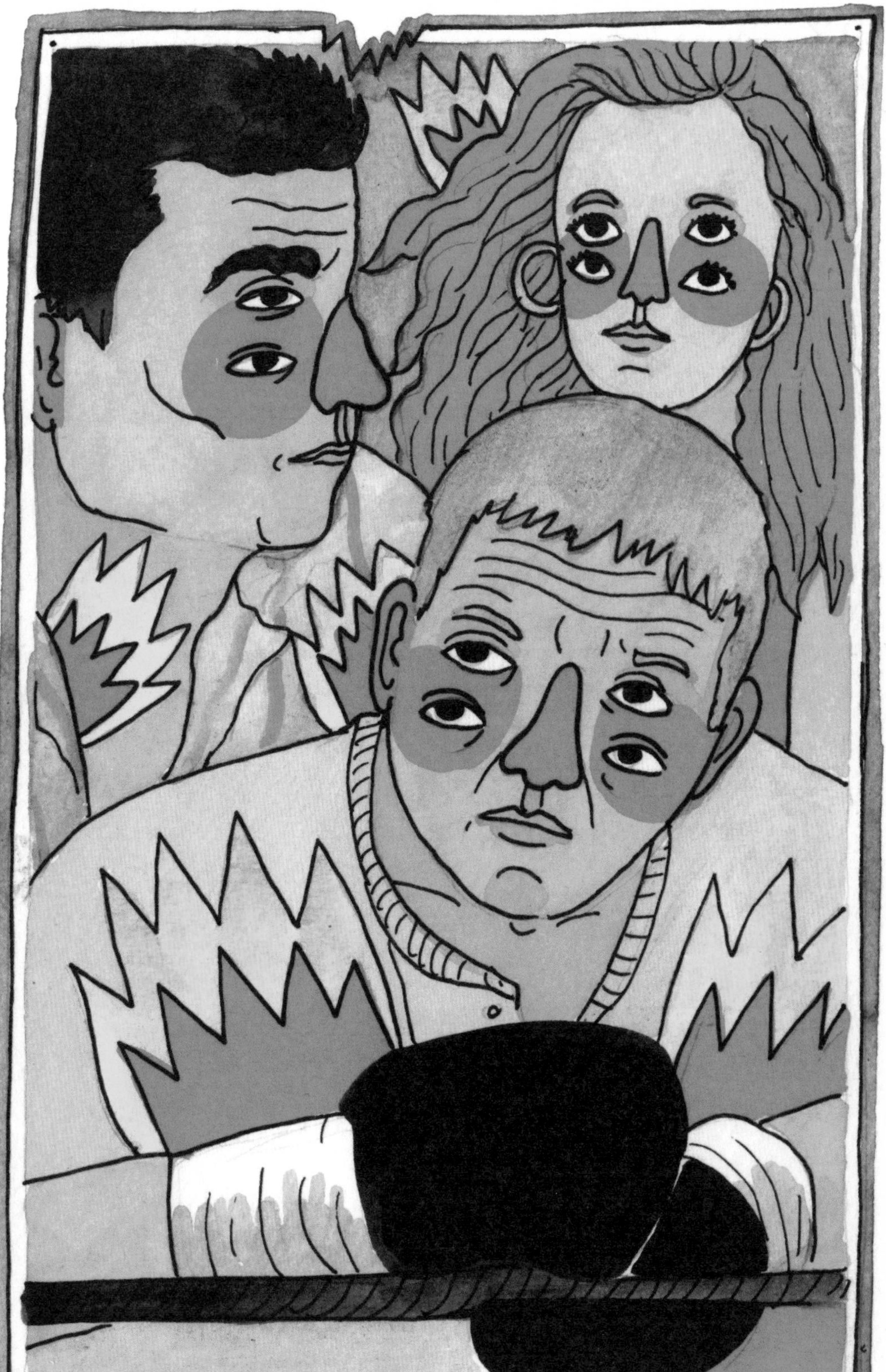

THE· FIGHTER

WINTER'S BONE

(2010)

IF I HAD TO CHOOSE JUST TEN MOVIES FROM THIS BOOK, I THINK THIS WOULD MAKE THE CUT. IT'S A PEERLESS PORTRAIT OF DEEP AMERICA. THE COLD, MUDDY AMERICA OF METH COOKING IN MAKESHIFT LABS. IT'S ALMOST A MODERN WESTERN, IN WHICH THE HEROIC DEED OF A TEENAGER (A FLAWLESS JENNIFER LAWRENCE — I STILL CAN'T UNDERSTAND WHY THEY DIDN'T GIVE HER THE OSCAR), MAKES HER WAY THROUGH TERRIBLE WOODS, FULL OF MONSTROUS MEN AND DIABOLICAL WOMEN, SNOW, DRUGS, SILENT KILLINGS... IT'S A WHITE TRASH ODYSSEY. AND BY NOW YOU MIGHT HAVE REALIZED THAT I'M A MAJOR FAN OF THAT WHOLE WORLD. IT'S LIKE "THE TRAVELS OF MARCO POLO", ONLY IN THE GREY WOODS OF MISSOURI AND FOLLOWING A SEVENTEEN-YEAR-OLD GIRL WHO HAS TO FIND HER MISSING FATHER IN ORDER TO SAVE THEIR HOUSE AND WHAT LITTLE THEY HAVE. WHEN I SAW IT, I FELT LIKE SOMEONE HAD HIT EXACTLY THE RIGHT BUTTON.

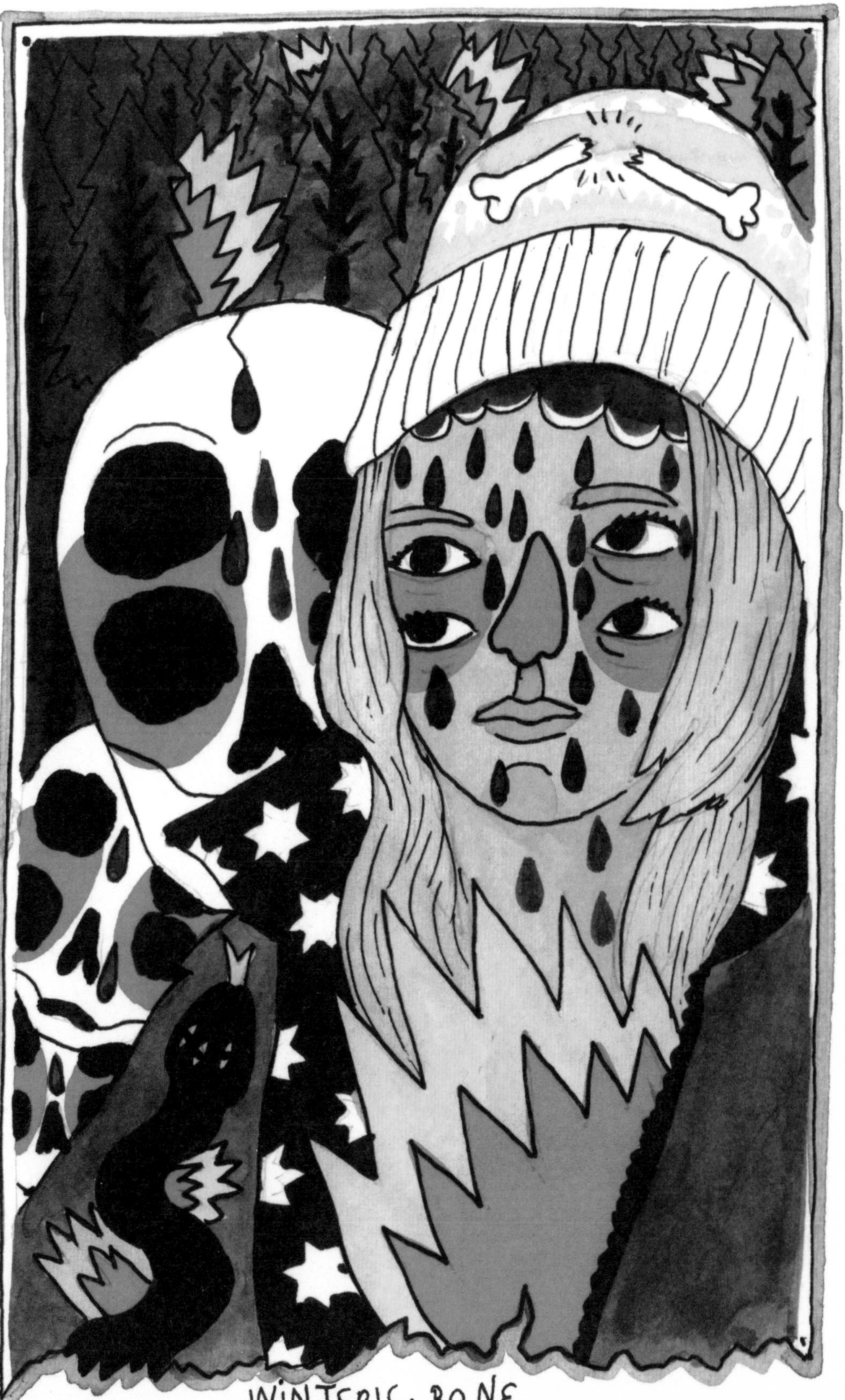

WINTER'S · BONE

Drive

(2011)

ANOTHER MINOR STORY, ABOUT CHARACTERS THAT NO ONE WOULD BAT AN EYELID AT IN REAL LIFE, BUT WITHIN THEIR SMALL UNIVERSE YOU FIND METEOR SHOWERS, BLACK HOLES, SUNS AND COLLIDING STARS. AESTHETICALLY SPEAKING, IT'S A MASTERPIECE. THE COLOURS ... ALL OF IT. PURE "STYLE" IN A MOVIE. AND OF COURSE THE STORY ITSELF IS ALSO MASTERFUL. THE PLOT ISN'T GOING TO CHANGE THE WORLD, BUT WILL ALTER THE FATE OF TWO OR THREE CHARACTERS IN THE MOVIE. BLOW AFTER BLOW OF LOVE AND VIOLENCE. A SIMPLE PLOT LIKE THE KIND YOU GOT IN 1940s FILM NOIR. RYAN GOSLING IS PERFECT. ANOTHER OF MY CHOICE ACTORS. AND AS IF THAT WEREN'T ENOUGH, FOR THOSE OF YOU WHO DON'T KNOW, HE HAD A BAND (DEAD MAN'S BONES), WHICH IS ONE OF MY FAVOURITE GROUPS FROM RECENT YEARS. i PUT THEIR ALBUM ON EVERY WEEK. DEFINITELY A GOSLING FAN! ♥

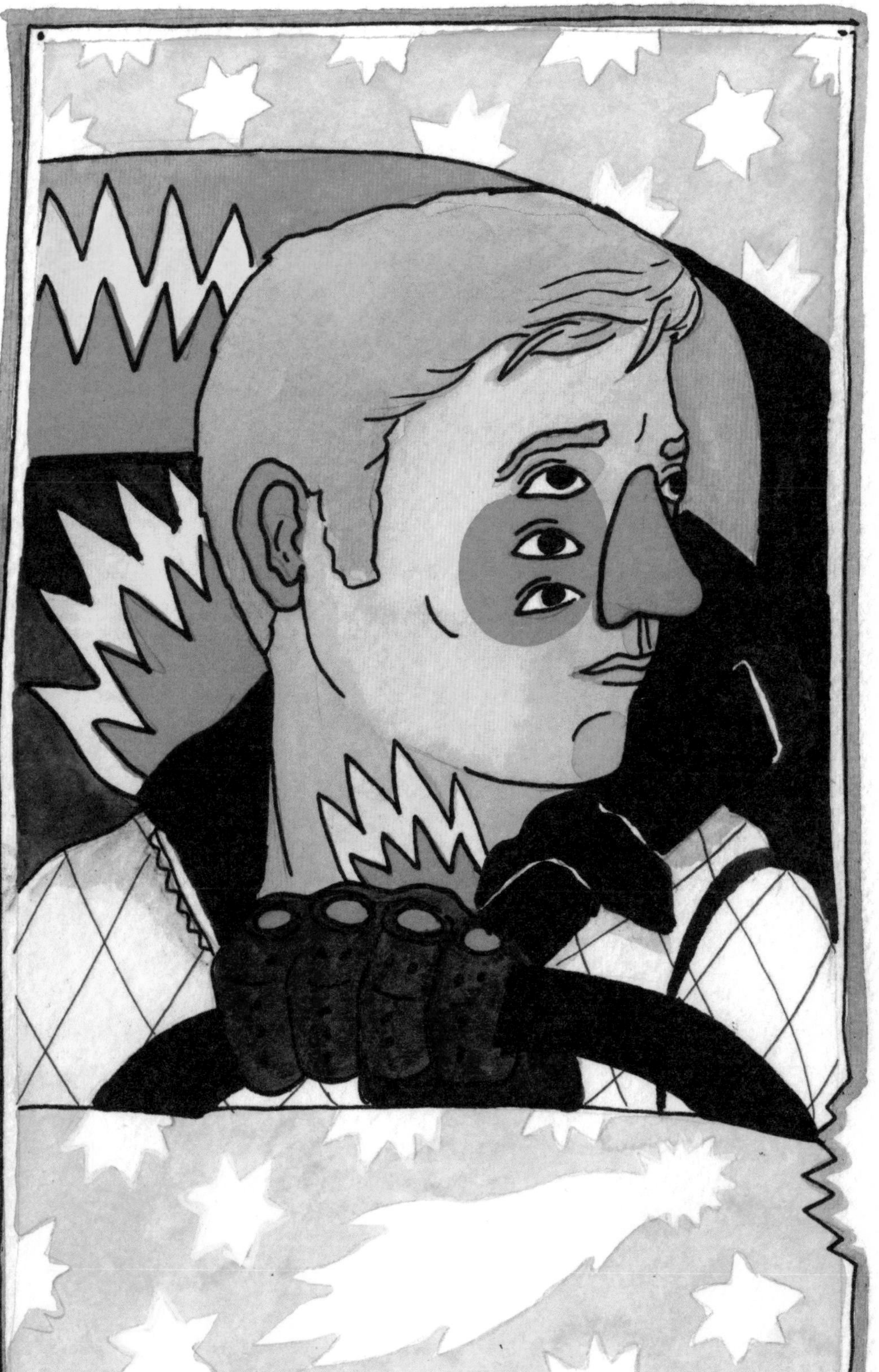

DRIVE

Moonrise Kingdom

(2012)

GUESS WHO'S BACK... WES... ANDERSON!
I COULDN'T NOT INCLUDE THIS MOVIE. IN MY
OPINION THIS ONE IS THE ZENITH OF HIS
UNIVERSE. I THINK THIS TIME HE'S OUTDONE
HIMSELF. UNTIL NOW THERE WERE ALWAYS KIDS
IN HIS MOVIES, BUT THE MAIN PARTS WERE CARRIED
BY ADULT CHARACTERS. IN MOONRISE KINGDOM THE
KIDS ARE THE SHINING STARS AROUND WHICH THE
REST OF THE CAST ORBITS.
IT ALSO SEEMS HERE LIKE WES ANDERSON MOVES
FURTHER AND FURTHER AWAY FROM THE REAL
WORLD TO RECREATE HIS OWN IDEAL SETTINGS. I
THINK ONE OF THE THINGS I MOST LIKE ABOUT
WES ANDERSON'S MOVIES ARE THESE ALMOST STATIC
IMAGES. I LIKE HOW HE CREATES AN ENTIRE
ENVIRONMENT AS IF FOR A PHOTO OR A PAINTING
AND HIS CHARACTERS MOVE AROUND WITHIN IT AS
LITTLE AS POSSIBLE. THIS APPEALS TO ME BECAUSE
I TRY TO ACHIEVE THAT ALMOST MEDIEVAL OR
BYZANTINE FEEL TO MY ART SO THAT EACH FIGURE
APPEARS IN THE MOST MEMORABLE AND EPIC WAY.
AND I STILL GET A KICK OUT OF THE PLEASURE WES
SEEMS TO TAKE FROM EACH AND EVERY DETAIL IN
THE FRAME. THAT'S ANOTHER THING I TRY TO
REPLICATE IN MY OWN DRAWINGS.

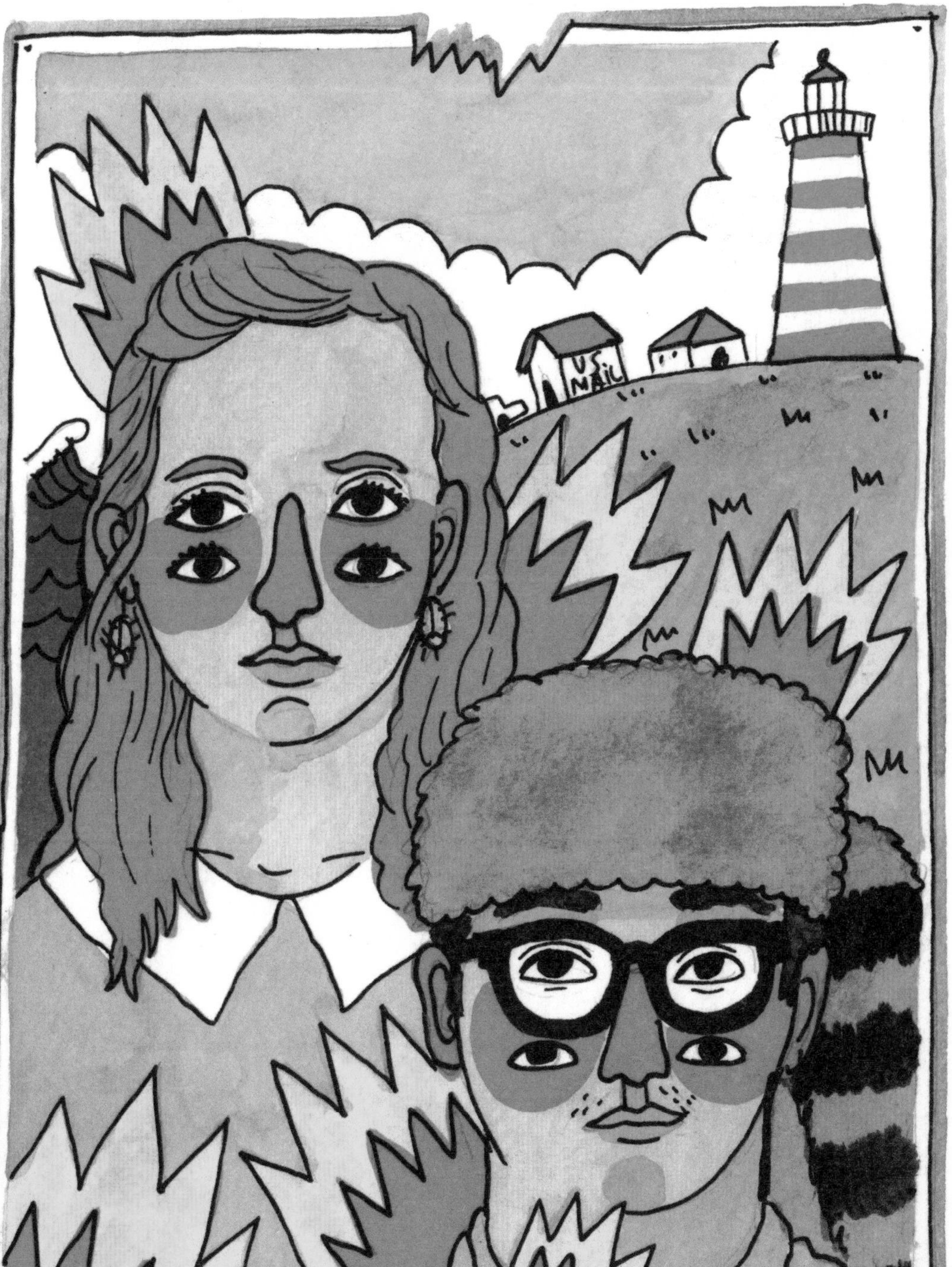
U.S. MAIL

MOONRISE · KINGDOM

THE WOLF
OF · WALL · STREET

(2013)

IT'S BEEN TOO LONG SINCE I MENTIONED MARTIN SCORSESE. I THINK HE MUST HAVE HAD A LOT OF FUN MAKING THIS MOVIE. IT'S TOTAL PANDEMONIUM, ONE LONG ORGY. EVERY TIME I WATCH IT I SPEND THE WHOLE THREE HOURS WITH MY MOUTH OPEN, EITHER LAUGHING HYSTERICALLY, OR FLIPPING OUT AT SOME CRAZY THING LEO DICAPRIO IS DOING. IT'S LIKE WE'VE TAKEN THE SAME SUBSTANCE HE HAS. WE WATCH HIM CLIMB THE RANKS AND GAIN MORE AND MORE SUCCESS, ALL IN THE MIDDLE OF A PILL, ◆ BOOZE AND COCAINE-FUELLED HAZE. I ALWAYS FINISH THE MOVIE EXHAUSTED BUT REALLY SATISFIED. ONCE AGAIN, SCORSESE OPENS THE DOOR TO ONE CHARACTER'S LIFE FOR US TO SEE THEIR ODYSSEY, FROM START TO FINISH, AND SOMETIMES RIGHT BACK TO WHERE THEY STARTED. IT'S A LESSON IN ~~ENTIRE~~ EXCESSIVE FLAMBOYANT FUN. UNCLE MARTIN RETURNS TO THE FORM OF HIS BIGGEST HITS, GOODFELLAS AND CASINO. KEEP THEM COMING, MARTIN!

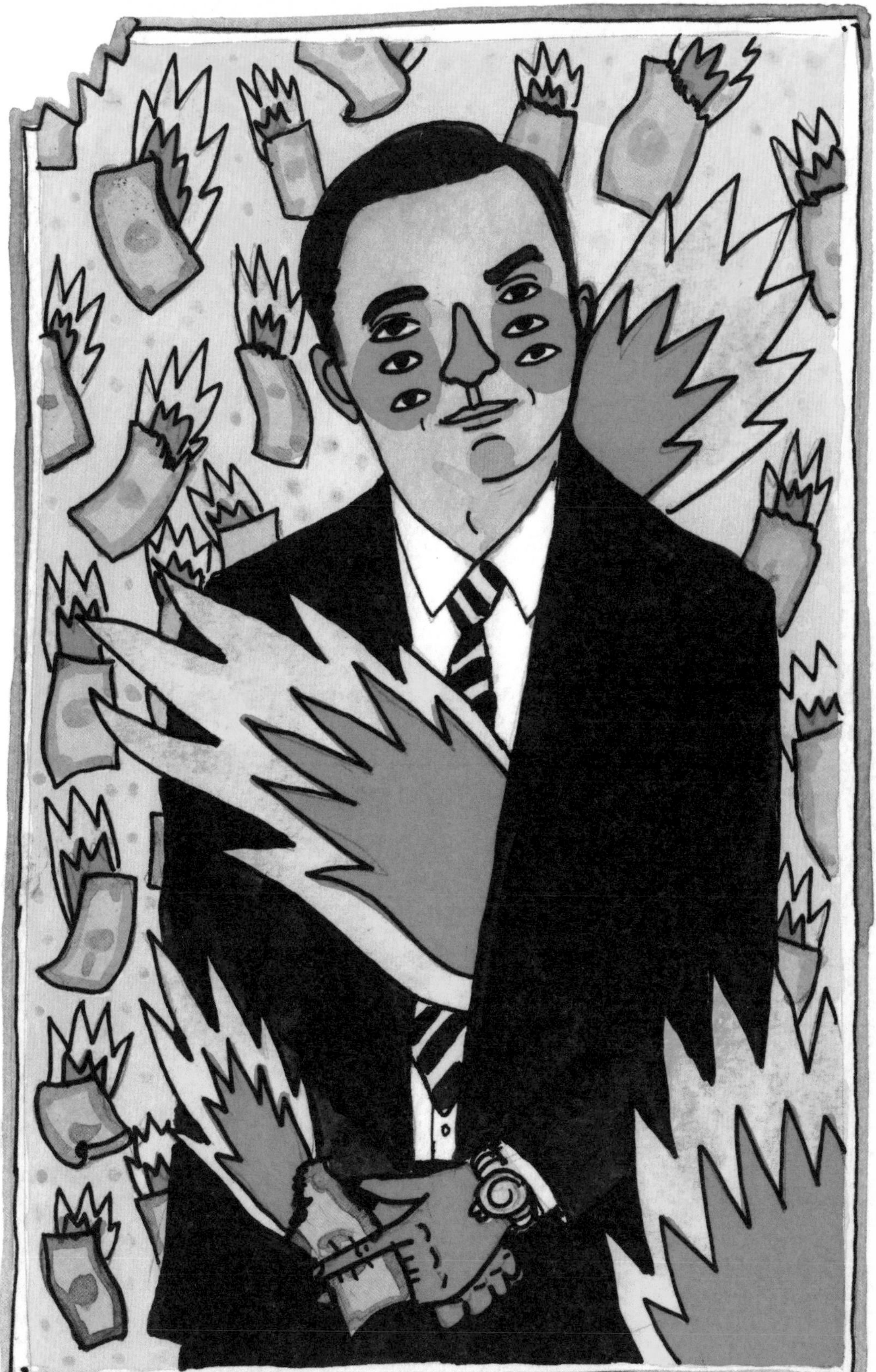

THE · WOLF · OF · WALL · STREET

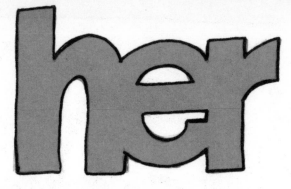

her

(2013)

AS YOU CAN SEE, I'M PRETTY LOYAL TO THE DIRECTORS I LIKE, WHICH IS WHY I CAN'T HELP RETURNING TO SPIKE JONZE. THIS MOVIE REALLY IS AMAZING. THE DIRECTOR BUILDS A STORY THAT PROVOKES A KIND OF NERVOUS SMILE. WHAT HAPPENS TO THE MAIN CHARACTER SEEMS REALLY NUTS. BUT GIVEN WHAT WE'VE SEEN SO FAR, AND WHERE WE'RE HEADING, MAYBE IT'S NOT SO CRAZY ~~XX~~ AFTER ALL. WE ALL LOOKED AT EACH OTHER ON LEAVING THE CINEMA WITH A FACE LIKE "SHIT, THE MOVIE WAS GOOD, BUT ALL THIS IS A LITTLE SCARY, RIGHT?" IT'S PRETTY POWERFUL STUFF WHEN A MOVIE CAN PRODUCE A REACTION LIKE THAT. AND BEYOND THE MESSAGE, VISUALLY SPEAKING THE MOVIE IS WORLD-CLASS. IT'S GOT THAT CONTAINED JAPANESE VIBE BUT WITH WARMER, FRIENDLIER TOUCHES. PHOENIX WEARS RED A LOT, AND HE'S ALWAYS AROUND RED THINGS. IT'S A COLOUR THAT USUALLY CONNOTES STRENGTH. BUT I THINK IN THIS CASE IT'S MORE LIKE THE RED OF A TARGET. SOMEONE IMPERFECT.

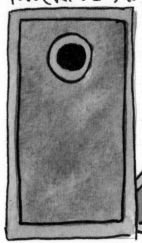

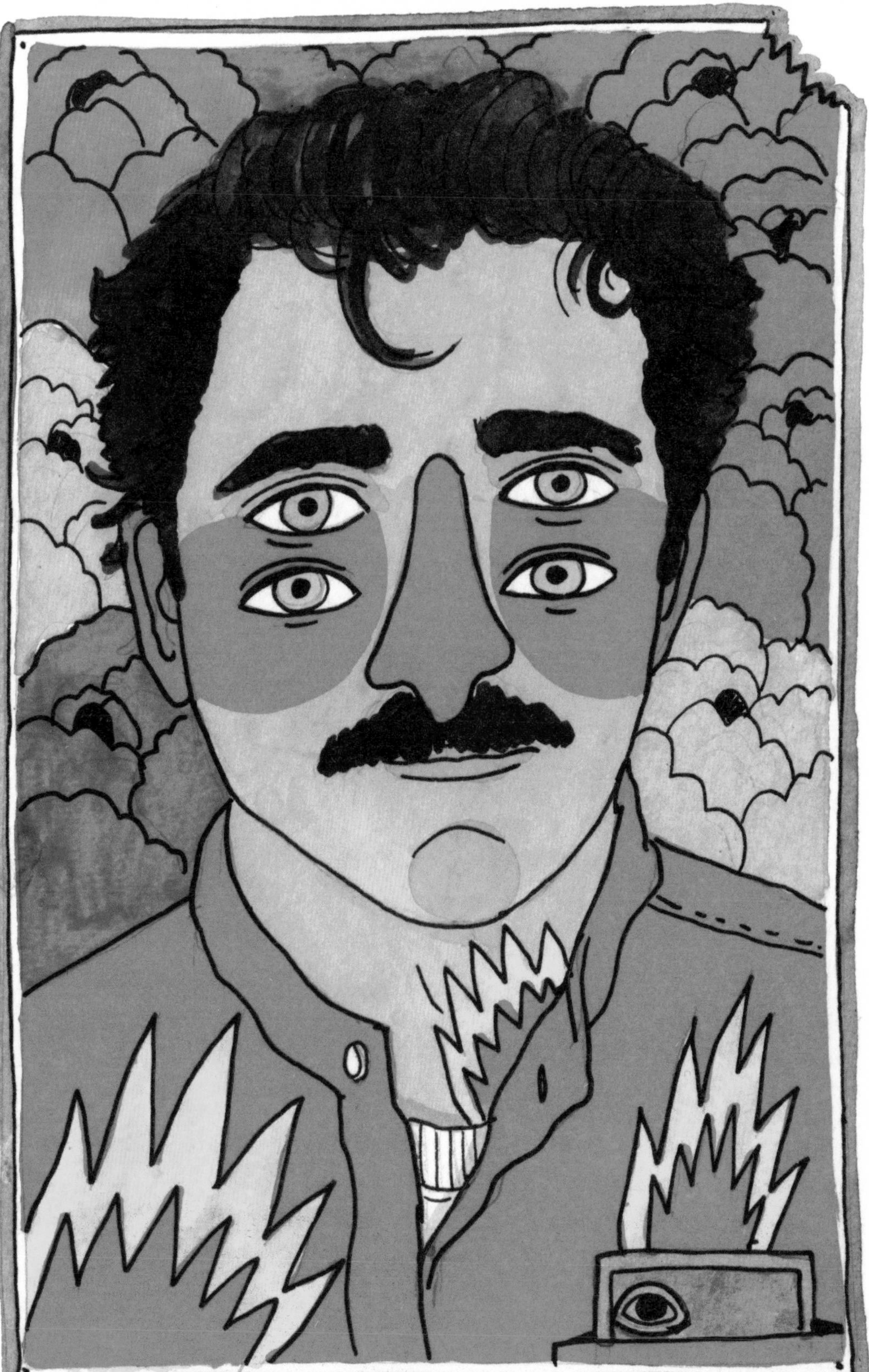

HER

INTERSTELLAR

(2014)

CHRISTOPHER NOLAN AGAIN, OF COURSE.
THERE MIGHT █ NOT BE THAT MANY SCIENCE
FICTION MOVIES IN THIS BOOK, BUT i SHOULD
SAY THAT it'S A GENRE i LOVE. AND THIS
MOVIE IS LIKE A NEW BENCHMARK FOR SCI-FI.
i THINK THAT NOLAN RECEIVED THE BATON
FROM KUBRICK AND HIS "2001: A SPACE ODYSSEY".
THE INITIAL PREMISE IS BRILLIANT, BUT THE
BEST THING OF ALL IS THAT THIS IS REALLY
JUST THE BASE ON WHICH THE REAL STORY
RESTS IN ALL ITS COMPLEXITY.
TALKING ABOUT THIS MOVIE ALSO GIVES ME
THE OPPORTUNITY TO PRAISE MATTHEW
MCCONAUGHEY. i'VE BEEN PRAISING HIM FOR
YEARS, BUT IN INTERSTELLAR HE'S REALLY
OUTDONE HIMSELF. THE MOVIE IS EVEN ~~A████~~
ABSTRACT AT TIMES, AND THAT'S PERFECT,
BECAUSE SURELY THAT'S HOW WE SEE THE
UNIVERSE — BOTH GEOGRAPHICAL AND CONCEPTUAL.
i'M NOT GOING TO RUIN THE END, BUT... HOLY SHIT.

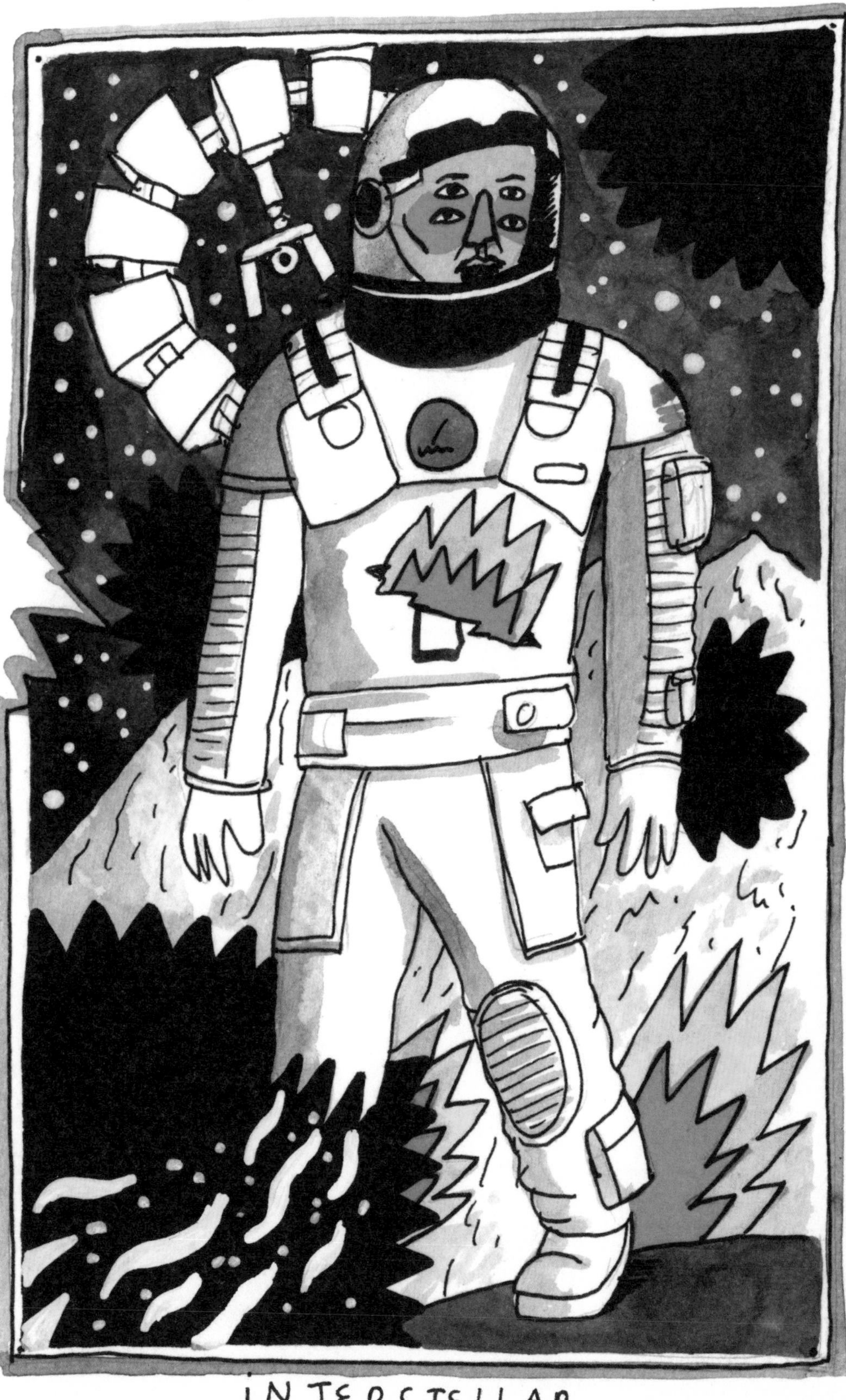

INTERSTELLAR

THE · REVENANT

(2015)

AND MY LIST CLOSES WITH AN UNBEATABLE COLLABORATION BETWEEN TWO NAMES YOU'LL RECOGNIZE FROM THIS BOOK: ALEJANDRO GONZÁLEZ IÑÁRRITU DIRECTING LEONARDO DICAPRIO. I STILL CAN'T GET THAT FIRST SHOT FROM THE START OF THE MOVIE OUT OF MY HEAD — HALF WESTERN, HALF WAR MOVIE. I THINK I'D PUT IT UP THERE WITH THE SCENE I MENTIONED FROM GOODFELLAS. ARE YOU SURE, RICARDO? HELL, YES. AND THAT'S JUST THE START OF THE MOVIE. I'M REALLY INTO ODYSSEYS, AS YOU WILL HAVE NOTICED BY NOW. AND THIS STORY IS ONE OF THE LONGEST AND MOST GRUELLING IMAGINABLE. THIS TIME IT'S SET IN THE NINETEENTH CENTURY WITH EUROPEAN SETTLERS ON WILD NORTH AMERICAN SOIL.
THE WHOLE VOYAGE WE TAKE WITH DICAPRIO IS FULL OF SUFFERING (BOTH PHYSICAL AND MENTAL). IT'S ALMOST LIKE A "VIA CRUCIS" OF THE GENESIS OF THE USA.
THE REVENANT IS FEROCIOUS AND EPIC, AND IN IÑÁRRITU'S HANDS, IT BECAME A MAJOR MOVIE IN CINEMA HISTORY. OR AT LEAST IN MY PARTICULAR HISTORY.

214

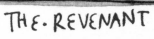

THE·REVENANT

APPENDIX

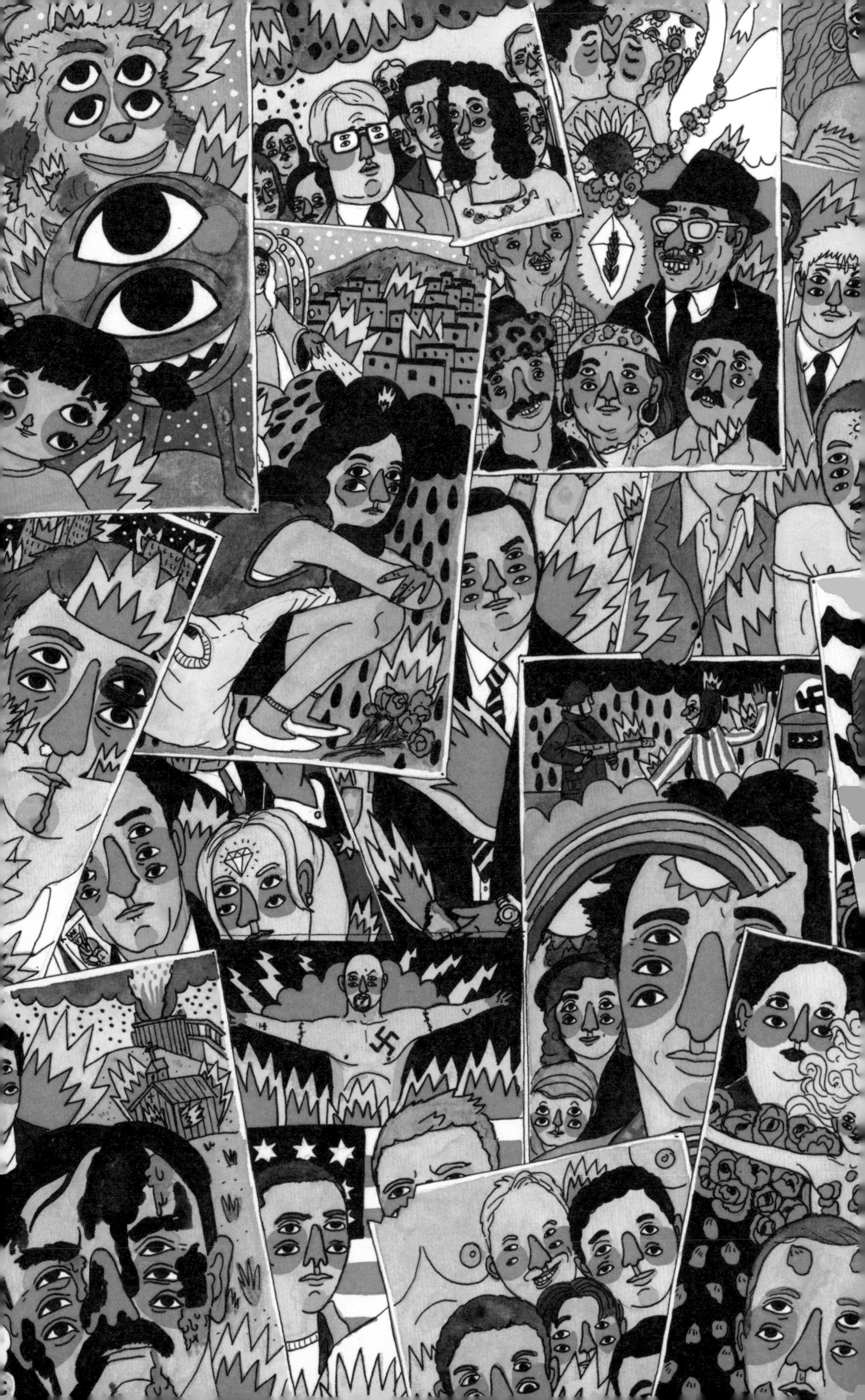

ALSO AVAILABLE:

101·ARTISTS·TO·LISTEN·TO·
BEFORE·YOU·DIE·

RICARDO·CAVOLO

NOBROW

A NEW YORK TIMES BESTSELLER
ISBN: 978-1-910620-00-7

RICARDO·CAVOLO

BORN IN HIS FATHER'S PAINTING STUDIO, RICARDO
CAVOLO HAS GROWN UP SURROUNDED BY ART AND
IS NOW ONE OF THE MOST EXCITING AND SUCCESSFUL
YOUNG ILLUSTRATORS TO COME OUT OF SPAIN.
CAVOLO'S INFLUENCES RANGE FROM OUTSIDER ART
TO MEDIEVAL PAINTINGS AND HIS WORK HAS BEEN
EXHIBITED IN SOLO SHOWS ACROSS THE WORLD.

TO MY PARENTS WHO HAVE PLAYED ME
MOVIES SINCE I WAS BORN

TO MARIA FOR EVERYTHING AND FOREVER

TO MARTIN SCORSESE

HUMPHREY BOGART

i WANT TO EXPLAIN TO HUMPHREY WHY
MY FATHER CALLED ME "JAMFRY". i'M SURE
WE'D BE BEST BUDDIES. ☺

CHARLIE CHAPLIN

i WANT TO TELL CHAPLIN THAT HE WAS MY
BEST FRIEND WHEN i WAS A BOY. AND ASK HIM
TO TEACH ME TO SING AND DANCE ALONG TO THE
SONG FROM MODERN TIMES.

RYAN GOSLING, LEONARDO DiCAPRIO,
BRAD PITT, MATT DAMON AND GEORGE CLOONEY

I'D LIKE TO HIT UP LAS VEGAS WITH THIS LOT
ONE WEEKEND. THE QUESTIONS WOULD COME
TO ME ALONG THE WAY.

223

SOFIA COPPOLA

i WANT TO ASK SOFIA IF SHE'LL SHOW ME
THE MAP OF PEOPLE'S INNER LONELINESS, SO
THAT, IF ONE DAY i FIND MYSELF IN THERE,
i KNOW HOW TO GET BACK OUT.

ALFRED HITCHCOCK

I NEED TO ASK ALFRED HOW I CAN THROW ALL MY FEARS AND OBSESSIONS INTO MY WORK, JUST AS HE DID.

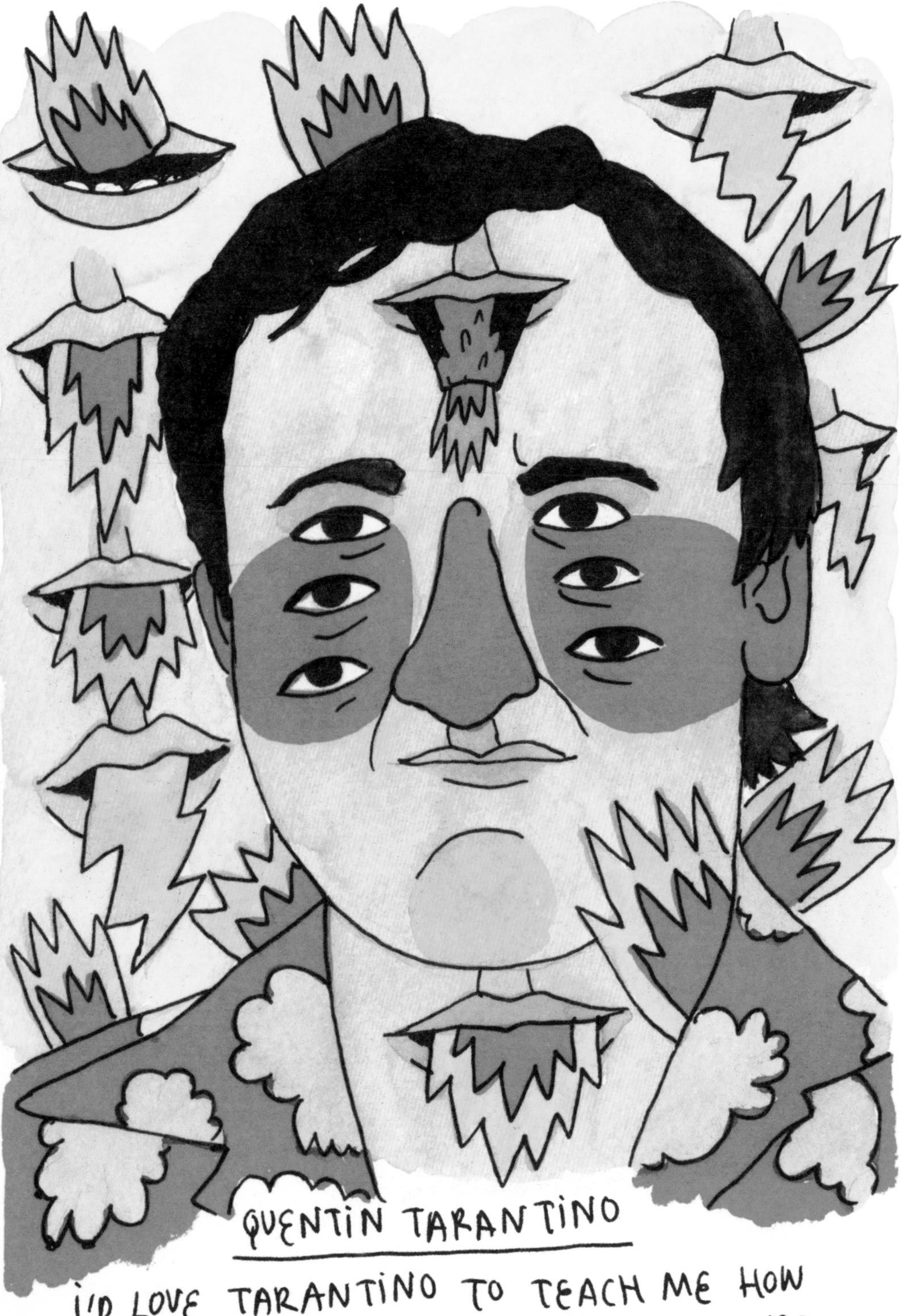
QUENTIN TARANTINO

I'D LOVE TARANTINO TO TEACH ME HOW TO HAVE CONVERSATIONS LIKE THE ONES HE WRITES IN HIS MOVIES.

FRANCIS FORD COPPOLA

I WANT COPPOLA TO TELL ME EVERYTHING
HE KNOWS ABOUT THE RELATIONSHIP
BETWEEN THE MAFIA AND THE MOVIES.

MARTIN SCORSESE

I REALLY NEED MARTIN SCORSESE TO TALK
TO ME ABOUT VIOLENCE IN MOVIES.
HE'S A MASTER AT IT. BANG! BANG!

218

EIGHT·PEOPLE

FROM·THE·MOVIE·WORLD

i·WISH
WERE·MY·FRIENDS ☺
♥